Endor

"A compelling read that challenges com true
meaning of Christianity. It sounds a wal
- Peter DeHaan, author of *Jesus's Broke*

"*Beneath the Graffiti, a De-churched Christians Search For Christianity* for those who have been turned off, or wounded by modern Christianity. It thoughtfully and effectively highlights the flaws in too much Christian doctrine. CJ peels back the layers and uncovers what is hidden beneath: Jesus' version."
- Rev. Dr. Sheri Pallas, author of *We Have Ruined God*, and host of live stream *Fireside Creators*.

Beneath the Graffiti

A De-churched Christian's Search for Christianity

CJ Penn

Beneath the Graffiti

A De-churched Christian's Search for Christianity

ISBN-13: 979-8-9916272-3-8

Cover photo: mosaic by Giacomo Raffaelli (1816), copy of Leonardi da Vinci painting of *The Last Supper*, licensed by iStock.com/sedmak.

People's names have been changed and some of their stories slightly modified to protect their privacy.

Thanks

To Debi and Alison, whose professional editing filled those double-spaced pages with golden comments, corrections, and suggestions. Thank you so much for helping make this book what it has become.

And what's a book without a cover? To Jersey M., a cover designer on Fiverr, who created a cover that exceeded anything I had previously imagined.

Dedication

"Whatever you do, do it all for the glory of God." (1 Corinthians 10:31)

May God be glorified within these pages.

I also dedicate this book to those who read it, with the hope that you'll find freedom in the truth of Christianity, a truth that though not always visible, is still within reach, just beneath the graffiti.

"Then you will know the truth, and the truth will set you free."
(John 8:32)

Contents

1. Wake Up

"Wake up CJ. The Matrix has you."

Like Neo in the movie *The Matrix*, was I living in a world of deception? Neo was an unwitting prisoner in a computer-generated, virtual reality world—the Matrix. While Neo may have suspected something was wrong with his reality, he didn't know there was another world out there, the *real* world, beyond the virtual world of his experience. Then Morpheus, another *Matrix* character, called Neo to wake up to the truth.

About twenty years ago, I first suspected I was living in a human-generated version of Christianity, where though it was put forth as true to what Jesus lived and taught, it wasn't. I began to sense another Christianity out there, a *real* Christianity, beyond the Christianity of my experience. And it felt like Morpheus was calling me to wake up to the truth, a truth hidden beneath the graffiti of church history and human nature.

I struggled through those years, trying to understand what I was feeling and why. At first, I didn't know what to do about my feelings, or how to respond to that imagined Morpheus voice. Then, realizing that "Christianity" and "Christian" are manmade terms subject to human definition and manipulation, I felt a growing desire to know how Jesus would define Christianity. What would Jesus say it means to be a Christian? So, I listened to the voice.

Eventually, a new image seeped into my mind, an image that helped solidify my resolve to search for the truth of Christianity. Picture a Bible resting on a table. The Bible—the collection of historical documents that defines Jesus' version of Christianity—was compiled a few centuries after Jesus showed us His Christianity. Then, as the centuries ticked by, men added other books.

Where Jesus' Christianity and what it means to be Christian is defined by God's word as recorded in the Bible, manmade versions of Christianity are often defined and governed by those manmade rulebooks. Now, looking at that pile of books, where's Jesus' Christianity?

Having spent my formative years on the outside, I was in my early thirties when I first ventured inside the Christian world. With no other purpose than to follow my wife and two kids, I initially limited myself to one church. I sat through lots of sermons, though I didn't always listen. I read the entire Bible, yet like with those sermons, I wasn't always paying attention. I did get involved though, like when I volunteered to help with the church youth group.

Shortly after I accepted the youth group challenge, a co-worker asked me about the church I was attending. He wanted to know what kind of Christianity they promoted. What kind of Christianity? Hmm, I had thought Jesus envisioned only one kind of Christianity.

Then, a couple years later, the suspicions began creeping in, and the feeling that the world of Christianity, at least the small corner of it I lived in, was some kind of manmade construct, a Christian establishment matrix. However, was it all my imagination? I knew I was broken. I knew I was a victim of my past, a past that had bruised my mind. Maybe my thoughts about a false, manmade version of Christianity came from one of those black-and-blue patches of gray matter.

Well, whether my suspicions came from imagination or reality, my past was real, as were the questions that haunted me. Questions like, would my stepfather Henry really go to hell because his mother and the Catholic Church had told him so? And if his destiny was hell, what about mine? There were lots of things in my past I wished I could forget, but … could God?

In my early search for answers, I returned to the Bible—this time with more serious intention. I initially found more questions than answers. For example, the Holy Spirit's mentioned a lot in the Bible, though not often in sermons. What's up with that? The Holy Spirit was a mystery to me. Also, why was my stepfather doomed to eternity in hell? The Bible said his sins had been forgiven.

Stepping back to take in the bigger picture painted by the Bible, a new question snuck in. Why? Why are we the way we are? Why is there so much evil in the world? Why is life sometimes so difficult? Why is peace with each other, and even with God, sometimes so unattainable? And why is it so hard to believe? Without falling too deeply into philosophical notions, I guess I just wanted to know what life's all about—the elusive meaning of life.

So much of life felt either meaningless or perilous. I wanted something solid and unchanging to hold onto, a safe place in the midst of this conspiracy-theory-dominated, truth-starved, war-rattled, chaotic world. I was craving meaning and a purpose I could believe in without fear and doubts, and I wasn't finding that in the church I was attending.

Then it happened, a situation at church. I mean, this was a big deal. It wounded me and left me confused. *That's not true Christianity, is it?* I kept asking myself. *That can't be what Jesus has in mind.* The episode added to my sense of a false Christianity, a Christianity matrix that had been holding me, and those sitting in the pews next to me, captive.

I have friends who found freedom from similar situations by quitting Christianity. I wasn't interested in going that far. Instead, I quit that church. I visited other churches around town, yet nothing felt right, and I didn't know why. The whole experience was disorienting and depressing. I eventually decided to go it alone. However, as I later learned, I was never truly alone.

Soon after becoming a church refugee, I began spending all my spare time searching for the truth about the way of life that Jesus lived and taught, what I call Jesus' Christianity. I suspected I'd find it somewhere under the false Christianity that held me captive. Something told me it was there, like Morpheus sending me that cryptic message, "Wake up CJ. Manmade Christianity has you."

Early one morning, while waiting for the coffee to kick in, I grabbed a fresh notebook. During my search for Christianity, I used that now-dog-eared notebook to record ideas, Bible verses, quotes from others, and anything else I found helpful. The first entry in my notebook was a list of other things that fed my doubts about the truthfulness of the Christianity I'd experienced. The beginning of my list looked like this:

> Christianity seems to be all about rules, which if not followed, will send you to hell. But so many Christians don't follow their own rules. Hell must be full of delinquent Christians. Is Christianity really like that?
>
> Survey results show a growing number of church refugees. There seems to be a lack of power to improve people's lives and keep them coming back for more. Are Christianity and God really that weak?
>
> Church (while I was attending) felt like a club, yet run like a business. Corporate Christianity—that's how church sometimes felt. Is that really how it's supposed to be?
>
> And what about all the different denominations, each with their different doctrines, rules, beliefs, traditions, and bureaucracy? Why so many flavors? And which ones, if any, are closest to Jesus' Christianity?

That quiet voice in my head, the mysterious Morpheus-like voice, was telling me that Jesus' Christianity isn't as weak and confusing as the Christianity we often encounter.

Still, my idea of being caught in a matrix felt like a weak illustration. I needed a better way to visualize what I was experiencing. That's when I started seeing manmade Christianity as graffiti splattered on a painting, with Jesus' masterpiece hidden beneath. With that image in mind, what is Christianity really like under the accumulated graffiti of the past two thousand years?

One of the next entries in my notebook was a quote by Mohandas Gandhi:

> *"Oh, I don't reject Christ. I love Christ. It's just that so many of you Christians are so unlike Christ."*

Christians and their behavior are partially a product of the kind of Christianity they follow. What they're told, what they are led to believe, shows up in their behavior. Therefore, Gandhi's observation is a clue that much of modern Christianity is unlike Jesus' Christianity.

As I later learned, it's also our self-centered, prideful human nature—something we all suffer from—that makes Christians so unlike Christ. And since pride and personal opinion tend to distort the truth, I needed to be careful. I didn't want to splatter my own graffiti over whatever truth I might uncover. I didn't want to create a customized truth that satisfied my personal desires—there's already too much of that going on in this world.

Speaking of truth, another entry in my notebook came from the Apostle John:

> *"I have no greater joy than this, to hear that my children are walking in the truth." (3 John 4 NRSV)*

Being a father, I, too, hope my children make decisions based on truth rather than lies, pride-influenced beliefs, conspiracy theories, and fake news. I bet God feels the same way about His children.

Entering the campus of Trinity College in Dublin, Ireland, my wife and I followed the herd of other tourists through Library Square when I looked up to see a large sign saying, *"Falsehood flies, and truth comes limping after it,"* by Jonathan Swift. Yes, it seems that in our society, falsehoods often prevail far more than truth. What matters most to some people is *who* said something, rather than the trustworthiness of what they said. For many people, truth is whatever they decide it to be. But remembering that Jonathan Swift quote has fueled my desire to give truth—that is, Jesus' truth as defined in the Bible—a shoulder to lean on, especially when many people are kicking it in the shins.

Yet, I feared I was venturing into hazardous territory. I had a growing concern that what I end up discovering might offend churchgoing family and friends whom I dearly love. Maybe that's one reason it's taken me over sixteen years to finish writing this book. Many times, I've considered chucking the whole thing, though each time I felt God urging me to keep going, with such encouragement as:

> *"For whatever is hidden is meant to be disclosed, and whatever is concealed is meant to be brought out into the open." (Mark 4:22)*
>
> *"The spirit of the Lord God is upon me ... he has sent me to bring good news to the oppressed, to bind up the brokenhearted, to proclaim liberty to the captives, and release to the prisoners." (Isaiah 61:1 NRSV)*
>
> *"God our Savior, who wants all people to be saved and to come to a knowledge of the truth." (1 Timothy 2:3-4)*

So, why have I written this book, this record of what I found while searching for Christianity? I wrote it because I like the idea of helping Jesus bring hidden truths out into the open, truths that could help release the wounded and captive prisoners of manmade Christianity, at least those willing to be free.

Also, thinking back to survey results I've seen about the growing numbers of fellow de-churched Christians, I suspect some people who quit manmade Christianity started out looking for something, something they apparently couldn't find in church. Maybe that's why they quit. However, I believe Jesus' Christianity will give them what they were looking for, what manmade Christianity is lacking.

I'm not thinking only about church refugees. I know many non-Christians who are captive to a false, manmade image of Christianity. For those who remain curious, I hope to give them the chance to reconsider their opinion about God and Jesus, this time based on truth.

And what about you? Have you ever questioned the truth of the Christianity you've experienced? Have you ever wondered what Jesus might think about today's various forms of Christianity? Would you like to see His truth? If so, then as Jesus often said: come, follow me.

Several years ago, when my son and some friends climbed Mt. Whitney, they first stayed a day or two in a nearby town to get their bodies used to the high altitude. If they had skipped that step on their journey and had driven straight to the trailhead from their sea-level homes and begun climbing, they likely would have suffered from some form of altitude sickness.

I tell this story because on this journey you and I are about to embark on, it's just as important to not skip steps. Each step on this journey to uncover the truth of Christianity will prepare you for the steps ahead. And in many ways, what we're about to do will be like climbing a mountain, where some stages of the journey will be smooth and level, while others will be rough and steep. But first, the next few chapters will help you get acclimated and ready for the climb.

As I stepped off on my own journey many years ago, there was a new question loitering in my mind. Jesus had said, *"Then you will know the truth, and the truth will set you free"* (John 8:32). But, free from what? I suspected there was something more than freedom from wounds and captivity to a manmade Christianity. I suspected there was something else holding me prisoner that I wasn't aware of … like the matrix.

So, now it's decision time. Will you stop here and remain captive to a distorted, manmade image of Christianity, a Christianity that may be blinding you to the truth? Or, will you follow me at least a little farther on this journey to uncover the truth? For *Matrix* fans, this is the blue pill or red pill moment. And like Morpheus said, all I'm offering you is the truth. Nothing more.

2. *What Experts Have to Say*

Though the image of manmade graffiti covering the masterpiece of true Christianity works for me, there have been times when modern Christianity felt more like a wall, with Jesus' Christianity hidden behind it. The wall imagery works for another reason—walls can hold people prisoner, people like my stepfather, Henry.

Shortly after Henry and my mom were married, I overheard a conversation where Henry's devout Catholic mother told him he'd go to hell for divorcing his first wife. That memory represents one of the first times I hit my head on a stone in the wall, a stone placed there by the Catholic Church. It frightened me, added to the emotional bruises on my mind, and locked Henry in a prison of guilt and fear.

Later, in my early twenties, I ventured into the Bible for the first time, limiting my exploration to the New Testament. I wasn't yet sold on Christianity, just curious. That first read was hard, not because I had trouble understanding what I was reading, but because much of what I read didn't match up with what I'd seen from the sidelines of the Catholic Church.

However, many years later, after embarking on my journey in search of Christianity, I still had lingering doubts about the idea of a false Christianity with the truth hidden behind it. Again, was it all my imagination? Being cautious about jumping to conclusions, I wanted to hear what some experts have to say. I began with God.

What God has to say

God experienced corruption of His truth long before Jesus came on the scene, and He foresaw a need to warn future generations:

> "Thus says the Lord God: Because you have uttered falsehood and envisioned lies, I am against you, says the Lord God. My hand will be against the prophets who see false visions and utter lying divinations. ... I will break down the wall that you have smeared with whitewash, and bring it to the ground, so

> *that its foundation will be laid bare."* (Ezekiel 13:8-9, 14 NRSV)

I wasn't the only one who felt the presence of a wall of falsehood, and God seemed none too happy about it. Unlike God, however, I wasn't looking to break down the wall—I only wanted to see what's hidden behind it.

Realizing that God may have been talking about Old Testament falsehoods that no longer exist, I returned to the New Testament, where I found words of warning from the Apostles Peter and Paul:

> *"But there were also false prophets among the people, just as there will be false teachers among you. Many will follow their depraved conduct and will bring the way of truth into disrepute."* (2 Peter 2:1, 2)
>
> *"Even from your own number men will arise and distort the truth in order to draw away disciples after them. So be on your guard!"* (Acts 20:30-31)
>
> *"For the time will come when people will not put up with sound doctrine. Instead, to suit their own desires, they will gather around them a great number of teachers to say what their itching ears want to hear. They will turn their ears away from the truth and turn aside to myths."* (2 Timothy 4:3-4)

To hear only what you want to hear. Gee, I've never done that, have I? Hmm, anyway, based on these warnings from the Bible, I took another step toward being convinced that what I had experienced in church really may have been a false, distorted version of Jesus' Christianity.

What other experts have to say

Those Biblical warnings of lies and distorted truth were written a long time ago. Do they apply today? What do others think, respected authorities more contemporary than Peter and Paul? I soon learned my angst about what I saw on the surface of modern Christianity wasn't unique or new.

Starting with respected Christian scholar and author C.S. Lewis and his classic, *Mere Christianity*, I encountered a subtle clue that today's Christianity might truly be a distorted version of what Jesus intended:

> *"The Church exists for nothing else but to draw people into Christ, to make them little Christs. If they are not doing that, all the cathedrals, clergy, missions, sermons, even the Bible itself, are simply a waste of time. God became Man for no other purpose."* [1]

To make people little Christs—I hadn't met many of those. I certainly wasn't one. The scarcity of them made me wonder about the truthfulness, effectiveness, and value of modern Christianity.

Though I'd circle back to this idea of little Christs later in my journey, I quickly forgot about it and moved on. I next found a humble book by a humble 17th century monk we know as Brother Lawrence, who claims in *The Practice of the Presence of God*:

> *"It isn't necessary that we stay in church in order to remain in God's presence. We can make our hearts personal chapels where we can enter anytime to talk to God privately."* [2]
>
> *"He* [Brother Lawrence] *encouraged other Christians to rely on God's love to lead them in their spiritual lives, rather than the knowledge of learned men. He used to tell his brothers, 'It is the Creator who teaches truth, who in one moment instructs the heart of the humble and makes him understand more about the mysteries of our faith, and even about Himself, than if he had studied them for a long term of years.'"* [3]

Brother Lawrence is saying that we should rely *only* on our spiritual God for guidance in spiritual matters. Makes sense. Now, I realize this says nothing about a false Christianity, directly anyway. Yet, maybe this is another clue, and a warning—a warning that relying on the seminary-taught knowledge of learned men, rather than God, could result in a false manmade version of Christianity.

After discovering Brother Lawrence, I jumped ahead two centuries to Andrew Murray, a highly esteemed 19th century pastor and prolific author from South Africa. Murray gave clear answers to many of my questions, such as why the church and its messages appear so weak. Now some of this might rattle your core a bit, so be ready:

> "The reason for the weakness of your Christian life is that you try to work it out on your own, only allowing God to help you when you are desperate." [4]
>
> "God has called the church of Christ to live in the power of the Holy Spirit. But the church is living, for the most part, in the power of human flesh, and of will and energy and effort apart from the Spirit of God. I do not doubt that this is the case with many individual believers." [5]
>
> "I fear that if you ask why there is so little converting power in the preaching of the Word, why there is so much work and often so little result for eternity, why the Word has so little power to build up believers in holiness and in consecration—the answer will be that the power of the Holy Spirit is absent. And why is this? There can be no other reason except that the flesh and human energy have taken the place that the Holy Spirit ought to have." [6]
>
> "I might press still further in connection with the church. Does God have His full and rightful place there? Sadly, very seldom." [7]

According to Murray, God and the Holy Spirit are absent from many churches, pushed out by human effort. Since God doesn't have His rightful place in church, what's left must be manmade and weak. With that thought in mind, if God and His Spirit are missing, can you even call it Christianity?

Charles Spurgeon, another well-known 19th century preacher, also mentioned something that implied the presence of a false, weakened Christianity:

"Jesus said 'If ye love me, keep my commandments.' What a great amount of religion may be cast out as worthless by this text! Men may keep on going to church, they may be religious throughout their whole lives, and they may be apparently blameless in their moral conduct, and yet there may be nothing in them because there is no love for the ever blessed Christ at the foundation of their profession of faith." [8]

Then I jumped up a century to A.W. Tozer, an American pastor whom some called a 20th century prophet. In his book aptly titled *Reclaiming Christianity*, I found this:

"More young preachers imitate men in the world with a good deal more energy than they imitate the holy saints of God." [9]

Hmm, sounds like another clue. Then, from Tozer's book *Mystery of the Holy Spirit*, there's this:

"Many people know about God but do not know God. There is a difference." [10]

"You can discover more of the Holy Spirit in five minutes on your knees in adoring worship than five years at a seminary." [11]

That could explain a lot. Also, it's easy to see the difference between reading someone's biography verses personally knowing them, or learning about God from men verses learning from God Himself. God doesn't want us to know books; He wants us to know Him. God doesn't want us to rely on someone's seminary education; He wants us to rely on Him. However, Tozer's comments gave me another clue that today's Christianity, resulting from centuries of reliance upon manmade education, is not necessarily Jesus' Christianity. There is a difference.

Moving on, recently I read Tozer's classic, *The Pursuit of God*. Yet be warned, because Tozer is rather blunt:

"Every age has its own characteristics. Right now we are in an age of religious complexity. The simplicity which is in

> *Christ is rarely found among us. In its stead are programs, methods, organizations and a world of nervous activities which occupy time and attention but can never satisfy the longing of the heart. The shallowness of our inner experience, the hollowness of our worship, and that servile imitation of the world which marks our promotional methods all testify that we, in this day, know God only imperfectly, and the peace of God scarcely at all."* [12]
>
> *"The world is perishing for lack of the knowledge of God and the church is famishing for want of His presence."* [13]

The church is famishing because God is missing. Interesting. Have you seen any of the recent survey data showing the increasing number of churches that, starved by a lack of membership, are permanently closing their doors? Maybe those churches are starving for want of God's presence.

Looking for more opinions regarding the existence of a false Christianity, I bounced back a few centuries when Andrew Murray introduced me to William Law. Though Law lived in the 1700's, his messages were clear to my 21st century mind. I first read Law's book *The Power of the Spirit*, about fifteen years ago, as I was picking up momentum on my journey. I didn't have to read far when I ran into this:

> *"All true religion is, or brings forth, an essential union and communion of the spirit of the creature with the Spirit of the Creator; God in it, and it in God, one life, one light, one love. … A religion that is not wholly built upon this supernatural ground, but solely stands upon human powers, reasoning's, and conclusions, has not so much as the shadow of truth in it."* [14]

Law is saying that Christianity based on human effort with human reasoning—like seminary-inspired ideas and doctrines—is not a Christianity where we'll necessarily find the truth. How does that strike you?

I recently re-read Law's book, and here are other bits that passed under my highlighter:

"True Christianity is nothing but the continual dependence upon God through Christ for all life, light, and virtue; and the false religion of Satan is to seek that goodness from any other source." [15]

"If the faith of illiterate fishermen did more for the establishment of the church in a few years than centuries of prodigious scholarship, one may readily understand that a trust in the wisdom of men and the letter of Scripture has caused the church to fall from its first gospel state in much the way that Adam fell through eating of the same tree of knowledge." [16]

"But now corruption, sin, death, and every evil of the world have entered into the Church, the spouse of Christ, just as they entered into Eve, the spouse of Adam, in Paradise. And in the same way, and from the same cause, namely, a desire for knowledge other than that which comes from God alone." [17]

"If Christ had said to His disciples, 'Labor to be rich, indulge yourselves, be conformed to this world, enjoy its pleasures and see its honors,' nothing more need have been done to prove their faithfulness to such a master than popish and Protestant churches have been doing for centuries." [18]

"The one true proof of our being living members of Christ's Church on earth is our being inwardly of the Spirit and outwardly of the behavior which Christ manifested while in the world." [19]

"Christianity is nothing else than living unto God in the power of Christ as He lives in us." [20]

So, true Christianity amounts to living with the Spirit of God and Christ living within you. That's not what I'd heard from churches I'd attended.

But what do these insights from these long-dead Christians say about the condition of modern Christianity? If people like Law and Murray saw the church so messed up back in the 18th and 19th centuries, today's church could be even more off its foundation with the added influences of the 20th and 21st centuries.

What the people have to say

What does the health of 21st century churches say about the validity of the Christianity those churches promote? I initially found answers in the book *Churchless; Understanding Today's Unchurched and How to Connect with Them*. Drawing from research conducted by The Barna Group, this book focuses on the state of the Christian church in the US, and for me anyway, it contained some surprises, such as:

> *There are 18 million born-again Christians who no longer attend church.*
>
> *Barna Group research shows that 51% of unchurched adults are still looking for something better spiritually than they have seen so far.*
>
> *The Barna study found that 16% of non-churchgoers previously attended church and at one time made a personal commitment to Jesus. And though they've left church behind, they still believe they will go to heaven because of Jesus' sacrifice for them.* [21]

Eighteen million church refugees … and that was in 2014! Looking for more recent data, I found an article reporting that the Episcopal Church in the US has lost 400,000 members between 2012 and 2021. The refugee camp continues to grow.

Yet why have so many of those on the inside bugged out? Could the reason be related to why so many of those outside the church—at least a portion of those 51%—didn't like what they saw when they looked inside? Is there a common cause that's pushing insiders out and keeping outsiders away, a cause that's maybe hindering these people from finding the spirituality they seek?

Setting that question aside for now, in another book filled with Barna Group research—*unChristian; What a New Generation Really Thinks About Christianity*—I found the following:

> *"Our research confirmed that many young* [outsiders] *... were probing the Christian faith, trying it on for size, but they couldn't get past some of the mental, emotional, or spiritual barriers ... so they gave up."* [22]

Considering those 51% of unchurched adults I just mentioned, maybe what they saw when they peeked inside the church were mental, emotional, or spiritual barriers … so they gave up.

In my search for further insight, I then found some 2007 research data by the Schaeffer Institute, with more evidence of Christians escaping confinement:

> *"Every year, 2.7 million* [Christian] *church members fall into inactivity. This translates into the realization that people are leaving the church. From our research, we have found that they are leaving as hurting and wounded victims—of some kind of abuse, disillusionment, or just plain neglect!"* [23]

The picture of modern Christianity was becoming clearer. For those on the outside of Christianity curious enough to look in, many of them didn't like what they saw. For those on the inside, many have given up and escaped. Yet shouldn't Christianity be magnetic—like it was in the first century—attracting people, rather than repelling them?

Before leaving this chapter, consider this quote from the book *You Lost Me; Why Young Christians Are Leaving Church ... and Rethinking Faith*:

> *"The next generation is caught between two possible destinies—one moored by the power and depth of the Jesus-centered gospel and one anchored in a cheap, Americanized version of the historic faith that will snap at the slightest puff of wind."* [24]

There it is, the choice between Jesus' Christianity and a cheap, manmade version. My imagined graffiti was beginning to take form, painting a picture of a manmade false Christianity that's pushing people away, leaving many of them as hurting and wounded victims.

At this point in my own journey, I'd confirmed my purpose—to shine a light on the graffiti of the manmade version and uncover Jesus' truth hidden beneath. Again, my hope is that the truth will free those imprisoned or wounded by a false Christianity. Those willing to be free, that is.

3. What the Wounded Have to Say

Energized by a meaningful purpose—and a strong cup of coffee—I'm up long before sunrise, trying to get in some writing before opening my work laptop. My commute to work was much longer before the pandemic.

With a bit of gnawing reluctance, I accept what may have been inevitable. There really is a manmade version of Christianity—represented by my figurative graffiti—which in many ways hides the truth of Jesus' Christianity. Before looking beneath that graffiti, I want to hear what the wounded themselves have to say. What is their perception of and experience with manmade Christianity? First, there are the wounded unchurched, those who may have scars from a bad experience with a church or a Christian. Then there are the church refugees, the de-churched who may also suffer from church-inflicted wounds. And finally, there are current churchgoers who may have festering wounds of their own.

But first, consider this: If the Christianity someone experiences inflicts wounds, then that Christianity must be manmade. For Jesus' Christianity doesn't inflict wounds—Jesus' Christianity heals wounds.

The unchurched

I went back to the book *unChristian*, looking for more data on what unchurched outsiders see when they look inside today's Christianity. What I found may be surprising:

> 20% of all outsiders, regardless of age, admit they "have had a bad experience in a church or with a Christian that gave them a negative image of Jesus Christ."
>
> 25% of outsiders say that their foremost perception of Christianity is that the faith has changed for the worse. It has gotten off track and no longer seems Christian. [1]

No longer seems Christian—there it is, manmade Christianity. And what about the outsiders who've had a bad experience with a church or a Christian? What kind of bad experience? Here are some clues:

> In a survey of young adults who don't attend church, the Barna Group discovered the following:
>
> - 91% see Christians as anti-homosexual
> - 87% see Christians as judgmental
> - 85% see Christians as hypocritical
>
> More data from the Barna study shows that 80% of adults outside the church believe that "Christian churches do not accept and love unconditionally, regardless of how people look or what they do." And get this: 59% of Christian churchgoers believe the same thing. [1]

Anti-homosexual, judgmental, hypocritical, and unloving—that's not an attractive picture. Yet, isn't Christianity supposed to be all about love and acceptance? What many outsiders, and even current churchgoers, apparently see is a religion that no longer seems Christian.

The de-churched

Next, how do church refugees feel, those 18 million-and-counting who no longer go to church? I looked again in the *Churchless* book and found more disturbing survey results:

> Of American adults who don't attend church, 33% of those surveyed by the Barna Group once were active in a church, but attend no more. Barna calls these the "de-churched."
>
> 23% of de-churched people said the Bible isn't taught clearly or often enough.
>
> 20% of the de-churched said that "God seems missing from their experience of church."
>
> The majority of de-churched Christians leave church without finding a connection with God. [2]

God seems missing, and as A.W. Tozer said, "the church is famishing for want of His presence." Could there be a relationship between the presence of God—or lack of His presence—and the presence of churchgoers? That is, does less God equate to fewer churchgoers, and therefore more refugees?

Look again at that last survey comment. Most de-churched Christians didn't find a connection with God while attending church. However, as I learned throughout my journey, the sole purpose of a truly *Christian* Church is to help people find a connection with God. Yet from the perspective of the de-churched, it indeed looks like many churches no longer seem Christian.

Churchgoers

Finally, what's the perception of current churchgoers that may add to our evolving image of manmade Christianity? According to the data I cited above, most of them see Christian churches as unloving. I went back to the book *unChristian* for more, and found this:

> Two-thirds of churchgoing Christians said that following rigid rules is an important part of the life and teaching of their church. [1]

Maybe this is another reason most of the de-churched hadn't found a connection with God—all the rules got in their way. Besides following rules, what do churchgoers see as other important aspects of being Christian? The Barna survey reported this:

> When born-again Christians were asked to list two or three of the most important priorities for being Christian in terms of their faith:
> - 37% said being good and not sinning
> - 31% said learning about Jesus and the Bible
> - 25% said sharing their faith and helping others come to know Jesus
> - 25% said worshiping God and singing
> - 23% said loving others and making friends
> - 18% said helping the poor and serving other people

- 4% said giving money and time to bless others
- 1% said influencing and shaping the faith of family
- 10% aren't sure [1]

Great priorities, though many Christians apparently fail to live up to them. For if they did live by these priorities, why would so many outsiders see them as hypocritical, judgmental, bigoted, and unloving?

Stepping back, I looked again at the list, and groaned. I saw a possible reason why most de-churched Christians hadn't found a connection with God. I saw why 20% of the de-churched said God was missing from their experience of church. God was indeed missing. Look again at the list. Where's the Holy Spirit? God sent His Spirit to help and guide us. God sent His Spirit to be God within us. Shouldn't some mention of the Spirit be near the top of the list? Yet it looks like most churches aren't letting Him in the door.

What about those 10% at the bottom of the list? Are those people taking the name Christian—even calling themselves *born-again*—without knowing what that name stands for? Are they Christian in name only? Whatever the answer, I see those 10% as more wounded victims, suffering from some form of church neglect.

This list of priorities became something of a touchstone I kept returning to while on my journey in search of true Christianity. This list answers many questions about the state of today's Christianity, and how it's not a clear reflection of Jesus' Christianity. Therefore, you'll notice me periodically referring to this list as you follow me on this journey.

The path ahead

Hypocritical, judgmental, bigoted, abundance of rules, lack of love, where God and His Spirit are missing—this is what Christianity sometimes looks like from outside, and even inside, the church. This is some of the graffiti blocking the view of the truth of Jesus' Christianity. To keep track of all this, I started a list in my notebook and titled it "Perceptions of Christianity." These perceptions could be why millions of people are leaving churches. I had a feeling I'd be adding more to the list.

Before taking another step on this journey however, there's something I need to make clear, though you may have already figured it out. There's no seminary degree hanging on my wall. I'm just a searching wannabe Christian, maybe a lot like you. So, as you follow me on this path in search of Christianity, please know that I'm not necessarily ahead of you. In fact, sometimes I lose ground, falling back into old habits. Maybe that's because my own journey's not over. If it were, I'd be in heaven.

After several years of searching, questioning, and struggling, I accepted that most of the Christianity I had experienced was not Jesus' Christianity. Along with that acceptance came the understanding that many of Paul's warnings to first century Christians were also warnings for us. Paul was speaking to you and me when he said:

> *"Evidently some people are throwing you into confusion and are trying to pervert the gospel of Christ."* (Galatians 1:7)
>
> *"See to it that no one takes you captive through hollow and deceptive philosophy, which depends on human tradition and the elemental spiritual forces of this world rather than on Christ."* (Colossians 2:8)

In reading this book I hope you will see, maybe for the first time, the truth of Jesus' Christianity. In that truth, I hope you will find and experience a closer relationship with God and Jesus, an intimate relationship, filled with love, trust, peace, hope, healing, and freedom. As Jesus said,

"Then you will know the truth, and the truth will set you free" (John 8:32).

4. A Truth Disregarded

The truth is sometimes hard to find, especially during election years—the bluster of the 2024 US presidential election is at full volume as I take another editing pass over this chapter. Unlike politics, however, the truth of Jesus' Christianity, which by definition is contained in the Bible, is right out in the open, not at all hard to find. Yet with Jesus' truth so easily accessible, why is it often missing from churches and the lives of Christians?

As I begin to scrape away the layers of manmade graffiti that have accumulated over the past 2000 years, it may help you to understand some common reasons for the presence of that graffiti, and the absence of Biblical truth.

Lack of faith and trust

If you really want to see the truth of Christianity, you first need to trust the document that defines Christianity. I trust the Bible, so my own journey didn't include Bible validation. But not everyone shares that trust. A non-Christian friend once asked me, "The Bible's written by people, so why should I trust it?" Great question, as people often distort the truth, either intentionally or accidentally. There's plenty of historical support for the validity and trustworthiness of the Bible, but I'll give you the simple reason why I trust it.

For those who wrote the original documents that comprise the Bible and the scribes who copied those documents, the aspect of their personalities that would have motivated them to distort the truth is ego. It's easy to imagine prideful, ego-driven men seeking power over gullible believers by perverting the truth and promoting self-serving fiction. We see such behavior in certain politicians all the time.

However, that's not the case with the Bible, for the Bible gives no power, control, or authority of any kind to church leaders, churches, or anyone else. Though church history is full of men ignoring the Bible and grabbing power, the Bible clearly states that all power and authority reside where they originated, with God. For me, that's adequate evidence that the Bible is the truth as dictated to the writers by God, free from the corruption of power-hungry, ego-driven men.

Why else do I trust it? Because of faith, because I believe that, *"All Scripture is inspired by God"* (2 Timothy 3:16 NASB). And as Jesus said, *"The word which you hear is not Mine, but the Father's who sent Me"* (John 14:24 NASB).

Though non-Christians like my friend have no reason to trust the Bible, how do Christians feel about the book that defines Christianity? A 2008 PEW Research report claims:

> "While a large majority of Christians believe that the Bible is the word of God, the various Christian traditions are divided over whether or not the Bible should be interpreted literally, word for word." [1]

Is this saying that many Christians believe God inspired the words, yet they play this *non-literal* card to avoid believing the words? Looking for more details, I found this in a 2015 PEW Research report:

> 39% of Christians believe the Bible is the word of God and should be taken literally. The rest either believe the Bible is the word of God but should <u>not</u> be taken literally (36%), or the Bible is <u>not</u> the word of God (18%), or they don't know (7%). [2]

So, most Christians believe the Bible shouldn't be taken literally. And what about the 18% who also believe the Bible is *not* the word of God? If so-called Christians lack the willingness to take God's words literally, or lack the faith to believe God inspired the words—the words that define what it means to be Christian—why do they call themselves Christian? Are they Christian in name only?

Interpretation or modification

The Bible is at times confusing, as if portions were written in code. So, Christians often rely on seminary-trained code breakers and their seminary-inspired knowledge to interpret what they think the God-inspired words mean. An underlying theme of manmade Christianity is that Bible understanding comes from the interpretation of Bible scholars. Since each scholar has their own opinion—and therefore their own interpretation—as it says in the 2008 PEW Research report,

> "More than two-thirds of adults affiliated with a religious tradition agree that there is more than one true way to interpret the teachings of their faith, a pattern that occurs in nearly all traditions." [1]

However, since there can be only one true truth, how can there be more than one true interpretation? Regarding the concept of multiple interpretations, I found these warnings from Peter and Paul:

> "First of all you must understand this, that no prophecy of scripture is a matter of one's own interpretation, because no prophecy ever came by human will, but men and women moved by the Holy Spirit spoke from God." (2 Peter 1:20-21 NRSV)
>
> "Do not go beyond what is written." (1 Corinthians 4:6)

Interpretation sounds risky to me, since intentionally or by accident, a human-inspired interpretation of God-inspired words could end up going beyond what is written. Yet, what else is there to do when faced with scripture we don't understand? In Peter's advice above, he showed me the way, though I didn't see it at first.

In my search for a better understanding of all this, I found two basic reasons why interpretation is used as an excuse to go beyond what is written. First, as shown by the PEW research data, either you have the faith to trust the words in the Bible and take them literally, or you don't. When it's hard to believe and accept certain things in the Bible, some people make up something they can believe.

The second basic reason some people go beyond what is written is that they allow themselves to be moved by their ego rather than the Holy Spirit. Ego-driven modification can take several forms, such as those who modify scripture and go beyond what is written in a way that gives themselves power. Then there are those who add their personal spin to the word of God, customizing it in their image. Also, our ego can have a hard time accepting our inability to understand complex messages. So, ego makes up something it can understand—and believe—replacing God's meaning with its own.

Maybe some of those who believe the Bible *is* the word of God but should *not* be taken literally would rather trust their ego, than God.

Whether driven by a weak faith, a strong ego, or both, some people are using the word "interpretation" as license for them to modify Christianity and paint it in their image. Such interpretation that goes beyond what is written is one reason why easily accessible truth is often missing from churches and the lives of Christians.

Finally, since the words in the Bible contain the truth of Christianity, and since most Christians choose to selectively ignore or modify those words, the dominance of a false, manmade Christianity is guaranteed. As if I needed more convincing.

Unread and untaught

My stepfather Henry, who grew up in a devout Catholic family, once told me that as a boy he was discouraged from reading the Bible. How many Christians *do* read it? I found answers in the 2015 PEW survey:

> 25% of Catholics read the Bible weekly and 52% claim to read the Bible seldom or never. Mainline protestants are somewhat more Bible literate with 30% reading weekly and 44% seldom or never. [3]

Whatever those percentages are today, it looks like many Christians, especially my stepfather's fellow Catholics, seldom or never read the Bible. Also, as the Barna Group survey found, 23% of de-churched Christians said the Bible isn't taught clearly or often enough in churches.

So, another reason Christian truth is often missing from churches and the lives of Christians is that many Christians are unfamiliar with the book that defines that truth. Where the Bible isn't read or taught, manmade Christianity will flourish.

Understanding

As I asked earlier, for those of us who do read the Bible, what can we do when faced with Bible passages that are confusing and hard to understand? Check this out:

> In referring to Jesus after He was resurrected, Luke said: "Then <u>he opened their minds</u> to understand the Scriptures." (Luke 24:45 NRSV, emphasis added)

> *Paul said: "What we have received is not the spirit of the world, but the Spirit who is from God, so that we may understand what God has freely given us." (1 Corinthians 2:12)*

Understanding complex Bible passages doesn't come from study, intellect, cleverness, imaginations, or a seminary degree. Jesus told us where understanding comes from:

> *"I have much more to say to you, more than you can now bear. But when he, the Spirit of truth, comes, he will guide you into all truth." (John 16:12-13)*

The majority of PEW survey respondents believe there are many ways to interpret and understand the teachings in the Bible. The truth is, there's only *one* way, and that's with the guidance of the Holy Spirit. The oft-ignored Holy Spirit will reveal the truth of God and Christianity, not a scholar. Brother Lawrence said it this way:

> *"God alone is capable of making Himself known as He really is; we search in reasoning and in the sciences, as in a poor copy, for what we neglect to see in an excellent original. God Himself paints Himself in the depths of our souls."* [4]

The writers of the documents comprising the Bible needed God's guidance to know what to write, and we need God's guidance to understand what we read. That's why Peter said, *"No prophecy of scripture is a matter of one's own interpretation, because no prophecy ever came by human will, but men and women moved by the Holy Spirit spoke from God."*

If you want worldly knowledge, look to worldly people. If you want spiritual knowledge, look to the Holy Spirit. Without the Holy Spirit, truth and understanding will be missing.

I had begun what I set out to achieve. I'd scraped off some graffiti that depicts biblical understanding as coming from ardent study and the interpretation of scholars. Underneath I found the truth—that *true* understanding comes from the Holy Spirit, and only the Holy Spirit.

Yet I felt those simmering worries again, worries about offending Christians I care about. I saw how I was already challenging the Christian establishment. But how could I avoid doing that when the Bible itself challenges the establishment? How could I avoid finding fault with modern Christianity while uncovering the truth of Jesus' Christianity? Weighed down by those worries, I asked God if I should keep writing or stop. It became a frequent prayer along the way.

Finally, in picturing this journey as climbing a mountain, though this first part may have been rough at times, we've only cinched up our boots, strapped on our packs, and hiked a short distance to where we'll set up our base camp. Yet in completing these first steps on this journey, hopefully you now see that my idea of a false, manmade Christianity isn't just my imagination.

God, Jesus, and the Holy Spirit

5. Our Father

After twelve years of writing several revisions of this book, I was excited to start the final draft—*final* being a very inaccurate term, as it turns out. Then, 2020 attacked. My writing slowed to a crawl as I adjusted to working from home and coping with a pandemic and presidential election that competed for attention. I struggled through the first four chapters, then stopped.

It's now four years, a couple of cycles of professional editing, and four more revisions later, and though we're into another crazy presidential election year, I'm hopeful that *this* will be the final draft. Hey, it could happen. However, as I return to this chapter, I'm hesitant about the title. Some people are uncomfortable with a male God, so I'd like to say something about this gender issue.

I believe the concept of gender has no meaning when applied to God. After all, God is spiritual, not biological with a defined anatomy. Also, as it says in Genesis, "God created mankind … male and female He created them." God created gender. God is above gender. Nevertheless, to make my writing task a bit easier, I'm going to stick with the male pronouns used in the Bible. I hope that's okay.

Now then, in looking at God, people typically consider Him from a purely human perspective—it's the only perspective we have. But that's the problem, for from that perspective, some cross a line when they start to see God as an image of themselves. The graffiti obscuring the true image of God comes from painting Him in our image, seeing God as a depiction of defective humans, applying typical human characteristics to a spiritual God. Yet, God is not an image of flawed humanity. We are flawed images of Him.

It's time to start setting up our base camp, where we'll prepare ourselves for the rest of the journey in search of Christian truth. First, I'll highlight some of the images-of-man graffiti concealing God, and then see what lies beneath. In uncovering the true image of God, we can begin to see ourselves as He hopes we will be, as He created us to be, in His image.

Hateful?

There are some so-called Christians who were frequently in the news a while back, flashing their brightly colored signs proclaiming, "God hates _____" (fill in the blank with any chosen target). Their core message was that God hates sinners and condemns them to hell. That's a lot of hate because, as the Bible says, all of us sin. Though God obviously despises sin, does He actually hate and condemn all sinners to hell? Here's how Jesus and Paul might answer that question:

> *"For God so loved the world, that He gave His only Son, so that everyone who believes in Him will not perish, but have eternal life. For God did not send the Son into the world to judge the world, but so that the world might be saved through Him." (John 3:16-17 NASB, emphasis added)*
>
> *"But God demonstrates his own love for us in this: While we were still sinners, Christ died for us." (Romans 5:8)*

Jesus died for us sinners because God loves us sinners. For those who declare that God hates and condemns all sinners to hell, they're denying Jesus and His sacrifice, and possibly painting God in their own image, splattering their hate onto Him.

However, the Bible does talk about God hating sinners, such as in Proverbs 6:16-19 and Psalm 5:4-6. Some so-called Christians take these verses as license for them to shout out that God hates a particular person or group of people. Yet I have two thoughts regarding this.

First, maybe it's possible for God to both love and hate the same person. Maybe God can love the good, and at the same time hate the evil and sin within a person. I've felt that odd combination of emotions, and if I can, God certainly can do even better.

Second, it's not up to me or anyone else to declare who God hates. That privilege is reserved for Him, and Him alone. For me to declare a particular person or group of people as an object of God's hate is an act of judgment. Maybe that's one reason so many outsiders view Christians as judgmental.

Harsh disciplinarian?

Some Christians blame God for the sufferings of others, claiming it's His discipline for their sins. That could be true, though only God knows for sure. However, the Bible says this about God's discipline:

> *"For they* [earthly fathers] *disciplined us for a short time as seemed best to them, but He* [God] *disciplines us for our good." (Hebrews 12:10 NASB)*

For some parents, disciplining their child is a way to make the parent feel good—they vent their anger and remind their ego who's boss. Yet with God, discipline has nothing to do with Him. God's discipline is for *our* good, like the parent who disciplines their child only in a way that will help develop their moral character.

But what about all the talk in the Bible about fearing God, seemingly painting an image of a harsh disciplinarian? Well, I feared my first stepfather because of his abuse. I also feared my second stepfather, though for different reasons. I feared him because I respected him, admired him, and loved him. I guess I feared disappointing him. There's a big difference between fear of abuse and fear motivated by love.

Yes, the advice in the Bible is to fear God, such as:

> *"The fear of the Lord is the beginning of wisdom." (Psalm 111:10 NRSV)*
>
> *"The fear of the Lord is the beginning of knowledge." (Proverbs 1:7 NRSV)*
>
> *"The Lord has compassion on those who fear Him." (Psalm 103:13 NASB)*

For a long time, this fear of the Lord talk confused me. Then I realized it's a fear motivated by love, trust, admiration, and respect. To fear God is to love God, and the Lord has compassion on those who love Him. Yet regarding those Christians who claim God punishes sinners as a way to inflict fear and vent His anger; this is simply another example of people painting God in their image.

Unforgiving?

Tom always sat quietly during the first part of our small group Bible study meetings, listening, thinking, and staring into his empty coffee cup. Eventually he'd join the conversation, and what he'd say was always interesting, well thought out, and often unexpected. Then one night he declared, "I know I'm not going to heaven. I've done too many bad things in my life. God can't forgive me. I'm just not good enough."

Tom was captive behind a wall of guilt constructed by a church he once belonged to. He didn't meet that church's standard for forgiveness—he just wasn't good enough … for them. However, the goodness Tom believed he lacked isn't defined by manmade standards and doesn't come from behavior. As Paul said:

> *"This righteousness* [goodness] *is given through faith in Jesus Christ to all who believe. There is no difference between Jew and Gentile, for all have sinned and fall short of the glory of God." (Romans 3:22-23)*

As far as God is concerned, faith is what matters, not past behavior. Regarding all those, like Tom, who carry the guilt and regret of past sins, to such repentance Jesus might say:

> *"I tell you that in the same way, there will be more joy in heaven over one sinner who repents than over ninety-nine righteous* [good] *people who have no need of repentance." (Luke 15:7 NASB)*

It may be natural to assume God's criteria for forgiveness is the same as our criteria. But again, God is not an image of us.

Playing favorites?

Some Christians insist God is a white man's God, as they try to squeeze Him into their white supremacy box. Others brag about receiving preferential treatment from God, implying that they're somehow special. Like those who see a God who has tough standards for forgiveness, some claim that God has similar standards for earning His love. Does God really show such favoritism? Paul might answer the question this way:

> *"He* [God] *who is both their Master and yours is in heaven, and there is no favoritism with him." (Ephesians 6:9)*

Clear enough. Also, Jesus said, "For God so loved *the world*, that He gave His only Son, so that *everyone* who believes in Him will not perish, but have eternal life" Other than the requirement for faith—which applies to everyone—there is no favoritism in that statement.

As my friend Tom couldn't understand, God loves those who believe in Him, no matter how dark their past. Yet, what if you *don't* believe? Will God love you anyway? Jesus talked a lot about loving others, like when He said,

> "Love your enemies, do good to those who hate you, bless those who curse you, pray for those who mistreat you. ... Do to others as you would have them do to you. If you love those who love you, what credit is that to you? Even sinners love those who love them." (Luke 6:27-28, 31-32)

Would Jesus tell us to do something He's not willing to do Himself? Would God love only those who love Him, yet expect us to love more? Look, God isn't stingy or selective with His love; He doesn't apply conditions to it. God loves everyone, no matter how they feel about Him, no matter what they believe.

Did I just light a fuse under some so-called Christians? Hey, I didn't light it. Jesus did.

Impersonal force?

On our family vacations when I was a kid, while cruising down the highway in our simulated wood paneled station wagon, my mom often got the urge to take a detour, and check out some sight she'd seen advertised on a passing sign. However, set on sticking to his planned route and schedule, my stepfather (the good one) would say, "We can't get there from here." He'd then look over his shoulder and wink at us kids.

My Christian friend Dave once told me that God feels like an unapproachable king, impersonal and inaccessible—we can't get there from here. A 2008 PEW survey shows that Dave's image of an impersonal king isn't uncommon:

> 19% of all Protestants and 29% of Catholics see God as an impersonal force. [1]

An impersonal force, aloof, inaccessible, sitting on His throne in some far-off palace, isolated from the world He created. Is that God? Is God some force glaring down at us mundane earthlings from His throne on high? After all, why should God dirty His hands with all the chaos going on down here in the trenches?

To those who see God as impersonal, Jesus and others might say,

> *"Anyone who loves me will obey my teaching. My Father will love them, and <u>we will come to them and make our home with them.</u>" (John 14:23, emphasis added)*
>
> *"The Lord is near to all who call on Him, to all who call on Him in truth." (Psalm 145:18 NASB)*
>
> *"If anyone acknowledges that Jesus is the Son of God, God lives in them and they in God." (1 John 4:15)*

God, our heavenly King, doesn't behave as human royalty might behave. Beneath the graffiti is a God who wants to live *in* us, making His home with us. That's definitely *not* an impersonal relationship.

Evil?

After my friend Dave joined the ranks of the de-churched, he once asked me, "How can God be good if He allows bad things to happen to good people?" I've wondered the same thing. If God is truly good and all-powerful, why is there so much bad and evil in the world? In looking for an answer to Dave's question, I found this:

> *"For My thoughts are not your thoughts, nor are your ways My ways," declares the Lord. "For as the heavens are higher than the earth, so are My ways higher than your ways and My thoughts than your thoughts." (Isaiah 55:8–9 NASB)*

What God is saying is that He's spiritual while we're mortal, and that ungodly mortals can't possibly understand all the ways of our spiritual God. We're like the young child who can't understand the rational thinking of their parents.

With all the evil in the world, it can be easy to picture God as either evil Himself, or someone who doesn't care about what goes on down here. Yet, God's words in Isaiah are His warning about considering Him from a purely human perspective, picturing Him as an image of us. Just because many humans are at times evil and uncaring, that doesn't mean God is.

In His image

When I talk about the image of God and seeing God as an image of flawed humans, rather than referring to a physical image, I'm referring to an image of personality and character. I guess you could call it a spiritual image. Now, the graffiti hiding the true image of God comes from looking at Him through a human lens, and seeing God with natural human character traits. I want to emphasize that God doesn't behave as we do, and thank God for that. We'd be doomed if He did.

Having scraped away some of the graffiti that obscures the truth about God, in the next chapter we'll look at more aspects of God's character and purpose that will add to our evolving image of Him. In seeing a truer image of God, we can begin to see ourselves as God created us to be, as children are an image of their parents. Finally, as John said:

> *"No one has ever seen God; but if we love one another, God lives in us and his love* [i.e., His image] *is made complete in us. This is how we know that we live in him and he in us: He has given us of his Spirit."* (1 John 4:12-13 NIV)

Yes, God created humanity in His image, and though that image has been disfigured by sin and the ways of the world, by God giving us of His Spirit, we can get His image back.

6. God's Purpose and Character

Why did God create humanity? What was His original purpose, that is, before His image in humanity became disfigured by the failure of Adam and Eve at the tree? And what's God's purpose now? I believe there's a relationship between purpose and character, and I believe knowing one helps you see the other. So, let's look at some of God's purposes and see where they lead us.

To be a loving parent

"What do you want for your birthday?" I asked my wife, giving myself two weeks to shop.

"I just want to be with my children," she replied. God and my wife have that in common.

As I mentioned near the end of the last chapter, Jesus said, "*My Father will love them, and we will come to them and make our home with them.*" My wife and I relish those times when we can be with our children. God feels the same way, and whether we feel the reality of it or not, we *are* God's children, and He *is* our Father. All we have to do is believe that…

> "I will be a Father to you, and you will be my sons and daughters, says the Lord Almighty." (2 Corinthians 6:18)
>
> "Yet to all who did receive him, to those who believed in his name, he gave the right to become children of God—children born not of natural descent, nor of human decision or a husband's will, but born of God." (John 1:12-13)
>
> "For those who are led by the Spirit of God are the children of God." (Romans 8:14)
>
> "See what great love the Father has lavished on us, that we should be called children of God!" (1 John 3:1)

So, what type of parent is God? By looking at carefully selected examples of human parents, we can see an image—though faded—of God as our Father.

First, consider the parents of three children I know. One child has Down Syndrome, another child is struggling with their sexual identity, and a third child keeps getting in trouble at school and with the police. Despite such things, in all cases the love the parents have for their children is undiminished by their child's condition or behavior.

Closer to home, I was a challenge for my parents. For example, as a young boy, I once nailed my blankets and sheets to my dresser, the walls, anything in my bedroom that would hold a nail. It was the most awesome tent ever. Then one night, several years later, I blew up a neighbor's mailbox with a barrel bomb—I had accomplices, but I was the one who got caught. Still, it was so cool how all the rivets blew out, leaving the swollen shell still perched on the post. Although my mom was always disappointed and usually angry with my pranks, I never doubted her love for me.

As children of God, we're all suffering from the disability and struggles associated with our sinful human nature. Yet like the parents in my examples, our Father God loves us and accepts us just as we are. Some parents are great at such love—God is even better.

Finally, the Apostle John once referred to God in this way: *"God is love. Whoever lives in love lives in God, and God in them"* (1 John 4:16). Since God is love, by replacing one word in Paul's definition of love, we begin to see a vivid portrait of our heavenly Father, and His love:

> "**God** is patient, **God** is kind. **God** does not envy, **He** does not boast, **He** is not proud. **God** is not rude, **He** is not self-seeking, **He** is not easily angered, **He** keeps no record of wrongs. **God** does not delight in evil but rejoices with the truth. **God** always protects, always trusts, always hopes, always perseveres. **God** never fails." (1 Corinthians 13:4-8, "love" replaced with "God" and "He")

To bring about justice

My law-breaking half-brother first went to jail in his late teens and spent most of his remaining years in prison. He went to prison to pay a penalty, to fulfill the requirement for justice. Without justice, there's chaos, such as sometimes happens in cities that are lenient on criminals.

Now then, if one of God's purposes is to bring us home to live with Him in heaven after we die, why not just do it? Why the need for faith, forgiveness, and all the rest? Well, for all our sins, someone must pay a penalty or there's no justice, and as God said,

> "For I, the Lord, love justice." (Isaiah 61:8 NASB)

The amazing, and very un-human, aspect of Christianity and God's justice is that we don't' pay the penalty for our own sins. God's chosen one for bringing about justice is His Son, as He foretold in Isaiah:

> "Behold, My Servant, whom I uphold; My chosen one in whom My soul delights. I have put My Spirit upon Him; He will bring forth justice to the nations. ... He will faithfully bring forth justice. He will not be disheartened or crushed until He has established justice on the earth." (Isaiah 42:1, 3-4 NASB)

By Jesus' sacrifice on the cross, He fulfilled God's purpose for justice. However, though Jesus paid the penalty for the sins of humanity, and though this is a foundational truth of Christianity, it seems to be often forgotten by some churches. I wonder why. Regardless, how God chose to fulfill the need for justice tells us a lot about God's forgiveness.

To forgive us

My stepmother never gave up on my imprisoned brother. Her forgiveness and love for him kept her returning for those painful prison visits. Yet is it possible for my stepmother to love and forgive more than God?

Consider the story of the prodigal son, in some ways like my criminal brother, where the father in the story represents God. Jesus tells us that the rebellious run-away son eventually decided to return home to his father: *"So he got up and went to his father. But while he was still a long way off, his father saw him and was filled with compassion for him; he ran to his son, threw his arms around him and kissed him"* (Luke 15:20). The father acted as if his son had never rebelled. That's how God reacts to children who return to Him, for as God said:

> "I, I alone, am the one who wipes out your wrongdoings for My own sake, <u>and I will not remember your sins</u>." (Isaiah 43:25 NASB, emphasis added)

Will not remember your sins—that's forgiveness.

There've been times when the vast size of God's forgiveness left me wondering about the need for justice. I mean, why not forgive us our sins and leave out the punishment inflicted upon His Son? Then I realized that God's forgiveness takes the form of God's justice. You can't have one without the other. God forgives us by having Jesus pay the penalty for our sins, and with the penalty paid, God then looks at us and sees us as if we've never sinned.

To protect us

We were at a high school reunion picnic and my 2-year-old son was running around on the grass, giggling and often falling on the spongy turf. He then scampered straight for a portion of the lawn where a retaining wall dropped down to a road about a foot below the edge of the grass. I started running, and just as my son got to the drop-off, I scooped him up as I leapt off the retaining wall. Landing and slowing to a stop, I swung my son to my chest, wrapped him in my arms, and squeezed. He was giggling all the way, unaware how close he came to a face-plant on asphalt.

Even today I cringe, thinking about how that might have turned out. Yet the idea of getting hurt never occurred to my son, because he'd grown up relying on my wife and me to protect him from harm. He never had reason to doubt our love and protection. God wants to be that kind of parent, scooping us out of harm's way while we may never know the danger we're heading for.

Like the morning Rob, Bryce, and I were on our way to a work-related event. Rob was driving, Bryce was riding shotgun, and I sat in the backseat behind Bryce, munching on a bagel. The two-lane highway wound through the hills of northern California, with vineyards on both sides. The grape leaves were turning color in the chill and damp fall air. Then, for some reason, I turned my head and looked out the side window and saw nothing but … *dirt!? What the—*

My rattled brain soon caught up a bit with reality, and I realized the car was laying on its side, as was I, with my right shoulder pressing against the window. *Umm, I believe we've been in an accident,* my mind mumbled. I took a quick inventory and, other than a pain in my ribs where my body had slammed into the seatbelt buckle, I felt fine. I looked up to see Rob suspended in his seatbelt, fumbling with something, white dust floating in the air (I later realized the dust was from the airbags). *Oh, this is interesting*, I thought. With my brain still on slow, I glanced up at the left-side passenger door, now above me, and said to myself, *Hey, I'll just push that door open and climb out the top, like something I've seen in the movies. Cool.*

Then, "Bryce, you okay?" Rob asked. No answer. *Oh sh#*. Umm, that's right. We've been in an accident! Bryce, you okay?* Several seconds went by … then, "Yah, I think so." Bryce's delay was because the passenger airbag had knocked the air out of him. We all compared notes, and it seemed we were basically okay.

A car coming from the other direction had swerved into our lane, and if it hadn't been for Rob's quick reactions, it would have been a direct head-on collision. As it was, the near head-on, with the other car slamming into our front-left quarter panel, was bad enough. The impact sent Rob's car into a ditch.

After the paramedics arrived, they seemed shocked as they examined us. One of them said that by the looks of the wreck, we should all be going to the hospital. But all they could do was treat some cuts from broken glass and send us on our way (Rob had called a co-worker to come get us).

As stated in my altered version of Paul's definition of love, "God always protects." But, really? Though I believe that God has indeed protected me from harm at times in my life, like with that car accident, clearly He doesn't protect everyone from all harm. And I'm not sure why. It's just one of those things about God that I accept.

One thing I feel certain about though is this: God *wants* to protect us from all harm, just like a loving parent wants to protect their children from all harm. And as a loving parent may reluctantly launch their adult child out into the world, where the parent can't always protect them, God has sent us out into the world.

Back to the purpose question

I never understood the sadness until my own children were grown and out on their own. But giving me a preview of coming emotions, my mom showed me how sad she would become every time I left home after a weekend visit. I thought she was being overly emotional. I now share her feelings whenever my sons leave after a visit home.

My wife and I miss those days when our sons lived at home; we miss the closeness, and being a part of each other's lives. My purposes in my relationships with my sons have evolved as they've grown from babies into men. However, one thing that never changes is my overwhelming desire to be with them and to show my love for them.

God is patient, kind, compassionate, humble, unbiased, all-forgiving, and protective—such is God's character. God's primary purpose, the one that His character and other purposes point to, is to live *with* us and express His unconditional love for us. God's purpose is to have His children return home. As Jesus said, *"and we will come to them and make our home with them."* And God makes a way for us to return, to the way it was in the beginning, before Adam and Eve were kicked out of the Garden of Eden. As Andrew Murray said:

> "When God established the plan of redemption, His objective was to restore man to the place from which he had fallen." [1]

To restore us to the place from which humanity had fallen, to bring His children back home—this is what salvation, God's ultimate purpose, is all about.

> "My Father's will is that everyone who looks to the Son and believes in him shall have eternal life, and I will raise them up at the last day." (John 6:40)
>
> "For God has destined us not for wrath but for obtaining salvation through our Lord Jesus Christ." (1 Thessalonians 5:9 NRSV)

7. Son of God

In my effort to reveal an undistorted image of Jesus, I'll begin by discussing His identification as God's only begotten Son. Realizing that some who followed Him were uncertain about His identity, Jesus asked His disciples who they believed He was:

> "He said to them, 'But who do you say that I am?' Simon Peter answered, 'You are the Messiah, the Son of the living God.'" (Matthew 16:15-16 NRSV)

That's clear. Looking further, I saw something curious, something I hadn't noticed before. Once, as Jesus was approaching a demon-possessed man, the demon of Satan shouted out to Him, *"What do you want with me, Jesus, Son of the Most High God?"* (Mark 5:7). That's only one of several episodes in the Bible where Satan declared, through demon-possessed people, that Jesus is the Son of God. Though I don't think we should take the word of Satan, it's noteworthy.

Now, what do Jesus and God have to say?

> "And they all said, 'So You are the Son of God?' And He [Jesus] said to them, "You say correctly that I am." (Luke 22:70 NASB)
>
> "And a voice from heaven said, 'This is my Son, whom I love; with him I am well pleased.'" (Matthew 3:17)

Yet Jesus is more than the Son of God. When He walked the earth, He was both fully God and fully human. As John and Paul said:

> "In the beginning was the Word [i.e., Jesus], and the Word was with God, and the Word was God. ... And the Word became flesh and lived among us." (John 1:1, 14 NRSV)
>
> "For in Christ all the fullness of the Deity lives in bodily form." (Colossians 2:9)

Isaiah prophesied about Jesus this way:

> *"For to us a child is born, to us a son is given ... And he will be called Wonderful Counselor, Mighty God, Everlasting Father, Prince of Peace." (Isaiah 9:6)*

Son, Counselor, God, Father, Prince—sounds like the fullness of the Deity to me. However, even though Jesus was God in flesh, He didn't acknowledge His Godly side; He didn't call Himself the Son of God. Instead, He usually referred to Himself as the *Son of Man*. Maybe He emphasized His humanity because He foresaw people valuing only His divinity.

I believe that by accepting Jesus' human side, it's easier to relate to Him. His divine side can feel mysterious and intimidating. Also, to appreciate the gravity of Jesus' death on the cross, I think we need to accept both His divinity *and* his humanity. His death would mean less if He hadn't been fully human.

Before discussing His death, let's get a better understanding of Jesus and His reasons for coming to earth in the first place? I mean, just look around at what's going on in this world. Now imagine you lived in a better world, one that didn't suffer from the chaos and problems we suffer from. Would you want to come here?

To testify to the truth

The Son of God confined Himself to a human body for about 33 years, living as a peasant, dying as a criminal, enduring the most painful torture Roman soldiers could dream up. Why'd He go through it all? Why did He leave His home in paradise for the painful and filthy trenches of humanity? The answers begin with what I'm searching for … the truth.

> *"The law indeed was given through Moses; grace and truth came through Jesus Christ." (John 1:17 NRSV)*
>
> [Jesus said,] *"In fact, the reason I was born and came into the world is to testify to the truth. Everyone on the side of truth listens to me." (John 18:37)*

By the time Jesus jumped into the trenches, the ancient religious graffiti artists had put a lot of work into painting over God's truth with their manmade rules and traditions. Jesus came to earth to scrape off that graffiti and reveal God's truth. Yet, sometime after Jesus returned to heaven, new graffiti artists kicked into action, painting over Jesus' truth with their own image of Christianity. They've been painting away ever since. However, though Jesus's truth often appears to be hidden, everyone on the side of truth will go looking for it.

This reminds me of when I was in grammar school, where our favorite place to play hide-and-seek was the old cemetery up on the hill, amid the forest of eucalyptus trees. In the early evening, dense fog crept over the coastal hills, swallowing up the cemetery as it went. The fright-level was fantastic, especially as it began to get dark.

In the middle of the cemetery was a large statue we used as base. I'd hide behind a tree or gravestone, far from the statue though still within sight. When the kid who was "it" left the statue and went searching in the other direction, I'd scamper from one gravestone to the next, working my way toward the statue. If I got to the statue before "it" spotted me, I was safe.

I didn't see the symbolism in what we were doing until several decades later, when I remembered that our base was a statue of Jesus. Jesus came to earth to be our base, our source of truth, our safe harbor in the midst of this crazy, truth-starved world. And though Jesus has returned to heaven, His truth remains.

For love and compassion

The Jesus some of us imagine is the Hollywood Jesus: stoic, mild mannered, soft-spoken, somewhat dull and emotionless. Yet as the stories in the Bible make clear, Jesus was no otherworldly droid, immune to human emotions and pain, shuffling about dispensing miracles.

Jesus was a man who wept, like when He saw two sisters mourning the death of their brother, (Lazarus, in John 11:17-44). He suffered His own pain of loss with the murder of His cousin, John the Baptist. Jesus tried to escape to a quiet place to mourn, but being a celebrity, He couldn't dodge the crowds who followed Him. These people needed Him, and they begged Him for help. Instead of focusing on His own needs, Jesus gave the people the compassion they needed, (Matthew 14:1-23).

Then there's a story about a man suffering from leprosy: *"While Jesus was in one of the towns, a man came along who was covered with leprosy. When he saw Jesus, he fell with his face to the ground and begged him, 'Lord, if you are willing, you can make me clean'"* (Luke 5:12). Those stricken with leprosy were outcasts. People would have avoided this man. It may have been years since someone had touched him, since a hand had rested on his shoulder in a moment of comfort. "Lord, if you are willing, you can make me clean," he said to Jesus. He didn't doubt Jesus' ability, only His willingness to heal him. It had been that long since this man felt kindness and compassion from another person.

We know from other stories that Jesus could have instantly healed the man with a simple command, like "be healed." However, Jesus did something different. He did something radical. Jesus first gave the man what he needed most.

Picture the man on his knees with his face to the ground, perhaps afraid to look up, perhaps afraid he'd see Jesus turn His back on him and walk away. Now picture Jesus kneeling down in front of the man, and then … *"Jesus reached out his hand and touched the man"* (verse 13). I like to picture Jesus gently squeezing the man's shoulder, followed by the man tentatively lifting his head and looking up. Seeing the compassion in Jesus' face and feeling it in the hand on his shoulder, tears well up in the man's eyes, run down his leprosy-scarred cheeks and into his beard.

The point is, for the first time in perhaps years, another person touched this lonely, outcast of a human being. Jesus gave the man what he needed most—love and compassion. In the midst of the emotion swelling within the man, Jesus then said, *"I am willing. Be clean,"* and the man was immediately healed of leprosy.

To set us free

Some modern churches preach that Jesus came to condemn those who don't follow the rules, God's *and* their rules. Now, Jesus indeed came to condemn, but not us rule-breakers. As John said,

> "The reason the Son of God appeared was to destroy the devil's work." (1 John 3:8)

Satan has long held potent influence over humanity. He's the designer of false Christianity, the author of all lies, the patron of the graffiti hiding God's truth. Jesus came to condemn Satan, destroy his work, and set us free from Satan's influence. Isaiah foresaw this when he stated that Jesus would come … *"to open the eyes that are blind, to bring out the prisoners from the dungeon, from the prison those who sit in darkness"* (Isaiah 42:7 NRSV).

Imagine all humanity held captive in a dark prison, where Satan is the warden. We're blinded by Satan's lightless influence. Most people don't know that they're prisoners, because they don't realize that there's another world out there. All most of us know is this chaotic prison-world we live in, when all along God offers another option.

Now, Jesus didn't come to condemn us *because* of our captivity. Rather, He came to open our eyes and free us *from* our captivity. As Jesus said of Himself:

> "The Spirit of the Lord is upon me, because he has anointed me to bring good news to the poor. He has sent me to proclaim release to the captives and recovery of sight to the blind, to let the oppressed go free," (Luke 4:18 NRSV)
>
> "For God did not send the Son into the world to judge the world, but so that the world might be saved through Him." (John 3:17 NASB)

Jesus came to testify to the truth, and it's His truth that opens our eyes and sets us free. *"Then you will know the truth, and the truth will set you free"* (John 8:32). For Christians, I think it's important to also realize that manmade Christianity with all its variations is another aspect of the Satan-inspired prison, where Jesus' Christianity offers us freedom.

To be our friend

I haven't always started my day relaxing in my home office waiting for the coffee to take effect. Many years ago, I had a different morning routine, followed with a finely tuned lack of enthusiasm. Before the sun was up, I'd be contorting myself into a weight-training machine at a nearby gym.

One morning, as I sat considering laying my head down on the machine's arm pad, my eyes drifted to a young man gliding into a machine across from me. I didn't recognize him. He seemed peaceful and even joyful, unlike the usual early morning gym crowd. Then he looked at me as if he knew me. He wasn't going to talk to me, was he? Oh no, what was that he said? "Is Jesus your best friend?" Seriously? You ask me *that*, in the midst of all this clanging steel and dripping sweat, none of it coming from me, by the way.

I didn't know Jesus well at the time, however, I said yes. I was afraid the truth would spawn an evangelistic sales pitch, and I couldn't handle that at 6:00am in a gym. Thankfully my *yes*, quickly followed by my exaggerated efforts to work the machine, excused me from a sunrise sermon.

For me, that story represents a step in my journey, a step which led me to eventually realize that where God wants us to be His children, Jesus wants us to be His friend. As He said,

> "No one has greater love than this, to lay down one's life for one's friends. You are my friends if you do what I command you. I do not call you servants any longer, because the servant does not know what the master is doing; but I have called you friends." (John 15:13-15 NRSV)

Once, in responding to a snide remark from some religious leaders, Jesus said, *"The Son of Man came eating and drinking, and they* [the religious leaders] *say, 'Here is a glutton and a drunkard, a friend of tax collectors and sinners'"* (Matthew 11:19). Did Jesus deny it? His next words were, *"But wisdom is proved right by her deeds."* Jesus is a friend of sinners, our *best* friend, the kind of friend who would die for us, and *did* die for us.

In His image

As Gandhi once said, *"I love Christ. It's just that so many of you Christians are so unlike Christ."* Maybe another reason Jesus came to earth was to show us what it looks like to be a human image of God. Not to give us a goal to work toward, because we can't possibly get there on our own. Rather, Jesus came to show us how far off we are and convince us that, if we want to be an image of Him—and thus return to our originally-created image of God—we'll need His help. And help is just what He sent us.

Before getting to that, I still have a question. In coming down here to the trenches, why did Jesus subject Himself to the torture of a flogging and crucifixion? I've saved for last perhaps the most important purpose that motivated God to send His Son to the battlefront. Everything is pointing to the cross, and as I've come to learn, more than Jesus hung on that cross.

8. Why the Cross?

Jesus Christ, the friend of sinners, laid down His life for His friends, and what He subjected Himself to was vicious. Before nailing Jesus to a cross, Roman soldiers first flogged Him. Once on the cross—

No. I don't want to go there. Though I think it's important to understand and appreciate what Jesus went through, my question is, why. Why couldn't God forgive us and leave out the torture of His Son? Why couldn't Jesus be our friend without dying for us? Yes, I know, there's the requirement for justice—the penalty for all sins had to be paid. But my understanding of justice-by-crucifixion felt sketchy. So, I went looking for a clearer image of the meaning of the Cross.

Justice revisited

I was working in the garage on a sunny spring day, while my 5-year-old son played on the lawn with his neighbor friend. I stepped out of the garage to check on the boys—they weren't there. Movement drew my eyes to a house across the street. There they were, plastering mud on the house's garage door. A dark brown line covered the light tan door from about a foot off the ground to as high as their little hands could reach.

After I got over my bewilderment, calmed myself down, and consulted with my wife, our son was punished. On top of having to help clean the garage door, he was restricted from playing with his mud-slinging friend. Our son's friend didn't receive similar consequences. Instead, his mom yelled at him and confined him to the house for the rest of the day—no real discipline, no meaningful consequences. Mainly anger.

Other than the fact that God requires it, why is justice so important? Well, if you only yell at a misbehaving child, the message they receive is that there are no constructive consequences for misbehavior, and little motivation to change behavior. There's just temporary anger. That's no way to build character in a child.

God, as our heavenly parent, understands the need for consequences. For the benefit of His children, there must be justice. As Isaiah said,

> "The Lord longs to be gracious to you, and therefore He waits on high to have compassion on you. For the Lord is a God of justice." (Isaiah 30:18 NASB)

Notice how Isaiah uses the words compassion and justice in the same reference to God. Is he telling us that God-like justice is a form of compassion? Or maybe, God's justice is carried out with compassion.

Anyway, as I see it there are three steps to effective discipline and justice. Step 1 is the crime, or sin. Step 2, and the step often neglected in our society, is the acceptance that a wrong was committed, leading to a sincere feeling of remorse. Without remorse, a penalty won't provide any benefit, and may even make matters worse. Therefore, God won't take you to step 3 until you first show remorse, that is, repent.

Step 3 is the penalty or punishment, which Jesus has already taken upon Himself, on our behalf. However, the punishment He endured isn't credited to us until we first accept both His punishment and our guilt, and then express sincere sorrow for our sins. We aren't truly forgiven until we complete step 2.

Yet notice that God's justice isn't borne out of anger, but rather out of compassion and love. It's a love so powerful that it transfers the punishment due us to His Son. And God's justice, along with Jesus' sacrifice, is executed in a way to encourage us to admit our guilt and feel sincere remorse. It's God's love—the foundation of His justice—along with Jesus' sacrifice on our behalf, which are the best motivators for repentance. Understanding God's love, Jesus' sacrifice, and Their desire to forgive helps feed our desire to complete step 2.

Now I want to make a slight modification to my 3-step process. God's path to justice is as follows: 1. Our sin; 2. Our faith and remorse; 3. God's *forgiveness*. Forgiveness is the fulfillment of God's justice, since the punishment has already been carried out. Thanks to Jesus and His sacrifice, God's forgiveness is God's justice—they are one and the same.

And it's all because of love …

> "This is how God showed his love among us: He sent his one and only Son into the world that we might live through him. This is love: not that we loved God, but that he loved

> us and sent his Son as an atoning sacrifice for our sins." (1 John 4:9-10)

I've sometimes wondered if another reason Jesus died for our sins was to earn our gratitude and love. I suppose that's possible. However, the cross wasn't just a means to earn *our* love for Him. Rather, Jesus died that way because of *His* unearned love for us.

Again, why the Cross?

Still, why did the need for justice have to include Jesus' death? Couldn't a lessor penalty have sufficed? All the Hollywood movies told me was that, for reasons never clear, the Romans wanted to kill Jesus. I learned differently once I started reading the Bible. Though the New Testament holds the story of Jesus' death, I needed to go back to the Old Testament to see the reason.

Among other things, the Old Testament contains God's laws and the penalties for breaking those laws. Chapter 20 of Leviticus declares some of the penalties. They seem harsh to our modern views, with death being the punishment for several acts that are commonplace and readily accepted these days. For some of us, our past and present behavior has earned such death sentences, which have seemingly been ignored by God. Nevertheless, the penalties are still real and unavoidable, or there will be no justice. After all, there must be consequences, right? Yet I found what appeared to be a pardon when God said,

> "I have swept away your transgressions like a cloud, and your sins like mist; return to me, for I have redeemed you." (Isaiah 44:22 NRSV)

Through Isaiah, God later clarifies that He's not talking about a typical pardon, where the punishment is waived. Rather, He laid the penalties due us upon someone else:

> "He was pierced for our offenses, he was crushed for our wrongdoings; the punishment for our well-being was laid upon Him, and by His wounds we are healed. All of us, like sheep, have gone astray, each of us has turned to his own way; but the Lord has caused the wrongdoing of us all to fall

> on Him. ... because He poured out His life unto death, and was counted with wrongdoers; yet He Himself bore the sin of many, and interceded for the wrongdoers." (Isaiah 53:5-6, 12 NASB)

Isaiah was prophesying about Jesus, and Jesus was talking about Himself when He said:

> "...just as the Son of Man did not come to be served, but to serve, and to give His life as a ransom for many." (Matthew 20:28 NASB)
>
> "This is my blood of the covenant, which is poured out for many for the forgiveness of sins." (Matthew 26:28)

Peter added his voice, even quoting a bit from Isaiah:

> "For Christ also suffered for sins once for all, the righteous for the unrighteous, in order to bring you to God." (1 Peter 3:18 NRSV)
>
> "He himself bore our sins in his body on the cross, so that, free from sins, we might live for righteousness; by his wounds you have been healed." (1 Peter 2:24 NRSV)

If you or I commit a sin where the Old Testament penalty is death, Jesus already paid that penalty with His own death. And again, for His payment to be credited to us, all we need do is believe in it, and feel sincere regret.

Finally, some people think Jesus died only for those who believe in Him. That's like loving only those who love you first. Yet as Jesus said, *"If you love those who love you, what credit is that to you? Even sinners love those who love them"* (Luke 6:32). Jesus takes His own advice and loves everyone, even His enemies. And He showed His love for everyone by dying for everyone:

> "Jesus Christ the righteous; and he is the atoning sacrifice for our sins, and not for ours only but also for the sins of the whole world." (1 John 2:1-2 NRSV)

> "For the love of Christ urges us on, because we are convinced that one has died for all; therefore all have died." (2 Corinthians 5:14 NRSV)

Jesus *died for all*—that's a powerful truth that seems to be missing from some segments of manmade Christianity.

More than justice

In addition to justice, Jesus may have had another purpose in mind when He allowed His enemies to nail Him to the cross. I'll try to explain with an illustration, admittedly an "abbey normal" illustration.

Near the end of the movie *Young Frankenstein*, Doctor Frankenstein strapped his deranged monster and himself to Hollywood-gothic laboratory tables. Igor threw a series of switches (though, "not the third switch!"), electricity crackled, sparks flew, and the aggravated machinery transferred a portion of the doctors' goodness into his delinquent creation. The machinery also transferred something from the monster to the doctor.

We're God's delinquent creation. He allowed His Son to be nailed to the cross for the great exchange. God then transferred our sin to Jesus, and Jesus' righteousness to us. Our righteousness had to come from Jesus, for there's been no other human who was truly and completely righteous.

> "God made him who had no sin to be sin for us, so that in him we might become the righteousness of God." (2 Corinthians 5:21)
>
> "This righteousness is given through faith in Jesus Christ to all who believe." (Romans 3:22)

Remember the story I told in the last chapter about how Jesus healed the leper who had said, "Lord, if you are willing, you can make me clean." I now look at that story as a foretelling of what Jesus did for all of us when He died for us. He was willing to make us *all* clean, clean of sin, by exchanging his cleanliness for our sinfulness. Is this exchange of righteousness for sin new to you? It was to me. Maybe ponder it a bit.

Love hung on that cross

The night before Roman soldiers nailed Him to the cross, Jesus looked to His disciples and, *"He said to them, 'My soul is overwhelmed with sorrow to the point of death. Stay here and keep watch with me'"* (Matthew 26:38). While praying just moments before His arrest, *"and being in agony, He was praying very fervently; and His sweat became like drops of blood, falling down upon the ground"* (Luke 22:44 NASB).

With Google's help, I learned there's a medical condition called hematidrosis where, due to extreme stress, blood vessels can burst and the blood then mixes with sweat. Perhaps Jesus was suffering from such stress. And I suspect that in addition to the pain of physical torture and death, Jesus may have dreaded what waited for Him within the captivity of that death.

Several hours prior to that stressful moment, while praying Jesus said, *"I pray also for those who will believe in me through their message, that all of them may be one, Father, just as you are in me and I am in you ... that they may be one as we are one"* (John 17:20-22). "As you are in me and I am in you." As Jesus prayed these words, He knew that soon, for the first time in eternity, He and His Father would not be together, not be one. The death penalty Jesus was about to pay included separation from God—a definition of hell.

Jesus and God became separated so that those who believe could be united with God, "that they may be one as we are one." There's no greater love than the love God and Jesus showed for us by their mutual sacrifice. As Jesus said:

> "For God so loved the world, that He gave His only Son ..." (John 3:16 NASB, emphasis added)

Once, when I was helping with our church youth group, one of the kids shared a saying he'd heard: "Nails didn't hold Jesus to the cross—love did."

> "This is how we know what love is: Jesus Christ laid down his life for us." (1 John 3:16)

It is finished

According to the Apostle John, as Jesus hung on the cross His final words were, *"It is finished."* Jesus may have been referring to multiple things, though *it* likely also includes Satan's reign on earth and his hold on souls. As I mentioned in the last chapter, *"The reason the Son of God appeared was to destroy the devil's work"* (1 John 3:8).

I suspect that Satan, being the promoter of all sin, was delighted with the knowledge that the penalty for sin is hell. Maybe Satan had expected *all* humanity to end up as subjects of his kingdom. However, when Jesus paid the death penalty Himself, Satan's future kingdom was greatly reduced.

Oh sure, Satan can still have influence over our lives. Yet he no longer rules over our fate—his power over our fate *is finished*. By Jesus' death, He wrested our fate away from Satan, freeing us from Satan's grip. As the writer of Hebrews said,

> "Since the children have flesh and blood, he too shared in their humanity so that by his death he might break the power of him who holds the power of death—that is, the devil—and free those who all their lives were held in slavery by their fear of death." (Hebrews 2:14-15)

Thanks to Jesus, our fate is now in our hands.

The cross and the promise

Shortly before His death on the cross, Jesus said to His disciples,

> "I am sending upon you what my Father promised." (Luke 24:49 NRSV)
>
> "But I tell you the truth: it is to your advantage that I am leaving; for if I do not leave, the Helper will not come to you; but if I go, I will send Him to you." (John 16:7 NASB)

Jesus' death wasn't the finale, for death and hell couldn't hold Him captive. As Peter said of Jesus, *"He was put to death in the flesh, but made alive in the spirit" (1 Peter 3:18 NRSV).*

As a human, Jesus could teach His followers with only His personal example and spoken words, and His reach was limited to only those physically close to Him. The Holy Spirit has no such limits. With the death of Jesus, the promised Holy Spirit was poured out onto all who believe. As God said,

> *"I will pour out My Spirit on your offspring, and My blessing on your descendants." (Isaiah 44:3 NASB)*

Yet, if you feel slightly confused at this point, know that neither intellect nor emotions will fully open your mind to the realities and truths of God, Jesus, and Christianity. Only the Holy Spirit can do that. As Jesus said,

> *"I have much more to say to you, more than you can now bear. But when he, the Spirit of truth, comes, he will guide you into all truth." (John 16:12-13)*

9. The Spirit of Truth

In my early churchgoing years, I pictured Jesus in heaven, no longer involved in the battle down here in the trenches. He'd done His tour of duty and was now sitting out the rest of the war. I never gave much thought to the Holy Spirit, as the only times it was mentioned in church was in prayers or songs that included *Father, Son, and Holy Ghost*. Looking back to the survey results at the end of chapter 3, the Holy Spirit's the only member of the Trinity who's not mentioned in the list of priorities for being Christian. Is the Holy Spirit also sitting out the war?

The Holy Spirit is a facet of God who's often more mystery than reality. For a long time, I ignored the Holy Spirit, considering it a third-rate entity, the silent partner of the Holy Trinity. However, who was I ignoring? Well, according to Paul:

> "Now the Lord is the Spirit, and where the Spirit of the Lord is, there is freedom." (2 Corinthians 3:17 NRSV)
>
> "God sent the Spirit of his Son into our hearts." (Galatians 4:6)
>
> "You, however, are not in the realm of the flesh but are in the realm of the Spirit, if indeed <u>the Spirit of God</u> lives in you. And if anyone does not have <u>the Spirit of Christ</u>, they do not belong to Christ." (Romans 8:9, emphasis added)

So, the Holy Spirit is both the Spirit of God and the Spirit of Jesus—not someone I want to ignore. But wait! What about that last sentence in Romans 8:9? Is Paul saying that anyone who ignores the Holy Spirit isn't a true Christian? Hmm, that could explain a lot.

Ignoring that volatile question (for now), what's the Holy Spirit do, what's His purpose? The third member of the Holy Trinity must have some kind of holy purpose, right? As I quoted Jesus at the end of the last chapter, the Spirit will guide us into all truth, which is something we could all use more of these days. As if that's not enough, there's this promise from Paul:

> *"You were sealed in Him* [Jesus] *with the Holy Spirit of the promise, who is a first installment of our inheritance." (Ephesians 1:13-14 NASB)*

A first installment of our inheritance? What inheritance? Does life with the Spirit here on earth give us a preview of the life waiting for us with God in heaven? Again, that's not something I want to ignore. With all that's going on in this crazy world, I could use some heaven-on-earth right now.

Anyway, when Jesus returned to heaven, I suspect He knew that those He left in charge needed help, or His budding Church would wither and die. Attacks against Christianity began immediately, and enemies soon included the Roman Empire. Therefore, Jesus sent His Spirit to help protect His newborn Church. Some people believe that once Christianity survived those initial attacks and gained strength, the Spirit walked away from the battle. Yet, as Jesus said,

> *"I will ask the Father, and He will give you another Helper, <u>so that He may be with you forever</u>; the Helper is the Spirit of truth." (John 14:16-17 NASB, emphasis added)*

The Holy Spirit hasn't abandoned the war. He's still in the trenches, for those willing to look for Him. And while down here on the battlefield, the Spirit has a mission, a purpose. Let's look at that purpose.

Spirit of unity

Shortly before Jesus' death, He prayed for unity: *"... that they may be brought to complete unity"* (John 17:23). The "they" Jesus referred to is everyone who believes in Him:

> *"My prayer is not for them* [apostles] *alone. I pray also for those who will believe in me through their message, that all of them may be one, Father, just as you are in me and I am in you." (John 17:20-21)*

Notice that Jesus wasn't praying for the unity of a shared membership in a church, or even shared doctrines. He was praying for something deeper, greater, and more powerful. Jesus was praying for a unity of shared spiritual intimacy, just as He has with God, *"...that they may be one as we are one"* (verse 22).

Paul said, *"Make every effort to keep the unity of the Spirit through the bond of peace"* (Ephesians 4:3, emphasis added). If the Spirit is within you and me, then His presence makes a connection between the two of us. Using an image Jesus drew, it's like the Spirit is a vine, and believers are the branches connected to that vine. The vine connects all branches to each other. That's the unity of the Spirit, the unity Jesus prayed for.

Spirit of fruitfulness

> [Jesus said,] *"I am the vine; you are the branches. If you remain in me and I in you, you will bear much fruit; apart from me you can do nothing." (John 15:5)*

Beyond establishing Christian unity, our attachment to the Spirit of Jesus gives us the ability to bear fruit. As Jesus emphasizes, this fruit isn't limited to small things:

> *"If you remain in me and my words remain in you, ask whatever you wish, and it will be given you. This is to my Father's glory, that you bear much fruit, showing yourselves to be my disciples." (John 15:7-8, emphasis added)*

Being connected to the vine of the Spirit, you can bear the fruit of the Spirit, which Paul defined as:

> *"The fruit of the Spirit is love, joy, peace, patience, kindness, generosity, faithfulness, gentleness and self-control." (Galatians 5:22-23 NRSV)*

But, self-control … seriously?

Spirit of self-control

I'd read it before, though never in a coffee shop. With my medium coffee in hand—being a bit of a rebel, I refuse to say Grande, or whatever they call it—I plopped down at a table and opened my Bible to chapter 7 of Paul's letter to the

Romans. He was complaining about himself: *"I do not understand my own actions. For I do not do what I want, but I do the very thing I hate. ... I can will what is right, but I cannot do it. For I do not do the good I want, but the evil I do not want is what I do. ... Wretched man that I am! Who will rescue me from this body of death?"* (Romans 7:15, 18-19,24 NRSV). Sound familiar? It does to me.

Often in my relationships with God and others, I know what I want to do, *but I cannot do it.* Not enough self-control. Who will rescue me from my wretched self-out-of-control? Here's how Paul began to answer his own question:

> "The mind governed by the flesh is death, but the mind governed by the Spirit is life and peace. ... You, however, are not in the realm of the flesh but are in the realm of the Spirit, if indeed the Spirit of God lives in you." (Romans 8:6, 9)

While in grammar school, my friend Gary let me ride his mini motorcycle. Gary sat behind me while I took *control* (yah, right). I followed a dirt track over rises and through dips, with twists and turns and loose gravel, and I lost control, and we ended up in a pond. Really.

For me, that is a good picture of life. There are twists, turns, dips, temptations, frustrations, hardships, etc., and sometimes we lose control. Sometimes we crash. Yet we have a choice. Instead of trying to govern ourselves and steer ourselves through life, we could give the Holy Spirit control and let Him drive. We could then sit back, wrap our arms around Him, relax, and enjoy the ride. However, the Spirit won't take control—I must surrender it to Him. Until I do, He'll take the backseat and patiently wait for me to accept that I'm a wretched, out-of-control driver.

Looking back to chapter 7 of Romans, Paul said, *"So I find this law at work: Although I want to do good, evil is right there with me"* (Romans 7:21). This makes me think of something I've seen in cartoons where the character facing a dilemma finds his angelic conscience on one shoulder and a little devil on the other shoulder, both telling him to do opposite things, both arguing for control. That's us, stuck between our good-natured conscience and our sinful-natured self—good versus evil.

Where Jesus, by His death on the cross, freed us from the penalties of sin; His Spirit, by His life within us, can free us from the devilish dominance of our sinful-natured self. As Paul said right after acknowledging his sinful wretchedness,

> *"Therefore, there is now no condemnation for those who are in Christ Jesus, because through Christ Jesus the law of the Spirit who gives life has set you free from the law of sin and death." (Romans 8:1–2, emphasis added)*

Using our typical meaning of the term, self-control is an illusion, a hopeless goal. Our conscience isn't always strong enough to win control over our sinful self. But your conscience doesn't have to be alone in the fight. The Spirit of Jesus can be there too, ready for action.

> *"So I say, walk by the Spirit, and you will not gratify the desires of the flesh* [i.e., sinful nature]." *(Galatians 5:16)*

Spirit of understanding

When I was in college, my mom and I wrote letters to each other. Occasionally we'd talk on the phone, with her usually calling me since I couldn't afford the long-distance charges. I always looked forward to those phone calls, as they left me feeling closer to mom, and closer to the home I missed. Years later, when my sons were in college, it was emails and video calls. Video calls were the best since they conveyed more understanding, like how healthy my son looked and how filthy his dorm room was.

With the Bible, all we have are the written words which, like many texts and emails I've received, can be easily misunderstood. We're missing the audio and visual that would provide more understanding. That's where the Holy Spirit comes in. Though He may not speak to our ears and eyes, He goes deeper, to our heart and soul. I found promises of this throughout the Bible, with these being a few examples:

> *"In the same way no one knows the thoughts of God except the Spirit of God. What we have received is not the spirit of the world, but the Spirit who is from God, so that we may*

> *understand what God has freely given us."* (1 Corinthians 2:11-12)
>
> [Jesus said,] *"But the Helper, the Holy Spirit whom the Father will send in My name, He will teach you all things, and remind you of all that I said to you."* (John 14:26 NASB)
>
> *"I keep asking that the God of our Lord Jesus Christ, the glorious Father, may give you the Spirit of wisdom and revelation, so that you may know him better."* (Ephesians 1:17)

It takes more than the Bible, a book such as this one, or a well-worded sermon. Real understanding of Christian truth comes only from the Spirit of truth.

Spirit of truth

Jesus prepared His disciples to spread His truth by telling them as much as they could handle, as much as the spoken word can communicate to an open mind. However, He wanted to tell them more, as He said: *"I have much more to say to you, more than you can now bear"* (John 16:12). Jesus then promised: *"But when he, the Spirit of truth, comes, he will guide you into all truth"* (verse 13, emphasis added).

Again, reading the Bible or listening to sermons isn't enough. Complete truth only comes from a personal relationship with the Holy Spirit, for the Holy Spirit speaks to us at a level far beyond the reach of reading, listening, human vocabulary, and human reasoning. And as Jesus also said:

> *"When the Helper comes, whom I will send to you from the Father, namely, the Spirit of truth who comes from the Father, He will testify about Me."* (John 15:26 NASB)

In the movie *A Few Good Men,* there's a climactic moment near the end of the court martial scene. In response to Tom Cruise's character demanding, "I want the truth!" Jack Nicholson's character shouts, "YOU CAN'T HANDLE THE TRUTH!" Without the help of the Holy Spirit, we can't handle the truth. It's scope and meaning won't be fully grasped by our limited minds. Yet the Spirit of truth will open our minds to the truth:

> *"It is the Spirit who testifies, because the Spirit is the truth."* (1 John 5:6 NASB)

Without limit

My friend Phil believes the Holy Spirit is only available to clergy, like He's a seminary graduation gift. Even the twelve apostles initially thought access to the Spirit was limited to them. As one of the apostles asked, *"Lord, why do you intend to show yourself to us* [as the Holy Spirit] *and not to the world?"* (John 14:22). Jesus responded, *"Anyone who loves me will obey my teaching. My Father will love them, and we will come to them and make our home with them"* (verse 23, emphasis added).

Anyone can live with the internal presence of the Spirit of God and Jesus. There are no limits to Jesus' promise, for as He said,

> *"For the one whom God has sent speaks the words of God, for God gives the Spirit without limit."* (John 3:34, emphasis added)
>
> [and God said,] *"I will pour out my Spirit on all people. ... Even on my servants, both men and women, I will pour out my Spirit in those days."* (Joel 2:28 & 29)

In summary, Jesus sent the Holy Spirit to unify His Church, to help us bear fruit, to provide self-control, to fill us with understanding, and open our minds to all truth—without limit. Jesus sent the Holy Spirit to give us access to God, as Paul said,

> *"For through him* [Jesus] *we both have access to the Father by one Spirit."* (Ephesians 2:18)

God revealed this miracle of access the moment Jesus died. Within sight of the cross stood the Temple, and in the Temple hung a large curtain, maybe like you'd see in a theater. This curtain hung in front of the back room where sat the Ark of the Covenant and God's Spirit. Not just anyone could get past that curtain and into God's presence. With Jesus' final breath, He changed all that:

> "Then Jesus cried again with a loud voice and breathed his last. At that moment the curtain of the temple was torn in two, from top to bottom." (Matthew 27:50-51 NRSV)

This curtain represented sin, the barrier separating people from God. When Jesus died, paying the penalty for all sins, the barrier came down, opening access to God's Spirit for everyone.

Now back to the survey data showing that 20 percent of de-churched Christians felt that God was missing from their experience of church and that the majority of de-churched Christians left church without finding a connection with God. The Holy Spirit *is* our experience of God. The Holy Spirit *is* our connection with God. The Holy Spirit *is* the presence of God. Yet, even though Jesus' death tore down the barrier that had separated God's children from His Spirit, that barrier has since been replaced by the graffiti of manmade Christianity.

However, for those willing to believe and look beneath the graffiti, the Holy Spirit is there, waiting for you. He will guide and counsel you, giving you peace, understanding, access to God, and awareness of His truth. And again, as Jesus said, *"Then you will know the truth, and the truth will set you free"* (John 8:32).

Where our faith in Jesus assures our eternal life in heaven, our relationship with His Spirit will determine the quality of our life while still on earth.

10. Heaven on Earth

Jesus once said, *"This, then, is how you should pray: 'Our Father in heaven, hallowed be your name, your kingdom come, ... on earth as it is in heaven'"* (Matthew 6:9-10). God's kingdom is where He lives, His home. God's kingdom is defined by the presence of God. In instructing us to pray for God's kingdom on earth, Jesus is calling us to pray for God's Spirit to live on earth as He does in heaven.

Yet when it comes to many churches, God isn't home. The Holy Spirit is missing from many churches and the lives of their members. Just look at all the disunity, the lack of fruit—as evidenced by the ever-decreasing population of churchgoing Christians—and the lack of understanding and truth. But, why is the Spirit missing? Since answers aren't necessary in my search for true Christianity, I'll resist stepping into that quagmire … for now anyway.

Now consider this bit of insight from Andrew Murray:

> "Look in your heart, and your heart will find its Savior, its God. If you see and feel nothing of God, it is because you seek Him in books, in church, in outward religious exercises. You will not find Him there until you have first found Him in your heart. Seek Him in your heart, and you will never seek in vain, for He dwells there in His Holy Spirit." [1]

Yes, Murray did say that church isn't the place to look for God. That's because God's earthly home, His kingdom on earth, is where His Holy Spirit lives, within the hearts of those who believe and receive Him. Recall that Jesus said: "*My Father will love them, and we will come to them and make our home with them*" (John 14:23). Let's look further at God's earthly home, His heaven on Earth, and how His presence in our lives determines the quality of our lives.

Living through you

There I was, standing in front of church on a Sunday morning, telling the congregation the story of how I came to know Jesus. Speaking in front of crowds is hard for me, however, I was relaxed and thoroughly enjoying myself. You see, I wasn't alone. As my story smoothly flowed forth, the Holy Spirit was with me—I felt Him. I even started to feel detached from what I was saying, as if I were standing off to the side, listening to someone else speak. And the words sounded great—far better than anything I'd typed up.

Two weeks prior, the church I attended had invited me to tell my story to the congregation. Ignoring my fear, I said sure, and proceeded to type four pages of notes. Before leaving for church that nervous morning, I prayed once more, asking God to help me get through it without collapsing. I also prayed that the telling of my story would glorify God.

"If you really want to glorify me," God said, "leave the notes at home." I swear, those are the words that came into my head—not a voice, just a thought. Then I remembered something Jesus had said:

> *"Do not worry about what to say or how to say it. At that time you will be given what to say, for it will not be you speaking, but the Spirit of your Father speaking through you." (Matthew 10:19-20)*

So, I left my notes at home and went to church.

My point is, the Holy Spirit does more than live *in* us. He can live *through* us. Paul expressed it this way: *"For this purpose I also labor, striving according to His power which works mightily within me"* (Colossians 1:29 NASB, emphasis added).

Now consider the survey data showing the growing numbers of church refugees. Why do many churches appear so weak, ineffective, and unable to keep people coming back for more? Murray might answer the question like this:

> *"The church seems to have lost possession of what ought to be her secret of secrets—the daily, abiding consciousness that only as she lives in the power of the Holy Spirit can she preach the gospel with Spirit and power. Therefore, there is much preaching and working with little spiritual results."* [2]
>
> *"The Holy Spirit has not only the power, but He also has the Spirit of love. He is brooding over this dark world and every sphere of work in it, and He is willing to bless. And why is*

> *there not more blessing? There can only be one answer. We have not honored the Holy Spirit as we should have done. ... No wonder there is so much feebleness and failure in the church of Christ!"* [3]

Yes, churches are weak because the Holy Spirit and His power are missing.

WWJD 2.0

What Would Jesus Do? Somewhere around here, I may still have a colorful wristband with WWJD on it. That acronym became so popular that I think it sometimes lost its meaning, which is, if Jesus found Himself in my situation, what would He do? Interesting question, implying that we should always strive to do as Jesus would do. I hope you have better luck with that than I've had.

Whenever Jesus tells us to do as He would do, like when telling us to love our enemies, He knows how futile our efforts can be. However, rather than miring us in futility, Jesus wants His hard-to-follow-instructions to motivate us to accept our feebleness and rely on His Spirit to do the doing through us. By His Spirit, Jesus will do what only *He* can do, what's impossible for us to do. As He said, *"What is impossible for mortals is possible for God"* (Luke 18:27 NRSV).

WWJD is still a good slogan, though I think it needs an upgrade. Instead of What *Would* Jesus Do, how about What *Will* Jesus Do? Instead of being an idealistic yet doubtful question of what I might do under my own power, it becomes a confident question of what Jesus *will* do within me by *His* power.

How you choose to ask this WWJD question may indicate how you choose to consider the Holy Spirit. Is He passive in your life, or active?

The two will become one flesh

In chapter 5 of his letter to the Ephesians, Paul talks about husbands and wives, the whole time comparing their relationship to that of Jesus and the Church. In verse 31, Paul quotes from Genesis and defines the unity of a husband and wife—the two will become one flesh. As Paul then explains in verse 32, he's referring here to Jesus and His Church—the two will become one:

> *"'For this reason a man will leave his father and mother and be joined to his wife, and the two will become one flesh.' This*

> *is a great mystery, and I am applying it to Christ and the church." (Ephesians 5:31-32 NRSV)*

The Spirit of Jesus wants us to share our bodies and lives with Him—two in one flesh. Here are additional supporting passages, where I've underlined noteworthy parts:

> [Jesus said], *"On that day you will know that I am in My Father, and <u>you are in Me, and I in you</u>." (John 14:20 NASB) and "Remain in me, as <u>I also remain in you</u>." (John 15:4)*
>
> *"And <u>I will put My Spirit within you</u> and you will come to life, ... declares the Lord." (Ezekiel 37:14 NASB)*
>
> *"If anyone acknowledges that Jesus is the Son of God, <u>God lives in them and they in God</u>." (1 John 4:15)*
>
> *"Examine yourselves to see whether you are living in the faith. Test yourselves. Do you not realize that <u>Jesus Christ is in you</u>?" (2 Corinthians 13:5 NRSV)*

Jesus wants to walk the earth again, though this time within the bodies of those who believe. Also, recall what Jesus said in His prayer to God: *"I have made you known to them, and will continue to make you known in order that the love you have for me may be in them and that <u>I myself may be in them</u>"* (John 17:26, emphasis added). Think about this a moment. What would your life be like if you were sharing it with Jesus?

At the beginning of chapter 9, we saw that the Holy Spirit is both the Spirit of God and the Spirit of Jesus. As the Holy Spirit is Father and Son united as one, so too the Spirit will unite you and Jesus as one. It's just as Jesus promised, *"you in Me, and I in you."* As Jesus also said in his prayer to His Father, *"I have given them the glory that you gave me, that they may be one as we are one—I in them and you in me—so that they may be brought to complete unity"* (John 17:22-23).

Does it seem like I'm overemphasizing this? I think I'm not stressing it enough. By the time I completed my journey in search of truth, I realized that this is the heart of Christianity. Jesus' Christianity *is* the Holy Spirit living within you, making you one with Jesus—two in one flesh.

> *"For it is said, 'The two will become one flesh.' But whoever is united with the Lord is one with him in spirit." (1 Corinthians 6:16-17)*

The Spirit who gives life

Many of us live most of our lives with puppet strings attached. Here's an example of what I mean, an example my sisters particularly enjoy recalling. When I was five or six years old, at the dinner table my older sisters knew the right string to pull at just the right instant to get milk squirting out my nose. To my sisters I was very much like a puppet, so easy to manipulate.

The world is full of influential string-pullers controlling our thoughts, feelings, and actions. Consider the advertisers, media outlets, podcasters, talk radio hosts, and politicians, and how they elicit reactions with catch phrases, exaggerations, conspiracy theories, and lies.

Yet we need not exist as lifeless puppets controlled by others. As God said, *"I will put My Spirit within you and you will come to life."* And Paul promised:

> *"If the Spirit of him who raised Jesus from the dead is living in you, he who raised Christ from the dead will also give life to your mortal bodies because of his Spirit who lives in you." (Romans 8:11)*

The Holy Spirit offers us a life free from the worldly strings that often control us. Plus, as Jesus said:

> *"The Spirit gives life; the flesh counts for nothing." (John 6:63)*
>
> *"I have come that they may have life, and have it to the full." (John 10:10)*

Children contain the life of their parents. The Spirit's presence fills us with the life of our heavenly Parent. With the Spirit of God, we become more like Jesus, a true child of God. Paul said so:

> *"For those who are led by the Spirit of God are the children of God. ... The Spirit himself testifies with our spirit that we are God's children."* (Romans 8:14, 16)

The Spirit transforms us into truly reborn and completely alive children of God. Maybe this is what born-again really means, born-again into our originally intended and originally created image of God, as true children of God.

Now regarding this born-again idea, consider this:

> *"He* [God] *saved us, not because of righteous things we had done, but because of his mercy. He saved us through the washing of rebirth and renewal by the Holy Spirit, whom he poured out on us generously through Jesus Christ our Savior."* (Titus 3:5-6)

The way to all truth

In the past six chapters, we've set up our base camp of foundational truths, truths which will help us as we continue our journey in search of Christianity. With a firm grasp on the truths of God, Jesus, and the Holy Spirit, we're ready to embark on the next leg of this journey. As we start off, please remember what Jesus said:

> *"I have much more to say to you, more than you can now bear. But when he, the Spirit of truth, comes, he will guide you into all truth."* (John 16:12-13)

My hope is that the Spirit of truth will guide you the rest of the way on this journey, along the path to all truth.

Finally, consider this, from Andrew Murray:

> *"God will take upon Himself the responsibility of making you full of the Spirit, not as a treasure that you must carry and keep, but as a power that is to carry and keep you."* [4]

So, if the climb up this metaphorical mountain of truth feels daunting at times, know that the Holy Spirit will help you, and even carry you, especially up the steep parts. By the way, what do you think waits for you at the top?

Church

11. What Do You See When You Look At Church?

It's Saturday afternoon and I'm lounging in the living room with my computer on my lap. My wife is reading some headlines from a news feed she's scanning. Many of the stories include acts prompted by bigotry and arrogance, with plenty of hypocrisy generously thrown in. And that includes stories about some so-called Christians and their churches. Bigotry, arrogance, and hypocrisy—that's an example of what many people see when they look at church.

What do *you* see when you look at church? What graffiti blocks your view of how Jesus would define church? With those questions hanging in the air—deep breath, heavy sigh—it's time to begin a more perilous part of this journey. Well, it feels perilous to me. As we leave base camp and continue our search for truth, portions of this next leg of the climb may be more difficult than what you've traversed thus far.

First, some definition: I'll be using Church with an upper case "C" when referring to Jesus' Church, the Church He founded. I'll use church with a lower case "c" when referring to human-founded and managed churches that are often more worldly than Christian.

Now then, regarding my list of perceptions of Christianity that I introduced in chapter 3, so far it contains the following: hypocritical, judgmental, anti-homosexual, unloving, a negative image of Jesus, where rules rule, it no longer seems Christian, and God is missing. That's what many people see when they look at church. That's the graffiti that leaves many people as wounded and hurting victims of manmade Christianity. My purpose with the next several chapters is to spotlight more worldly church graffiti, and then remove that graffiti to reveal the truth of what Jesus wants His Church to look like.

The Jesus Club

July in Chicago—hot and muggy. Thankfully, the conference was confined to an air-conditioned hotel on Michigan Avenue. During the conference, I studied my new business colleague as he spoke with potential customers. Sometimes he was all business; other times folksy with his sentences laced with profanity. He adjusted his style depending upon his audience.

As the day of meetings ended, he invited me to dinner at his private men's club. After walking several blocks from the hotel to his club, I reluctantly put my sport coat back on, re-fastened the top button of my shirt, cinched up my tie, and followed my friend through the heavy glass doors.

It was a scene from a 1940's movie. There was the great foyer with polished wood paneling and the wide staircase leading to the second-floor dining room. The maître d' greeted my friend as Mister Johns, and then led us to our table near the windows, with an expansive view of the lake.

I fell into a well-padded red leather chair as the waiter arrived, also greeting my friend by name. And my friend—who was he? His tone and style changed again. He had taken on his club persona. Serious, yet cordial, a bit aloof, with that look of superiority I'd seen on faces of some college professors. Not at all like the bulldog businessman I knew outside his club.

Speaking of clubs, many years earlier, when my wife and I were engaged, we both liked the idea of getting married in the local Presbyterian church. So we started attending, at least for the final few months before our wedding. My wife had attended a Presbyterian church when she was a little girl, so unlike me, she knew what to expect.

They had their own language with big words I didn't understand, like sanctification, justification, and righteousness. They adhered to a seemingly sacred routine, with those on the inside flawlessly following each step of the dance—standing, singing, and repeating phases, all on queue. I was like a dancer with my feet stuck in the mud. I felt lost and very much an outsider. After the wedding, we didn't go back, to that church anyway.

Yet during those handful of Sundays before our wedding, Christianity felt like a club—the Jesus Club, where many of the club members spoke that "churchy" language. Much of it sounded meaningless to me, as if they were reading from a script.

Like my multi-persona business colleague, later in life when I started to regularly attend church, I, too, was tempted to take on a dual personality, putting on my church club persona whenever I walked through those church doors. Perhaps the temptation to adopt such a persona is prompted by the exclusive club atmosphere that pervades some churches, with their club dress code, language, and implied policy of acceptable behavior.

A Barna Group study from 2015 shows my sense of a Jesus club isn't unique:

> *In a survey of young adults, 44% say, "The church seems too much like an exclusive club."* [1]

I added exclusive club to my list of perceptions of Christianity. But is that how Jesus wants His Church to be perceived?

Club walls

At times my church felt like a family. We had picnics together, dinners together, we laughed, and we cried together. However, there was a darker side. Some in our cozy church family had adopted an isolationist policy. We were all very comfortable with each other, and some members were reluctant to disrupt that comfort by changing the family dynamics. There was no room—in their minds anyway—for new family members.

The isolationist gang had built figurative walls around the church and volunteered for guard duty, protecting us against enemy intrusion. Maybe you've come across such gatekeepers, with their plastic smiles and scripted greetings. They're good at their job, for they never resort to overt tactics. But, an isolationist church … really? Though I suspect this is unusual behavior for a church, I added it to my list of perceptions.

However, what does Jesus think about figurative walls intended to keep out riffraff who might upset the church family dynamic? Jesus' brother James saw similar behavior and gave this warning:

> *"My brothers and sisters, believers in our glorious Lord Jesus Christ must not show favoritism. Suppose a man comes into your meeting wearing a gold ring and fine clothes, and a poor man in filthy old clothes also comes in. If you show special attention to the man wearing fine clothes and say, "Here's a good seat for you," but say to the poor man, "You stand there" or "Sit on the floor by my feet," have you not discriminated among yourselves and become judges with evil thoughts?" (James 2:1-4)*

God doesn't show favoritism. Neither should churches.

The *Divided* church of Jesus Christ

"I find it fascinating how many versions of Christianity exist and how different they are from each other," a friend once told me. "And it's like there's a competition for the greatest number of butts in pews." In support of my friend's perception, the 2008 PEW survey states:

> *"Moreover, the Protestant population is characterized by significant internal diversity and fragmentation, encompassing hundreds of different denominations."* [2]

Recent centuries have bred a rampant mutation of Christianity into thousands of variants—that's quite a prolific virus. Sorry, would you prefer a different metaphor? Anyway, instead of displaying a Christianity that's attractive, those fragmented denominations present a jumbled mess of conflicting beliefs, priorities, doctrines, and traditions. Of course, there's also the sense of a competition. I added "mutated denominations" and "competing for butts" to my list of perceptions.

But it gets worse. I know of at least two variants who proclaim that if you don't become a member of their elite denomination, you'll go to hell. To me, that sounds like a high-pressure tactic to get your butt in their pew. So, I added that to my list.

Divided denominations—each with their own church hierarchy and pecking order, beliefs and traditions, rules and doctrines. It didn't start out this way, though Paul saw it coming, and he saw the reason. Some people weren't content to follow and serve Jesus—they preferred to lead and serve themselves. So Paul warned,

> *"I urge you, brothers and sisters, to watch out for those who cause divisions and put obstacles in your way that are contrary to the teaching you have learned. Keep away from them. For such people are not serving our Lord Christ, but their own appetites." (Romans 16:17-18, emphasis added)*

Jesus once said, *"A house divided against itself will fall"* (Luke 11:17). With all the divided denominations built on foundations of sand, it's amazing that Christianity is standing at all.

Now consider this: as Jesus prayed shortly before His arrest, He knew a mob would soon be coming for Him with swords and clubs. He foresaw the pain and torture that waited for Him with the rising of the sun. Yet, rather than focusing His prayers on His own fate, He ignored the torment He knew He was about to face, and instead asked His Father on behalf of all believers …

> "… that they may be brought to complete unity. Then the world will know that you sent me and have loved them even as you have loved me." (John 17:23)

With only a few hours left to live, Jesus' concern in that moment wasn't for Himself. All He cared about was the unity of His Church. Paul later took up the call:

> "Make every effort to keep the unity of the Spirit through the bond of peace. There is one body and one Spirit, just as you were called to one hope when you were called; one Lord, one faith, one baptism; one God and Father of all, who is over all and through all and in all." (Ephesians 4:3-6)
>
> "Therefore if you have any encouragement from being united with Christ, if any comfort from his love, if any common sharing in the Spirit, if any tenderness and compassion, then make my joy complete by being like-minded, having the same love, being one in spirit and of one mind." (Philippians 2:1-2)

As I pointed out in chapter 9, the unity Jesus prayed for isn't a worldly unity based on worldly criteria. Jesus prayed for our unity with His Spirit—He is the vine, and we are the branches. As a vine unites the branches, the Spirit unites believers.

However, the mere existence of diverse denominations seems to reject the possibility of unity. And rather than uniting themselves to the Spirit, many denominations have united themselves to their manmade doctrines, traditions, and rules. Those hundreds of fragmented denominations are more evidence of the absence of the Holy Spirit, the Spirit who would otherwise unite them.

Does it appear to you that there's currently an epidemic of division in the world, and not only within the church, but throughout society? Shouldn't Jesus'

Christianity be different? Shouldn't Jesus' Christianity bring people together? Shouldn't Jesus' Christianity be a haven of unity amidst a world of division? After all, Jesus prayed for such unity. Yet, all the divided denominations only affirm my conviction that what we often see on the surface isn't Jesus' Christianity.

Distorted baptism

My stepmother and stepfather were both Catholic. I've already mentioned a few of my encounters with Catholic doctrine while living on the sidelines. I now want to share a few more, beginning with baptism.

My friend Pat once told me his newly-converted Catholic parents believe that since he isn't baptized, he'll go to hell. I've heard this before, from other Catholics. What's the truth about baptism and its relationship to salvation? John the Baptist, who should be an authority on such things, mentions two types of baptism:

> *"I baptize you with water for repentance, but one* [Jesus] *who is more powerful than I is coming after me; I am not worthy to carry his sandals. He will baptize you with the Holy Spirit and fire." (Matthew 3:11 NRSV)*

And as Jesus said:

> *"John baptized with water, but you will be baptized with the Holy Spirit." (Acts 1:5 NRSV)*

Water baptism is a symbolic act of faith conducted by man, with all the saving power of any other human-managed endeavor. Yet, the baptism that changes lives is the baptism of the Holy Spirit, washing over us and renewing us, making us into a new creation. As Paul said in his letter to Titus:

> *"But when the kindness of God our Savior and His love for mankind appeared, He saved us, not on the basis of deeds which we did in righteousness, but in accordance with His mercy, by the washing of regeneration and renewing by the Holy Spirit, whom He richly poured out upon us through Jesus Christ our Savior." (Titus 3:4-6 NASB)*

Faith saves us, not symbolic acts. It's our faith in Jesus that opens our souls to receive the baptism and presence of the Holy Spirit, the Spirit who will bring about our rebirth and renewal.

Catholic confession

Forgive me father, for I have sinned. Yet why should my friend Nancy see a priest to confess her sins? She once told me she didn't like the idea of a middleman. To her, the confessional felt like an obstacle, hindering her from being close to God. Since she craved closeness with God more than closeness with a priest, Nancy left the Catholic church.

What might Jesus think about the practice of going to a middleman to confess sins? Afterall, our sins are against God and Jesus, not a church. Also, since Jesus died to pay the penalty for our sins, shouldn't we go directly to Him when wanting to confess and repent of those sins? As Jesus said in His instructions for prayer:

> "But when you pray, go into your room, close the door and pray to your Father, who is unseen. Then your Father, who sees what is done in secret, will reward you." (Matthew 6:6)

Jesus tells us to go directly to God, not a middleman. He even tells us what to say:

> "When you pray, say: 'Father, hallowed be your name, ... Forgive us our sins, for we also forgive everyone who sins against us.'" (Luke 11:2, 4)

Forgive me father, for I have sinned—great words, though often spoken to the wrong person.

The top of the org chart

"The Pope enjoys, by divine institution, supreme, full, immediate, and universal power in the care of souls" (Catechism 937 of the Roman Catholic church). You don't get any higher on the church org chart than that. Along with this chart-topping, apparently God-given power comes the title "Vicar of Christ." Vicar means someone who's authorized to act on behalf of another. However, did Jesus intend to assign a man to be a lone representative for Himself?

You've seen these words from Jesus already, and they're worth repeating:

> *"I will ask the Father, and He will give you another Helper, so that He may be with you forever; the Helper is the Spirit of truth." (John 14:16-17 NASB)*
>
> *"But the Helper, the Holy Spirit whom the Father will send in My name, He will teach you all things, and remind you of all that I said to you." (John 14:26 NASB)*
>
> *"I have much more to say to you, more than you can now bear. But when he, the Spirit of truth, comes, he will guide you into all truth." (John 16:12-13)*

The *Holy Spirit* is Jesus' earthly representative, our helper, teacher, guide, and caretaker of our souls. The Holy Spirit is the true and only Vicar of Christ.

Now, what about the various ways those of us on the lower levels of the church org chart pay special respect to those higher up? For example, there's kneeling and kissing the Popes ring, giving extra honor to pastors and priests, and praying to saints, like the familiar Catholic prayer that starts out, "Hail Mary, full of grace." What does God think about such behavior?

The tendency to praise someone you respect and are grateful for is natural. A Roman Centurion was grateful to Peter for going out of his way to visit him. *"When Peter entered, Cornelius met him, and fell at his feet and worshiped him"* (Acts 10:25 NASB). Seems okay. After all, Peter was one of the pillars of the early Church, and supposedly the first Pope. If Peter had a ring, Cornelius might have kissed it. Nevertheless, as the next verse says, *"Peter helped him up, saying, 'Stand up; I, too, am just a man'"* (verse 26).

But what about worshipping an angel? That should be okay, right? Yet as the Apostle John prepared to fall on his knees before the angel who'd opened his mind to all those revelations, John tells us: *"But he* [the angel] *said to me, 'You must not do that! I am a fellow servant with you and your comrades the prophets, and with those who keep the words of this book. Worship God!'"* (Revelation 22:9 NRSV).

Also, regarding praying to saints, Jesus calls us to pray directly to God—no go-between required. Though we should be grateful for people like Mary, praying to them is a form of worshipping them, and as the angel declared to John, *"You must not do that! ... Worship God!"*

As organizational charts naturally do, they elevate some people above others. Sometimes those of us near the bottom of the religious ladder give special respect to those higher up, without regard for God and Jesus and their rightful position within that hierarchy. When higher-ups are elevated above God and Jesus, whether intentionally or by accident, that's a problem. To this, Jesus might say:

> "Very truly, I tell you, servants are not greater than their master, nor are messengers greater than the one who sent them." (John 13:16 NRSV)

In referring to Jesus, John the Baptist said, *"He must become greater; I must become less"* (John 3:30). That's good advice for all who call themselves Christian, especially those near the top of a manmade religious org chart.

Finally, Jesus doesn't rely on those near the top of a manmade organization to represent Himself to those at the bottom. Jesus showed this truth by His actions. In reading about His life, we see He didn't hang out with the church elite. If anything, Jesus was closest to the bottom-dwellers, like me. Maybe that's still the case today.

Did Jesus die for nothing?

My father and mother got divorced when I was five. My dad eventually remarried, and many years later decided to join the Catholic church of my stepmother. However, before the church could accept him, the sin of his divorce from my mom needed to be erased. So, my dad signed a pile of Catholic forms resulting in the annulment of his marriage to my mom. From the Catholic church's perspective, since my dad's first marriage never happened, neither did the sin of divorce. And since he and my mom were never married in the eyes of the church … well, you know what that makes me.

Then there's a notorious church in Topeka, Kansas, that claims that God hates homosexuals and condemns all sinners to hell. Does the Catholic church have something in common with them, in that neither will accept someone unless they're sin-free?

If that's the case, then why? Jesus accepts sinners. However, instead of accepting sinners, the Catholic church finds creative ways to ignore or erase sin, while the Topeka church ignores Jesus. Neither of them appears to accept that Jesus already paid the penalty for our sins. Churches such as these, who claim the authority to decide who qualifies for salvation, ignore the fact that Jesus already paid our entrance fee into heaven.

In the Catholic church, that Topeka church, churches who claim you'll go to hell if you're not a member of their club, and perhaps many more, it looks like Jesus died for nothing. As Paul stated,

> *"I do not set aside the grace of God, for if righteousness could be gained through the law* [rather than by Jesus' sacrifice]*, Christ died for nothing!" (Galatians 2:21)*

Also, Jesus didn't discriminate, like those churches do. He died for everyone, whether they're a member of a church or not. As Jesus said,

> *"For my Father's will is that <u>everyone</u> who looks to the Son and believes in him shall have eternal life, and I will raise him up at the last day." (John 6:40, emphasis added)*

Also, I've heard some churches claim authority to decide who qualifies to be a Christian. However, in referring to Jesus, John said:

> *"Yet to all who did receive him, to those who believed in his name, he gave the right to become children of God—children born not of natural descent, <u>nor of human decision</u> or a husband's will, but born of God." (John 1:12-13, emphasis added)*

I'm starting to recognize a characteristic of some churches and denominations. They've assumed authority that belongs only to God and Jesus, and because of that, to them Jesus died for nothing.

God seems missing, revisited

He'd attended a mainline denomination for many years, and then finally gave up. "I never felt any real effect on my life," my friend Dave confided. "I'd expected God to change my life somehow, to make things different. But there was nothing. So forget it. I quit." God was missing from Dave's experience of church. I already had "God missing" on my list of perceptions of Christianity. Yet, since I saw this as a problem worth emphasizing, and to honor Dave and his feelings, I underlined it.

According to the Barna Group survey I cited earlier, 20% of de-churched Christians had the same experience as Dave—God was missing. With God missing, as Andrew Murray said:

> "Church life will profit us very little unless it leads us closer to God, to have larger expectations from God, and closer fellowship with God." [3]

But why is God often missing from the church experience? Here's one reason: Jesus frequently left the crowds of His followers to be alone with God, yet how often are today's pastors able to do the same thing? The pastors I know have so many demands on their time, I've heard some complain about having no time left for God. The church structure and bureaucracy—the worldly institutional ways of church—won't allow for God time, and hence, God is missing. Where God is missing in the life of the pastor, He will likely also be missing in the life of the pastor's church.

Why else is God missing? Well, according to the findings of a Barna Group survey, the Holy Spirit is dead:

> Almost 60% of Christians see the Holy Spirit as "a symbol of God's power or presence but is not a living entity." [4]

That explains a lot. That's what happens when churches don't let the Holy Spirit in the door. Yet, why don't they? There's that question again.

Maybe churches don't introduce their congregants to the Holy Spirit because they don't know Him themselves. Or, perhaps some churches see the living Holy Spirit as a threat, much the same way the power-hungry religious establishment 2000 years ago saw the living Jesus as a threat. They pushed for the death of Jesus, while today's establishment seems to resist the life of His Spirit. Again, why? Well, with a personal relationship with the *living* Holy Spirit, people no longer need a relationship with a church. They don't need a human counselor, comforter, or guide, because that's the role of the Holy Spirit.

Yes, God is missing, as the survey data shows. And whatever the reason, to a majority of Christians the Holy Spirit is dead. Therefore, when people look at church, what they often *don't* see is the presence of God's Spirit. RIP, Holy Spirit.

12. Institutional and Worldly

It had been a long day-and-a-half of hastily booked airline flights, hectic travel, and emotional stress, only to reach the hospital an hour after our father died. We spent time with his body, and then my two sisters and I went to the grocery store. Upon arriving at his house, one of my sisters retrieved the hidden key, and we stumbled through the door. I unpacked groceries and started fixing dinner.

I found myself thinking about the time dad converted to the Catholicism of my stepmother. As far as I knew, he never attended church before he married her. Leaving the spaghetti sauce simmering, I wandered into his bedroom and spotted a Bible on his bedside table. I didn't know he owned a Bible. In that moment, I knew the Catholic church had been good to my dad.

Just two days after my father died, the small Catholic parish he and my stepmother had belonged to pulled together a memorial service. After a very thoughtful service attended by a surprising number of people, they provided a beautiful potluck luncheon. Everyone was wonderfully kind, compassionate, and generous.

I tell this story to make a point. In all my whining about modern churches, especially the Catholic church, I suspect I sometimes give the impression that I see nothing good in such institutions. Yet, as Luke told his father Darth Vadar, in *Star Wars, Return of the Jedi*, "I know there is good in you." Yes, the institutions aren't perfect—they have flaws, just like any other manmade institution. But there is good in them. And often, the kindness of the people makes up for some of the institutional flaws.

Now, regarding institutional and worldly churches, I have a theory that the decline of church membership in the US might be linked to a church's relationship with Jesus and His Christianity, and how it compares to their relationship with the world. Which relationship is stronger? Topping the list of membership losers is the Catholic church. As some PEW research explained:

> "Within Christianity the greatest net losses, by far, have been experienced by Catholics. Nearly one-third of American adults (31.7%) say they were raised Catholic. Among that group, fully 41% no longer identify with Catholicism." [1]

That's what happens when a church has a stronger relationship with worldly ways, rather than with Jesus Christ. That's what can happen when there's too much focus on worldly traditions and manmade doctrines, and not enough focus on Jesus, His Spirit, His Christianity, and His truth. It can be hard to see the truth of Christianity in institutional churches, especially when what's most visible are the traditions, rules, and doctrines.

What else do we see when we look at institutional and worldly churches? Since the Barna Group was way ahead of me in their curiosity and research, I checked out another book affiliated with them, focused on the perceptions of Millennials. Here are some highlights:

> *"Most young Christians are struggling less with their faith in Christ than with their experience of church."*
>
> *Young exiles* [Millennials] *sense God moving "outside the walls of the church." 33% say it's completely or mostly true that God is more at work outside the church than inside, and they want to be a part of that.*
>
> *21% say it's completely or mostly true that though they are Christian, the institutional church is a difficult place for them to live out their faith.* [2]

These insights into the perceptions of Millennials may be clues why, when you walk into some churches, it looks more like the clubhouse of an over-55 community. Since a third of young Christians don't see God when they walk into church, they go looking for Him elsewhere.

Now, continuing where I left off with the last chapter, what are more examples of characteristics that make a church more institutional and worldly than spiritual and Godly? And what truth lies hidden beneath that graffiti?

The sacred-secular dilemma

In his book *The Pursuit of God*, A.W. Tozer describes what he calls the sacred-secular dilemma. The *sacred* represents the spiritual and Godly with a focus on people, while *secular* represents institutional and worldly with a focus on the material.

Following the example of their church, many Christians divide their time and activities between the sacred spiritual world, and the secular material world. Tozer claims that such separation isn't necessary, for as he says, *"It is not what a man does that determines whether his work is sacred or secular, it is why he does it. The motive is everything."* [3] The problem, as Tozer explains, is that the sacred-secular dilemma creates a complete separation between the worlds of worship and daily life, when they should be blended.

However, the institutional church seems to promote one sacred day each week, followed by six secular days. Tozer points out that the original Church didn't start this way. They didn't set aside special places or days of the week as holier than others. Jesus didn't promote special days and places for worship. In fact, Jesus said,

> "Believe Me, a time is coming when you will worship the Father neither on this mountain nor in Jerusalem. ... But a time is coming, and even now has arrived, when the true worshipers will worship the Father in spirit and truth; for such people the Father seeks to be His worshipers." (John 4:21, 23 NASB)

Worship the Father in spirit and truth. Hmm, it looks like true worship has nothing to do with particular days or locations. Paul also had something to say about the sacred-secular dilemma:

> "But now that you have come to know God, or rather to be known by God, how is it that you turn back again to the weak and worthless elementary principles, to which you want to be enslaved all over again? You meticulously observe days and months and seasons and years. I fear for you, that perhaps I have labored over you in vain." (Galatians 4:9 -11 NASB)
>
> "So whether you eat or drink or <u>whatever you do</u>, do it all for the glory of God." (1 Corinthians 10:31, emphasis added)

Whatever you do, do it all for the glory of God. That's the motive Tozer was talking about. We can worship and glorify God in whatever we do and wherever we are. For worshipping and glorifying God are acts of the mind and soul, which cannot be bound by time and place. Maybe that's what Jesus meant when He advised us to worship the Father in spirit and truth.

Church of the rulebook

It was another Tuesday night leadership meeting, and each of the church elders had already put in a full day's work, with another workday less than nine hours away. In the third hour of the one-hour meeting, the pastor was again lecturing on the supremacy of the Presbyterian Book of Order. The elders had heard this sermon before, about how important it is that all their decisions are in accordance with the Presbyterian rulebook. At a pause in the sermon, my friend Chris slowly stood, raised his Bible as if to show it to everyone, hesitated, then slamming his Bible on the table he declared, "THAT's my Book of Order!"

Not to single out the Presbyterian church, here's a piece of Catholic rulebook doctrine to consider: "As a result the Church, to whom the transmission and interpretation of Revelation is entrusted, does not derive her certainty about all revealed truths from the holy Scriptures alone. Both Scripture and Tradition must be accepted and honoured with equal sentiments of devotion and reverence" (Catechism 82 of the Roman Catholic church, emphasis added). God's word as recorded in the Bible, and Catholic tradition as defined in the Catechism, are equal in importance, according to the Catholic rulebook.

However, by creating and elevating their own rulebooks, churches give less honor to God's rulebook. I mean, by elevating manmade rules and traditions to the same level as God's laws, churches in effect lower God-made laws to the level of manmade.

Maybe that's one reason why Jesus lashed out at the religious leaders of His day who held tightly to their manmade rules and traditions. Try reading the following as if Jesus is speaking to modern institutional churches:

> "Why do you break the commandment of God for the sake of your tradition? ... You hypocrites! Isaiah prophesied rightly about you when he said: 'This people honors me with their lips, but their hearts are far from me; in vain do they

> *worship me, teaching human precepts* [e.g., rules and traditions] *as doctrines.'"* (Matthew 15:3, 7-9 NRSV)
>
> *"Neglecting the commandment of God, you hold to the tradition of men."* (Mark 7:8 NASB)

Moses also had a warning about church rulebooks and traditions:

> *"Do not add to what I command you and do not subtract from it, but keep the commands of the LORD your God that I give you."* (Deuteronomy 4:2)

It looks like many churches ignore these warnings.

If you ever feel a church pressuring you to elevate the authority of their rules and traditions, maybe respond as Peter and John did when pressured by the traditionalists of their day: *"Peter and John replied, 'Which is right in God's eyes: to listen to you, or to him? You be the judges!'"* (Acts 4:19). At that meeting of Presbyterian church elders I mentioned, my friend Chris chose to listen to God.

Finally, please keep in mind Paul's warning:

> *"See to it that no one takes you captive through hollow and deceptive philosophy, which depends on human tradition and the elemental spiritual forces of this world rather than on Christ."* (Colossians 2:8)

Christianity Incorporated

I'd gotten everything on my grocery list and was heading for the checkout line, hungry and in a hurry to drive home and fix dinner. When I saw that familiar face, I knew dinner would be delayed. We hadn't seen each other since I quit attending church, so as I'd experienced several times before, she gave me the obligatory sales pitch, trying to convince me to return. She then excitedly told me about the churches progress in searching for a new pastor. "And you know how important it is to find someone with a strong business sense," she said, "for a church is a business."

I just nodded my head and said something about my ice cream melting. Then, on the drive home, I was troubled. Not by the fact that I lied about the ice cream, but by the concept of church as a business. Is that what church is really supposed to be, Christianity Inc.?

A couple of years later, I found an Associated Press article that said the following: "Shrinking mainline Protestant denominations are turning to marketing to help stem decades of membership losses and stay afloat."[4] Yep, Christianity Inc. in action. It seemed churches, such as the United Methodist church, believed large amounts of advertising dollars would help fill the pews again. The Methodists planned to spend $20 million on their ad campaign. However, judging by recent surveys showing the continuous decline in church attendance, I'd say that money was wasted.

Jesus' apostles took a different approach. In a single day the Church in Jerusalem added 3000 new members (Acts 2:41). Later, and contrary to Caesar's efforts to reduce membership, Christianity rapidly grew throughout the Mediterranean, and without the help of modern advertising techniques. So how did Jesus' disciples increase membership so quickly? Well, it wasn't elaborate traditions, preaching popular opinion, a solid business plan, or slick ads. It took more than that to motivate first century believers to risk their lives.

Churches in decline

Why is today's institutional church in decline, as all the survey data shows? Other than the negative perceptions of church that we've seen so far, is there one underlying reason, a deeper root cause of all the rest? Jesus might answer with this:

> "I am the vine; you are the branches. If you remain in me and I in you, you will bear much fruit; apart from me you can do nothing. If you do not remain in me, you are like a branch that is thrown away and withers." (John 15:5-6)

Apart from Jesus, a church will wither and die. Since God, and therefore Jesus, are missing from people's experiences of church—as indicated by the Barna survey data—it's no surprise churches are dying. Want a different illustration? How about this, also from Jesus:

> "Everyone then who hears these words of mine and acts on them will be like a wise man who built his house on rock. The rain fell, the floods came, and the winds blew and beat on

> *that house, but it did not fall, because it had been founded on rock* [i.e., Jesus]. *And everyone who hears these words of mine and does not act on them will be like a foolish man who built his house on sand. The rain fell, and the floods came, and the winds blew and beat against that house, and it fell—and great was its fall!" (Matthew 7:24-27 NRSV)*

Yes, storms often rage against Christian churches, and woe be it to those who ignore the words of Jesus, and build their church on the shifting-sand foundation of worldly ways and manmade traditions. Thriving Churches—and yes, there are thriving Churches—are likely built on the firm foundation of faith in Jesus, His Spirit, and His truth. Declining churches have moved to weaker ground, and great is their fall. And as Paul said:

> *"They perish because they refused to love the truth and so be saved." (2 Thessalonians 2:10).*

Now back to my question: how did Jesus' disciples increase membership so quickly? Short answer: the disciples didn't do it, the Holy Spirit did. However, since God is missing and His Holy Spirit is considered dead—as the surveys show—today's churches are declining.

False prophets

Have you heard that Jesus wants you to be rich? So say the promoters of a variant of Christianity that critics call the Prosperity Gospel. The idea is that God rewards people with some form of prosperity, though not necessarily financial. Just what our itching ears want to hear.

Preaching what people want to hear can indeed be profitable. Years ago, I read about one Prosperity Gospel pastor who had a 6-million-dollar house and 80-million-dollar sanctuary. Peter warned us about such preachers: *"In their greed they will exploit you with false words"* (2 Peter 2:3 NASB). Jesus warned us as well: *"For where your treasure is, there your heart will be also"* (Matthew 6:21 NASB).

A churches character is a reflection of those who are in charge. Pastors who treasure wealth spread a virus of greed, infecting the character of their church and their members. However, should pastors and their congregations treasure money, or Jesus? Also, what happens when the preached promises of prosperity, financial or otherwise, don't become reality? Many people may give up on Jesus, unable to recover from the disappointment of unfulfilled promises.

Now consider these warnings from Jesus and Paul:

> *"No one can serve two masters; for either he will hate the one and love the other, or he will be devoted to one and despise the other. You cannot serve God and wealth."* (Matthew 6:24 NASB)
>
> *"Take care! Be on your guard against all kinds of greed, for one's life does not consist in the abundance of possessions."* (Luke 12:15 NRSV)
>
> *"But those who want to get rich fall into temptation and a trap, and many foolish and harmful desires which plunge people into ruin and destruction. For the love of money is a root of all sorts of evil."* (1 Timothy 6:9-10 NASB)

Here's some advice for certain pastors:

> *"Shepherd the flock of God among you, exercising oversight, not under compulsion but voluntarily, according to the will of God; and not with greed but with eagerness."* (1 Peter 5:2 NASB)

In addition to greed being a motivator for false preaching, some pastors believe their opinion is more worthy than God's truth. Or they preach what people want to hear to make themselves popular. You may recall what Paul said about that: *"For the time will come when people will not put up with sound doctrine. Instead, to suit their own desires, they will gather around them a great number of teachers to say what their itching ears want to hear. They will turn their ears away from the truth and turn aside to myths"* (2 Timothy 4:3-4). Jesus also warned us about preachers who don't preach His truth:

> "Beware of false prophets, who come to you in sheep's clothing but inwardly are ravenous wolves." (Matthew 7:15 NRSV)
>
> "For they loved the approval of people rather than the approval of God." (John 12:43 NASB)

Others spoke out against preaching popular opinion:

> "Even from your own number men will arise and distort the truth in order to draw away disciples after them." (Acts 20:30)
>
> "Yes," declares the LORD, "I am against the prophets who wag their own tongues and yet declare, 'The LORD declares.' Indeed, I am against those who prophesy false dreams," declares the LORD. "They tell them and lead my people astray with their reckless lies." (Jeremiah 23:31-32)
>
> "But there were also false prophets among the people, just as there will be false teachers among you. ... Many will follow their depraved conduct and will bring the way of truth into disrepute." (2 Peter 2:1-2)
>
> "Evidently some people are throwing you into confusion and are trying to pervert the gospel of Christ." (Galatians 1:7)

As Paul added in his message to the Galatians, *"Am I now trying to win the approval of human beings, or of God? Or am I trying to please people? If I were still trying to please people, I would not be a servant of Christ"* (Galatians 1:10). Paul didn't care about popular opinion and preaching what itching ears want to hear.

So, considering modern churches, how much of a problem is the preaching of personal preferences and popular opinion? The Cultural Research Center of Arizona Christian University provides the following insight:

> *Overall, 37% of American Christian pastors possess a biblical worldview, that is, they have consistently biblical beliefs and behaviors. 62% have what's called a hybrid worldview, one that represents their personal preferences.* [5]

It looks like most American pastors put more value in their worldly opinion than God's truth. Spouting personal preferences, popular opinion, and wild ideas without regard for facts and truth—an all-too-common practice these days. Yet, shouldn't Christianity be different than politics?

Greed, selfishness, self-centeredness, materialism—all common human traits. Yet Jesus calls Christians and His Church to be different. The real problem with the Prosperity Gospel and other forms of false teaching is that they appear to be all about self, and where self is all, God is missing.

On a positive note: *"How blessed is the man who has made the Lord his trust, and has not turned to the proud, nor to those who become involved in falsehood"* (Psalm 40:4 NASB).

A matter of degree?

In most churches, to be a pastor you need that piece of hallowed paper, the Master's in Divinity degree, or similar academic honor. However, though required by most institutional churches, is a seminary education what God requires of His preachers?

When Jesus was looking for preachers, *"He appointed twelve, so that they would be with Him and that He could send them out to preach"* (Mark 3:14 NASB, emphasis added). The apostles spent about three years with Jesus, though that wasn't the entirety of their education. When Jesus returned to heaven, He sent His Spirit to continue their schooling. As He said,

> *"But you will receive power when the Holy Spirit has come upon you; and you will be my witnesses* [i.e., preachers] *in Jerusalem, in all Judea and Samaria, and to the ends of the earth." (Acts 1:8 NRSV)*

Seminary ordained, or Holy Spirit trained? The twelve apostles learned from the source, as can anyone who desires to be a witness for Jesus. Yet, regarding those who follow the seminary path, consider this, from William Law:

> "A specified education and acquired degrees are the measure of a minister's qualifications, while that enduement with power from on high that made apostles out of fisherman is scarcely known and often explained away. This is the root cause of the great apostasy in Christendom." [6]

My dictionary defines apostasy as, "a total desertion of or departure from one's religion." Is that what getting a seminary degree really amounts to? I think I warned you this leg of the journey might get rough.

Moving on, try this, from Brother Lawrence:

> "It is the creator who teaches truth, who in one moment instructs the heart of the humble and makes him understand more about the mysteries of our faith and even about Himself than if he had studied them for a long term of years." [7]

Brother Lawrence seems to agree that a seminar education isn't necessary. Additionally, Andrew Murray said:

> "Every minister of the gospel is called to rest content with nothing less than the indwelling life and power of the Holy Spirit. ... Nothing less than having Christ speaking through us in the power of His omnipotence will make us able ministers of the New Testament." [8]

Christ speaking through able ministers—sign me up for that church.

Now back to William Law, but be warned, because I'm about to repeat something Law said that may be as disturbing as that *great apostasy* remark. Ready?

> "If the faith of illiterate fisherman did more for the establishment of the church in a few years than centuries of prodigious scholarship, one may readily understand that a trust in the wisdom of men and the letter of Scripture has caused the church to fall from its first gospel state in much

> *the way that Adam fell through eating of the same tree of knowledge.* [9] *... But now corruption, sin, death, and every evil of the world have entered into the Church, the spouse of Christ, just as they entered into Eve, the spouse of Adam, in Paradise. And in the same way, and from the same cause, namely, a desire for knowledge other than that which comes from God alone."* [10]

Maybe read that again. According to Law, those who pursue a seminary education are eating from the same tree of knowledge that got Adam and Eve booted out from the Garden of Eden.

Pause. Deep breath. Ponder what I just said. I'm sorry if it disturbs you. I know it disturbs me. Here's something that may be easier to handle, from Murray:

> *"No outward instruction, even from Christ himself, or His words in Scripture, can bring us to the full blessing—until the Holy Spirit works it in us.* [11] *... The mighty power of the Holy Spirit can do it. The Holy Spirit makes Jesus present within us."* [12]

I have a friend who, upon beginning his seminary education, worried about a trend he'd heard of. It's apparently common for graduates to feel less connected to God upon graduation than they felt when they started. That's because looking for insight into God at a seminary is looking in the wrong place, for as Paul said,

> *No one knows the thoughts of God except the Spirit of God. (1 Corinthians 2:11)*

Many pastors preach not by the power of the Holy Spirit working within them, but by the seminary degree hanging on their office wall. Just look at the accomplishments of the Holy Spirit in the first century compared to the struggling seminary-fortified churches today. Again, churches are in decline because the Holy Spirit is missing.

Finally, Paul also said,

> *"Where is the one who is wise? Where is the scholar? Where is the debater of this age? Has not God made foolish the wisdom of the world?" (1 Corinthians 1:20 NRSV)*

The wisdom of the world—such is the problem with many churches. They rely too much on the wisdom of the world, and not enough on the Holy Spirit.

What do we see when we look at church?

After adding more observations to my list of perceptions of Christianity, the next thing I did was change the title. Now, what do we sometimes see when we look at church? Here's my revised list:

Manmade

Flaws and Perceptions of ^ Christianity

- From what I had gathered in earlier chapters, churches are seen as: Hypocritical, judgmental, anti-homosexual, un-loving, negative image of Jesus, rules rule, no longer seems Christian, and God is missing
- An exclusive club
- Isolationist, sometimes
- Divided and mutated denominations competing for butts in pews
- Not a member, go to hell
- Usurping God's authority
- Institutional and worldly
- Manmade rulebook and traditions more important than the Bible
- Christianity Incorporated, in constant need of revenue
- Jesus died for nothing
- The Holy Spirit is dead

The flaws and perceptions on this list paint an image of churches that are known more for their worldly weaknesses than for God's spiritual presence. I think Andrew Murray saw the same thing when, in referring to churchgoing Christians, he said:

> *"They do not see that the spirit of the world permeates the church and takes possession of it to a far greater extent."* [13]

Where manmade churches decline thanks to their reliance upon the spirit of the world, Jesus' Church survives and grows under the guidance of the Holy Spirit. Now consider this, from the PEW Research Center:

> "Between 2007 and 2014, the overall size of the U.S. adult population grew by about 18 million people. ... But the share of adults who identify as Christians fell ... (by) about 5 million." [14]

That's what happens when the spirit of the world permeates the church more than the Spirit of God. That's what happens when the worldly graffiti—represented by my list of flaws—hides the truth.

Before moving on, something drew me to a passage I'd copied to my Christianity notebook:

> "The prophets prophesy lies, the priests rule by their own authority, and my people love it this way. But what will you do in the end?" (Jeremiah 5:31)

As you turn the page and continue along the path to truth, the question I ask you to carry with you is this: what will you do in the end?

13. What the 91% See

What do you see when you look at church? According to the Barna Group survey data I frequently mention, 91% of young adults who don't attend church see Christians and their churches as anti-homosexual.

Though I've struggled with this topic and have often been tempted to ignore it, I believe I feel God prodding me to uncover the truth of His view of homosexuality. Besides, I want the truth, especially for those 91%. Before getting to that, here's a little perspective, some of which paints the image those 91% see when they look at certain Christians and churches.

The other night my wife was reading to me some headlines from her news feed. One of those headlines was about an evangelical pastor who declared to his congregation that LGBTQ people should be lined up and shot. Then there's the notorious Topeka church that for years has spewed a venomous message of hate and condemnation of homosexuals. Yet these people call themselves Christian.

As an example of a different perspective, many years ago I came across some articles in the *New York Times* about the 2009 General Convention of the Episcopal church and its resolution accepting homosexuality. The articles were full of opinions on both sides of the issue, though no mention of God's opinion. There was talk about being authentic to each other, but no mention of being authentic to God. There was concern about offending others within the Episcopal church, yet no concern about God. In my effort to find God's view of homosexuality, these guys were as useless as those who hate homosexuals.

Looking for more information, I found the convention resolution on the Episcopal website. The resolution appeared to boil down to a buzzword, "inclusivity." Now that's a great word, and a concept that's painfully lacking in many parts of society. However, it appears that word is more important to the Episcopal church than God's word.

But like that life-threatening evangelical church or the hate-filled Topeka church, other churches reject LGBTQ people, not even letting them in the door. If a church rejects those guilty of the sin of homosexuality, why don't they lock the doors to everyone? For as the writer of Ecclesiastes said, *"Indeed, there is not a righteous person on earth who always does good and does not ever sin"*

(Ecclesiastes 7:20, NASB). And as Paul said, *"... for all have sinned and fall short of the glory of God"* (Romans 3:23).

We're all doomed to behave in ways God doesn't approve of, and rejecting one group of sinners while welcoming others is just another sin, for it rejects the love Jesus calls us to have for one another. Yet, for LGBTQ people knocking on a church door and getting no answer, they're in good company. For standing right next to them is the Holy Spirit, knocking and getting the same response.

Anyway, what *is* God's view of homosexuality? Because of how volatile this topic feels, with each new draft of the book, I considered pressing the delete button on this chapter. Then one day, an obvious truth took shape in my mind—obvious, though I previously hadn't seen it. Read on, and you too will see that truth.

Is homosexuality a sin?

God begins to answer that question in the Old Testament. Some people insist that the Old Testament rules don't apply anymore, that Jesus replaced the old laws with His message of love and forgiveness. However, in referring to those Old Testament laws Jesus said:

> "Do not think that I have come to abolish the Law or the Prophets; I have not come to abolish them but to fulfill them." (Matthew 5:17)

So much for that theory.

One of God's Old Testament laws is, *"Do not have sexual relations with a man as one does with a woman; that is detestable"* (Leviticus 18:22). There are many other "do not's" in chapter 18 of Leviticus, which focuses on sexual relations, such as: do not have sex with your mother, your sister, your child's daughter, your aunt, your daughter-in-law, your sister-in-law, both a woman and her daughter, a woman during her period, a neighbor's wife, and finally, an animal. Though most people don't challenge these "do not's," some challenge verse 22, and claim that homosexuality is *not* a sin.

Jumping forward to the New Testament, Paul had this to say: *"Their women exchanged natural intercourse for unnatural, and in the same way also the men, giving up natural intercourse with women, were consumed with passion for one another. Men committed shameless acts with men"* (Romans 1:26-27 NRSV). In his letter to the church at Corinth, Paul went further:

> *"Do not be deceived; neither the sexually immoral, nor idolaters, nor adulterers, nor homosexuals, nor thieves, nor the greedy, nor those habitually drunk, nor verbal abusers, nor swindlers, will inherit the kingdom of God." (1 Corinthians 6:9-10 NASB)*

Therefore, a homosexual and I have this in common: I happen to be heterosexual, yet I'm also a sinner, and at times in my life I've committed maybe three of the sins in Paul's list. From this perspective, the only difference between a homosexual and me is the nature of our sins.

Now, for all who have committed one or more sins on Paul's list, his statement seems to say that we won't go to heaven. However, check out what Paul said next:

> *"Such were some of you; but you were washed, but you were sanctified, but you were justified in the name of the Lord Jesus Christ and in the Spirit of our God." (verse 11)*

Sounds like forgiveness to me, forgiveness that re-opens the gates into heaven.

Moving on, what did Jesus say that might give us clues as to His opinion of homosexuality? First, looking at His definition of marriage, Jesus said, *"But from the beginning of creation, 'God made them male and female. For this reason a man shall leave his father and mother and be joined to his wife, and the two shall become one flesh.' So they are no longer two, but one flesh. Therefore what God has joined together, let no one separate"* (Mark 10:6-9 NRSV). Marriage, being between a man and a woman, hints at Jesus' view of homosexuality, or at least same-sex marriage.

Jesus also said, *"For from within, out of the hearts of people, come the evil thoughts, acts of sexual immorality, thefts, murders, acts of adultery, deeds of greed, wickedness, deceit, indecent behavior, envy, slander, pride, and foolishness"* (Mark 7:21-22 NASB). Now I realize that Jesus didn't mention homosexuality specifically. Yet, it's important to acknowledge that Jesus never accepted sins of any form. He just accepts the sinner, and the penalty for their sins.

Adultery vs. Homosexuality

I asked a Christian friend, who sincerely believes that homosexuality is *not* a sin, what she thought about adultery; is adultery a sin? "Well, of course," she replied. Most Christians I know would agree, as does the list of sexual sins in Leviticus chapter 18.

Jumping back to Leviticus, God also said this about adultery: *"If a man commits adultery with another man's wife—with the wife of his neighbor—both the adulterer and the adulteress are to be put to death"* (Leviticus 20:10). Wow, that's harsh. Would God judge homosexuality as harshly? Three verses later God said, *"If a man has sexual relations with a man as one does with a woman, both of them have done what is detestable. They are to be put to death"* (verse 13).

God judges adultery and homosexuality as deserving the same punishment. However, as Paul said above, *we were washed, we were sanctified, we were justified in the name of the Lord Jesus Christ and in the Spirit of our God.* Jesus already paid the death penalty for the sins of adultery and homosexuality. He didn't come to abolish those penalties, but to fulfill them.

Finally, to believe that homosexuality isn't a sin, or to declare that all homosexuals will go to hell, is the same as declaring that Jesus died for nothing.

The heavenly truth

Ask a parent of a homosexual how they feel about their child. For many, they'll tell you about their special love and compassion for them. They see the challenges and pain their child may face in our society. Also, their love for their child is more powerful than whatever they might think about homosexuality.

God's love is more powerful than that.

Are you homosexual? The heavenly truth I referred to at the beginning of the chapter is this: though God's response to homosexuality is disapproval—like with any other sin—His response to you is love. His love is more powerful than the sin. Your Father God loves you just as you are. As the worn-out saying goes, God hates the sin, but loves the sinner. He hopes you love Him too.

14. Manmade Verses God-Made

It wasn't what I started out looking for. However, while searching for Jesus' Christianity, I'm beginning to see a more vivid image of the manmade version. What I see is a religion of divided and dissimilar denominations, putting their trust in traditions, ritual, self-reliance, human reasoning, and the ways of the world. The focus is often on obedience and judgment, hierarchy and structure, where God is missing and the Holy Spirit is dead.

As James described it, God's version is less complicated:

> *"Religion that is pure and undefiled before God, the Father, is this: to care for orphans and widows in their distress, and <u>to keep oneself unstained by the world</u>." (James 1:27 NRSV, emphasis added)*

God originally made humanity in His image, though that image has long been stained by pride and the ways of the world. Jesus then made what we call Christianity in His image, and that's become stained by the same things. To better understand and appreciate Jesus' Christianity, it might be helpful to further compare it to the stained, manmade version.

Shallow and short-lived

Manmade Christianity is like most movies in that it's fiction, and its impact on your life is often temporary. Each Sunday, you sit in the theater pews and enjoy the religious movie until you go home, where worry, stress, and distractions team up to shove the joyful memory out of your mind. Any positive effect of manmade Christianity on people's lives is often shallow and short-lived.

In contrast, Jesus' Christianity is a relationship with God, not a scripted act. Jesus' Christianity is a life lived with the Spirit of Jesus within you, cleansing you of the stains of the world. And like its creator, Jesus' Christianity and its influence on your life are real and eternal.

Ground Hog Day church

My friend Dave left manmade Christianity because sermon after sermon left no lasting impact on his life, like seeing the same movie week after week. Dave and I both attended *Ground Hog Day* churches. In case you haven't seen it, *Ground Hog Day* is a movie where Bill Murray lives the same exact day over and over again. He felt trapped in that one day.

To better understand what I mean by a *Ground Hog Day* church, pretend you're in school and you have a class that meets once a week. Let's say its geometry. As the semester progresses, you hear a variety of lessons. When the next semester rolls around, you find yourself back in the same class, hearing the same lessons. This continues, from one semester to the next, one year to the next. You feel trapped in geometry, unable to move up to the next level of math.

Many churches are like that. They keep repeating the same series of messages, from one year to the next. They bring you to a certain level of understanding, then go no farther. Christianity 1A is all they teach. But not so in Jesus' Church, where the Holy Spirit will take over and guide you to the next level, into all truth.

Confinement

The religion of manmade Christianity is a vessel built by man to contain God—as if that were possible. Churches define God within the boundaries of this container. Yet, since God can't be confined, this manmade religion has become more of a prison, holding people captive in a world where God and His truth are missing. The walls of this prison are all the manmade rules, doctrines, traditions, and obligations.

Those on the outside can be prisoners too, prisoners of past experiences that hindered them from seeing Jesus' Christianity. If you're such a person, you're not alone. According to a Barna Group survey:

> "37% of non-churchgoing Americans said they avoid Christian churches because of a negative past experience in churches or with church people." [1]

That's a lot of collateral damage, inflicted by a stained and flawed manmade Christianity and overly religious church people. Yet, whether you're wounded and confined within the walls of a false Christianity, or wounded by past experiences bumping against the outside of those walls, the truth of Jesus' Christianity can set you free. For where manmade Christianity inflicts wounds, Jesus' Christianity heals wounds.

Performance Christianity

On a recent Sunday morning I came across these words from Jesus: *"God is spirit, and his worshipers must worship in the Spirit and in truth"* (John 4:24). I thought of other Christians in town that morning, the ones getting ready to go to church. I knew what their times of worship would be like.

Some would be standing, others sitting, while they all sang worship songs led by the worship band, praise band, worship team, or whatever they call it. Other than the lyrics and the intended meaning behind those lyrics, the experience might not be much different than attending a concert, especially for the bigger churches with the professional sounding band. Some churches have such polished musical performers and sound systems that I've heard it called *performance Christianity*.

A.W. Tozer had this to say about such methods of worship:

> "A church fed on worldly excitement is no New Testament church at all. The desire for surface stimulation is a sure mark of the fallen nature—the very thing Christ died to deliver us from. A curious crowd of baptized worldlings waiting each Sunday for the quasi-religious needle to give them a lift bears no relation whatever to a true assembly of Christian believers." [2]

Many churches worship God in a very worldly way, with worldly methods, worldly music, and worldly traditions. That's not necessarily bad, as such forms of worship can be helpful elements of a Christianity 1A education. But worship shouldn't stop there, in the middle of the concert hall/sanctuary.

Contrary to the worldly methods, Jesus said to worship in a spiritual way, to go into our room, close the door, and pray to God in private. Jesus calls us to worship God not from the center of a sanctuary or concert hall surrounded by the sights and sounds of the material world, but from the center of our souls surrounded by the presence of the Holy Spirit. That is, *worship in the Spirit and in truth*.

Assumed authority

Back in chapter 12, I cited Catechism 82 of the Roman Catholic church, which starts out with, "As a result the Church, to whom the transmission and interpretation of Revelation is entrusted …". I suspect the Catholic church isn't alone in their assertion that they have sole authority to interpretate the truths of God and Jesus as revealed in the Bible.

But … that's the Holy Spirit's responsibility. As Jesus made very clear:

> "But the Helper, the Holy Spirit whom the Father will send in My name, He will teach you all things, and remind you of all that I said to you." (John 14:26 NASB)
>
> "I have much more to say to you, more than you can now bear. But when he, the Spirit of truth comes, he will guide you into all truth." (John 16:12-13)

Rather than directing wannabe Christians to some human authority, like himself, the Apostle Paul said:

> "I keep asking that the God of our Lord Jesus Christ, the glorious Father, may give you the Spirit of wisdom and revelation, so that you may know him better." (Ephesians 1:17)

The Holy Spirit provides revelation, not man, nor a manmade church. Paul was humble enough to accept this truth and direct people to God rather than to himself. Too bad more of today's churches don't do the same.

A walk through Galatians

The religion of manmade Christianity started infecting the newborn Christians of first century Galatia. Paul heard about it and sent them a warning. Let's take a very brief, highly paraphrased walk through Paul's letter.

> Hey! Beware of a perverted gospel that's beginning to infect you. The cure for this infection comes from God and your faith in His Son, not man. You'll not find what you seek in following manmade rules. You'll only find it in a close, personal relationship with God.
>
> Please, don't be a slave to a manmade religion and its manmade rules. Rules count for nothing. The only thing that counts is love, a love born out of true faith in Jesus Christ.

Yet are you having trouble breaking the shackles of manmade Christianity? If so, look to the Holy Spirit; He'll break your bonds, knock down the prison walls, and set you free, free to live life as God intended, filled with the fruits of His presence. And these fruits are love, joy, peace, patience, kindness, generosity, faithfulness, gentleness, and self-control. This is the truth of what Jesus' Christianity is all about.

I stress again, a manmade religion counts for nothing. What counts is a new you, living with the Holy Spirit.

Manmade and worldly, verses Jesus' Christianity

- Manmade Christianity is often an exclusive club;
  Jesus' Christianity is not.
- Manmade Christianity is often burdens and obligations;
  Jesus' Christianity is not.
- Manmade Christianity is complicated;
  Jesus' Christianity is simple.
- Manmade Christianity is, of course, manmade;
  Jesus' Christianity is God-made.
- Manmade Christianity is following rules and traditions;
  Jesus' Christianity is following Jesus.
- Manmade Christianity can be captivity;
  Jesus' Christianity is freedom.
- Manmade Christianity often inflicts wounds;
  Jesus' Christianity heals wounds.
- Manmade Christianity relies on human ability;
  Jesus' Christianity relies on the Holy Spirit.
- People oversee manmade Christianity;
  the Holy Spirit oversees Jesus' Christianity.
- God is missing from manmade Christianity;
  God's presence is the definition of Jesus' Christianity.

But why is manmade Christianity so different from what Jesus lived and taught? William Law might answer with this:

> *"The preaching of the gospel has become merely a work of man's wisdom, come forth in the power of human qualification, and is more or less full of itself, and trusting to its own ability. To this is the great apostasy of all Christendom to be attributed. This is the door through which the spirit of the world entered into possession of the Christian church."* [3]

What many of us experience is vastly different from what Jesus intended, because the spirit of the world has taken possession of Jesus' Church. Worldly verses spiritual, temporary verses eternal, imagined verses real, impersonal verses relational, false verses true; this sums up the differences between manmade and God-made Christianity.

Plus, God seems missing, which is the central flaw of the religion of manmade Christianity. However, as Oswald Chambers said,

> *"Many a soul begins to come to God when he flings off being religious, because there is only one Master of the human heart, and that is not religion but Jesus Christ."* [4]

Not religion, but Jesus Christ. True Christianity is not a manmade religion—it's a relationship with its founder.

15. The One True Church

According to an article I read many years ago, "Pope Benedict XVI has reasserted the universal primacy of the Roman Catholic Church, approving a document released Tuesday that says Orthodox churches were defective and that other Christian denominations were not true churches." [1] The Vatican document went on to say, "Christ established here on earth only one church. The other communities cannot be called 'churches' in the proper sense, because they do not have apostolic succession—the ability to trace their bishops back to Christ's original apostles." Since the Catholic church claims the Apostle Peter as its first Pope, that makes it the one and only "true" church, according to them.

Yet, what does Jesus think about this, and what does He consider *His* one true Church? First, here's a reminder of the convention I've been using. There's Church, with an upper case "C," which refers to Jesus' Church and the presence of the Holy Spirit. Then there's church, with a lower case "c," which refers to human-founded and managed churches where the Holy Spirit is often missing. Regarding Spirit-less churches, Andrew Murray said:

> "It is this Spirit that the church lacks so sadly; it is this Spirit she grieves so unceasingly. It is owing to this spiritual poverty that her work is so often feeble and fruitless." [2]

The first church building—though they didn't call it *church* back then—was the tabernacle, a tent built per instructions God gave Moses. The back section of the tent was the Most Holy Place, separated from the front section by a curtain. In the Most Holy Place sat the Ark of the Covenant and the Spirit of God.

When the Hebrews settled in Jerusalem, the stone Temple eventually replaced the tent, with the floorplan remaining the same. A curtain still separated the front section of the Temple from the Most Holy Place, and the presence of God. Yet whether tent or stone, this Old Testament *Church* was the earthly dwelling of God's Spirit.

Jesus' Church

Though Jesus' Church remains the earthly dwelling of God's Spirit, that dwelling is no longer manmade. In referring to Jesus and His Church, Paul said:

> *"And God placed all things under his feet and appointed him to be head over everything for the church, which is his body." (Ephesians 1:22-23, emphasis added)*
>
> *"And in him* [Jesus] *you too are being built together to become a dwelling in which God lives by his Spirit." (Ephesians 2:22)*

By Jesus' sacrifice on the cross, the Temple curtain—which represented the barrier of sin separating God from His children—ripped in two. With this barrier out of the way, the Spirit and God's children can unite into a new dwelling for both of them. Jesus wants us to become His Church, the One True Church, the dwelling in which God lives by His Spirit.

Now this novel definition of Church isn't some random idea mentioned in only one of Paul's letters. Here are a few more examples:

> *"But Christ is faithful as the Son over God's house. And we are his house, if indeed we hold firmly to our confidence and the hope in which we glory." (Hebrews 3:6)*
>
> *"Do you not know that you are God's temple and that God's Spirit dwells in you? ... For God's temple is holy, and you are that temple." (1 Corinthians 3:16-17 NRSV)*
>
> *"For we are the temple of the living God." (2 Corinthians 6:16 NRSV)*
>
> *"Do you not know that your bodies are temples of the Holy Spirit, who is in you, whom you have received from God?" (1 Corinthians 6:19, emphasis added)*

Since the Bible defines what I'm calling the One True Church as being the earthly dwelling of the Holy Spirit, without the Holy Spirit, there is no Church.

Without the Holy Spirit, a church is often feeble and fruitless, lacking the spiritual power to influence people's lives and hold onto members. Yet, as A.W. Tozer said:

> "If we cooperate with Him in loving obedience, God will manifest Himself to us, and that manifestation will be the difference between a nominal Christian life and a life radiant with the light of His face." [3]

A nominal Christian life—such is life in a church, lower case "c."

A new model for church, doing as Jesus did

As mentioned in the previous chapter, many churches do a good job teaching an introduction to Christianity, that is Christianity 1A, though the Holy Spirit is often absent from the lesson plan. Along with that, the bureaucracy, hierarchy, complexity, and politics that are part of institutional church often hinder people from graduating to Church. However, churches should do as John the Baptist and Jesus did.

John's job was to inspire people to repent of their sins and prepare them to accept Jesus. Once Jesus arrived on the scene, John humbly stepped aside and let Jesus take over. As John said in referring to Jesus, *"He must become greater; I must become less."*

Jesus then told His followers as much as they could understand, and having completed that, He stepped aside and returned to heaven. He then sent His Spirit to take over where He had left off. As Jesus said,

> "I have much more to say to you, more than you can now bear. But when he, the Spirit of truth comes, he will guide you into all truth." (John 16:12-13)

With these words, Jesus established the model for churches. They should teach as much as we can bear, all the while preparing us to receive the Holy Spirit into our lives. Churches should then step aside and let the Spirit take over our spiritual guidance and education. After all, that's what Jesus did.

Along with teaching Christianity 1A, churches should drop all the bureaucracy, hierarchy, complexity, and politics, and throw out the business model. Also, a church's success shouldn't be judged by how many students they have, but rather by their graduation rates.

Yet, how can a church organization survive if people keep graduating and leaving? Well, like any school, they need to bring in new students. But no worries, God will help. The Spirit-filled alumni will help too, like at other schools. Besides, when someone graduates from the school of Christianity 1A, they don't have to stop attending.

The bottom line is this: a church should do no more, *and no less*, than what Jesus did for His followers when He walked the roads of ancient Israel. Jesus was preparing them to receive the Holy Spirit. A church should do the same.

They call it fellowship

I sometimes run across folks still attending the church I had left. At first, there were the invitations for me to return. Eventually, the sales pitches stopped. That's when the greetings started with, "So, where are you going to church now?" or, "Where do you worship now?" Awkward. When I admit the truth, there's sometimes that judgmental glare, like they don't believe I'm a real Christian because I no longer attend church. Is that really the mark of a true Christian, a good Sunday attendance record?

There is something I occasionally miss, however. They call it fellowship; hanging out with other Christians, learning together, building relationships together. I have to be honest though. The fellowship I crave is found in my relationship with God and Jesus, via the Holy Spirit. Like the Apostle John said,

> "Our fellowship is with the Father and with his Son, Jesus Christ." (1 John 1:3)

Where a big part of church is fellowship with other churchgoers, the One True Church is all about fellowship with the Spirit of God and Jesus.

Church distilled to its essence

The One True Church is all the people who welcome Jesus' Spirit to live within them and through them, sharing their body with them, whether they consciously feel His presence or not. Jesus had painted a picture of the Church, where He is the vine and Spirit-filled believers are the branches attached to that vine. The Church is the entire plant.

Before leaving my quest for the truth about the Church, I decided to read the entire New Testament again, just to make sure I hadn't missed anything. I walked away from that multi-week detour with the following list, the true nature of Jesus' Christianity, and *His* One True Church.

Church is …

- Looking out for widows and orphans, and sharing with those who are in need,
- Loving God and all others,
- Preaching only the words of God and Jesus, not going beyond what is written,
- Praying for each other and those who are still lost,
- Serving God in the Spirit,
- Living sacrificially and living for the Spirit,
- Keeping oneself from being stained by the world,
- More than salvation,
- Teaching, encouraging, and spreading the truth, mercy, and love,
- Being united by our common connection with the Holy Spirit,
- Fellowship with God and Jesus,
- Worshiping God in spirit and in truth,
- Being God's Temple, the dwelling where His Spirit lives,
- Denying our self and surrendering to the Spirit of Jesus within us,

More than a description of Jesus' Church, this is a portrait of a true Christian, which of course is the same thing. With that understanding, you're now ready for the next leg of this journey in search of Christianity.

So-called Christian

16. Christian in Name Only

My wife and I watched a movie last night where a nineteen-year-old girl and her boyfriend discover she's pregnant. In one scene the boyfriend's mother, a hardcore institutional Christian, corners the girl, shoves her finger in the girl's face and screams that the girl is evil and the baby in her womb is going to shrivel up and die and the girl is going to hell because she sinned against God for having sex out of wedlock. Whether prompted by a movie or personal experience, this is an example of how some people see Christians.

Unfortunately, what we sometimes see in the behavior of so-called Christians is more graffiti hiding the truth of what it truly means to be Christian. Yet, I'm troubled by that phrase I've been using: *so-called Christian*. I've heard of RINOs, Republicans In Name Only. I now believe there are CINOs, Christians In Name Only. Actually, I know there are CINOs, because I used to be one.

Not many years ago, I reacted differently than I do now whenever I read this from Jesus: *"Whoever wants to be my disciple must deny themselves and take up their cross daily and follow me"* (Luke 9:23). Lacking desire, and maybe being afraid of how drastically such a commitment might change my life, I'd push Jesus' words out of my mind and shut my Bible. Though Jesus' criteria for being Christian is clear and direct in that statement, I sometimes imagined He was talking about a higher level of Christian than what He expected me to become. I guess I hoped He was referring to a black belt Christian, while only expecting me to be a yellow belt. I was wrong.

Yes, I've spent much of my Christian life as a CINO. It's only been in the past few years, during the writing of the last several drafts of this book, that I've learned what it means to deny myself and follow Jesus. So I apologize to those of you who may feel offended by the label I've been using. Maybe I can use something kinder. How about *aspiring* Christian, *apprentice* Christian, or even *Christianity 1A* Christian? Hey, we all have to start somewhere.

On our climb up the metaphorical mountain in search of Christian truth, we first set up our base camp, built on the truth of God, Jesus, and the Holy Spirit. We then traversed a somewhat difficult section of trail leading to the truth about Church. The next leg of our climb will take us to within sight of the top.

But before stepping back on the trail, in the next few chapters I want to show more examples of Christian behavior that doesn't appear very Christian, behavior of people who are Christian in name only. Later, with that image more clearly in mind, you'll be able to better appreciate the power and beauty of the truth that lies beneath that graffiti.

Why only a few?

First, what's the problem with being a CINO—sorry, I mean aspiring Christian? There's no problem, unless you're stuck there. I used to be a *stuck* aspiring Christian, and though I claimed His name, as evidenced by my behavior I didn't know the man. Jesus has a warning for such Christians:

> "Not everyone who says to me, 'Lord, Lord,' will enter the kingdom of heaven, but only the one who does the will of my Father who is in heaven. Many will say to me on that day, 'Lord, Lord, did we not prophesy in your name and in your name drive out demons and perform many miracles?' Then I will tell them plainly, 'I never knew you. Away from me, you evildoers!'" (Matthew 7:21-23, emphasis added)

Jesus is clearly addressing this warning to people who believe in Him, who call Him Lord and use His name, which is a common definition of a Christian. But then He said, "I never knew you." Lots of people know *about* Jesus. They know Him as much as they know any historical figure. According to Jesus, that's not enough.

Further up the page in my Bible, Jesus gives this warning:

> "Enter through the narrow gate. For wide is the gate and broad is the road that leads to destruction, and many enter through it. But small is the gate and narrow the road that leads to life, and only a few find it." (Matthew 7:13-14)

These words have always troubled me. I'd even penciled this question in the margin of my Bible: *Why only a few?* I'm beginning to see the answer.

Many aspiring Christians don't *know* Jesus. They take the name and not much more. They think they're in good with God because of a label they've adopted, a bit of faith, and devotion to rules. However, in the end will Jesus say to them, *"I never knew you. Away from me?"*

Yet, it's not their fault. According to the Barna Group survey data I'm fond of, most de-churched Christians leave church without finding a connection with God. So, it's no surprise many aspiring Christians don't *know* God and Jesus, since their church hadn't introduced them to each other.

Non-literal Christians

In chapter 4, I cited some PEW Research survey results showing that 35% of Catholics and mainline Protestants believe the Bible is the word of God, but *should not be taken literally*. It looks like they don't consider God's word as trustworthy or meaningful. Yet they call themselves Christian.

In the early days of Saturday Night Live, in a Weekend Update skit where Chevy Chase is the news anchor, Gilda Radner plays a character who goes into a long, flawed editorial. When corrected by Chevy, Gilda's character looks at the camera and in a whiny voice says, "Never mind."

Is that how these non-literal Christians see God and His word in the Bible? It appears that from their perspective, God defined and documented His Christianity and then, after handing them the document (the Bible), He says, "Never mind."

These 35% are more examples of Christians many outsiders see—Christians who can't possibly know Jesus because they won't give credence to what He says. Yet, I wonder how many of them, though they won't take the word of God literally, will happily accept every word from conspiracy theory promoters, fake news influencers, or lying politicians.

The politicization of Christianity

Some Christians very vocally and publicly support certain politicians. Since Jesus said to make disciples of *all* nations (Matthew 28:19), such public support of politicians presents a problem. Publicly taking a political side alienates those on the other side. This doesn't help achieve Jesus' mission. Rather, it likely pushes people away from Christianity—you've seen some of the survey data showing the growing exodus. Also, Jesus doesn't call His followers to preach civic issues or give their support to political leaders. He calls us to preach His gospel and give our support, in fact, our very selves, to God.

Along these lines, Paul had this advice: *"Join with me in suffering, like a good soldier of Christ Jesus. No one serving as a soldier gets entangled in civilian affairs, but rather tries to please his commanding officer"* (2 Timothy 2:3-4). According to Paul, Christians shouldn't get all wrapped up in civilian affairs and political issues, and their commanding officer should be Jesus rather than a politician.

By the way, in a Barna Group survey of young adults who don't attend church, 75% of them view Christians as too involved in politics, with 50% of young adult churchgoers feeling the same way. [1] And back in chapter 3, I cited other Barna Group survey results stating that about 25% of church outsiders felt that Christianity had gotten off track and *no longer seemed Christian*. The more political Christianity becomes, the less Christian it will be.

The war against Christianity

The war against Christianity periodically makes the news, like when certain secular groups protest against Christmas nativity scenes on public property. Many Christians feel under attack from secular society. They feel their right to believe as they choose is threatened, that their free will is threatened. I get it. I've sometimes been a victim of anti-Christian bigotry.

Some Christians fight back with their votes. As many conservative Christians proclaimed during the 2020 US presidential election, they relied on their candidate to protect them and their religion. But as God said through Isaiah,

> "I, even I, am he who comforts you. Who are you that you fear mere mortals, human beings who are but grass, that you forget the Lord your Maker." (Isaiah 51:12-13)

It's easy to understand why Christians are attracted to a friendly face when many others are scowling at them. But does God really need help keeping Christians and Christianity safe? God and Jesus have done fine on their own over the past 2000 years. Shortly after Jesus died on the cross, the same religious leaders who pushed for his death started trying to kill His newborn Christianity. Roman emperors took on the fight. Throughout the centuries, many others joined in. They all failed. And Christians of the past didn't have the opportunity to vote for friendly faces.

This suggests that many Christians trust politicians and their worldly ways more than the God they claim to follow. I wonder; is that how some outsiders see Christians—strong on attitude, weak on faith?

The real threat to Christianity

In defending themselves against anticipated secular attacks, some Christians are launching preemptive strikes by trying to force their values upon their perceived enemies, either directly or by how they vote. But their battle strategy is all wrong, and launched in the wrong direction. The attacks they should be concerned about are coming from within.

Christianity has been under attack since Jesus started preaching. At first, the attacks came from outside. Later, attacks started coming from inside, from worldly Christians. Their weapons have been such things as dictatorial attitudes, arrogance, lust for power and influence, and of course their judgment, hypocrisy, and bigotry. These character traits of some CINOs do more harm to Christianity than anyone in the secular world could ever do.

I feel sorry for these aspiring Christians, as they've fallen victim to a manmade religion that is more worldly than Godly, where God and His truth are missing. Nevertheless, like the father of the prodigal son, God is watching for them, hoping they'll turn around and return home, to the truth.

Defending against attacks

As I've quoted before, Jesus said,

> "Everyone then who hears these words of mine and acts on them will be like a wise man who built his house on rock. The rain fell, the floods came, and the winds blew and beat on that house, but it did not fall, because it had been founded on rock. And everyone who hears these words of mine and does not act on them will be like a foolish man who built his house on sand. The rain fell, and the floods came, and the winds blew and beat against that house, and it fell—and great was its fall!" (Matthew 7:24-27 NRSV).

Christians who've moved off the foundation of Jesus, to things like politics and manmade Christianity, will indeed suffer from the storms coming from the secular world. Yet, instead of fighting back, what if they moved onto the solid foundation of Jesus and His truth? As Jesus said, when they're anchored to the truth, when they listen to Him and act on His words, the winds of the external war against Christianity can't harm them.

Also, if the internal attacks would stop so that outsiders could see an unblemished image of Jesus' Christianity, the external attacks would diminish. Most of their reasons for attacking would no longer exist, like the hypocrisy, judgment, Christian arrogance, intolerance, trying to force their values on others, and all the other weapons wielded by CINOs and worldly Christians.

Finally, regarding the fear of attacks from outside of Christianity, Jesus might also say:

> "If your enemies are hungry, feed them; if they are thirsty, give them something to drink." (Romans 12:20 NRSV)
>
> "But to you who are listening I say: Love your enemies, do good to those who hate you, bless those who curse you, pray for those who mistreat you. If someone slaps you on one cheek, turn to them the other also. ... Do to others as you would have them do to you." (Luke 6:27-29, 31)

How do you think external enemies would respond if this were the behavior they saw from Christians? What would they think if they experienced Christians doing as Jesus would do?

Had enough?

The important reality I hope you take from this chapter is that the most harmful attacks against Christianity are coming from people who call themselves Christian. With that thought, I want to remind you of a question I invited you to consider:

> "The prophets prophesy lies, the priests rule by their own authority, and my people love it this way. But what will you do in the end?" (Jeremiah 5:31).

I know, this chapter may have been a bit difficult. Truth can be that way sometimes. Yet, if you're willing to continue following me on this journey, it's not just Christianity that's under attack from within.

17. The Other Enemy Within

Back in chapter 9, I used an image from cartoons where there's a little devil on one shoulder and our conscience on the other shoulder, both fighting for control of our feelings, thoughts, actions, and words. This dual aspect of the human personality is what Paul was complaining about when he said,

> "I do not understand my own actions. For I do not do what I want, but I do the very thing I hate. ... As it is, it is no longer I myself who do it, but it is sin living in me. ... So I find this law at work: Although I want to do good, evil is right there with me." (Romans 7:15, 17, 21)

Although my conscience wants to do good, my little devil is right there with me, tempting me to do something else. Many of us suffer from such an internal conflict. On one shoulder stands our worldly nature—our sinful, self-centered, image-of-the-world self. On the other shoulder is our Godly nature—our loving, humble, image-of-God Self.

But as Paul said, how can I, *"Put to death, therefore, whatever belongs to your earthly nature"* (Colossians 3:5). How can any of us find freedom from attacks by our devilish self, the self who often holds us captive to such things as fear, anger, anxiety, and depression? Yes, it's not just Christianity that's under attack from within. Everyone, whether Christian or non-Christian, is subject to captivity by their worldly nature.

Let's now look at some of the weapons wielded by that little devil on our shoulder. Then, we'll see how to defend ourselves against those attacks.

Hypocritical

As you've already read, 85% of unchurched young adults see Christians as hypocritical.[1] That's no surprise, since hypocrisy is a common weapon of our worldly self. Jesus saw hypocrisy in those who opposed him and his efforts, and He criticized them for it when He said such things as:

> "In the same way, on the outside you appear to people as righteous but on the inside you are full of hypocrisy and wickedness." (Matthew 23:28)
>
> "So when you give to the poor, do not sound a trumpet before you, as the hypocrites do in the synagogues and on the streets, so that they will be praised by people." (Matthew 6:2 NASB)

The budding Christian community wasn't immune either, as Peter warned:

> "Therefore, rid yourselves of all malice and all deceit, hypocrisy, envy, and slander of every kind." (1 Peter 2:1)

Peter made it sound easy, like telling us to take out the trash. However, such common ingredients of our human nature don't willingly let themselves be thrown away. I've tried, and failed. Yet, as I eventually learned, freedom from captivity to things like hypocrisy doesn't come by my efforts alone.

Judgmental

A Christian friend recently posted on Facebook about a CINO acquaintance who said my friend won't go to heaven because he's not doing God's will. My friend mentioned that others have started judging him in similar ways, and he doesn't know why. He's losing sleep over it and considering giving up on Christianity. In his words, "It feels like faith has been weaponized."

Another common weapon of our worldly selves is the tendency to be judgmental. That's why 87% of non-Christian survey respondents see Christians as such.[1] Judgment wielded like a club stands out in Christian circles, because, like with hypocrisy, even outsiders expect Christians to be different from the rest. Jesus, James, and Paul certainly did:

> "Do not judge, and you will not be judged; do not condemn, and you will not be condemned. Forgive, and you will be forgiven." (Luke 6:37 NRSV)

> "Judgment without mercy will be shown to anyone who has not been merciful. Mercy triumphs over judgment!" (James 2:13)
>
> "Brothers and sisters, do not slander one another. Anyone who speaks against a brother or sister or judges them speaks against the law and judges it. ... But you—who are you to judge your neighbor?" (James 4:11-12)
>
> "Therefore let's not judge one another anymore, but rather determine this: not to put an obstacle or a stumbling block in a brother's or sister's way." (Romans 14:13 NASB)

That's only a small sample of Bible warnings against being judgmental. And as usual, Jesus led by example, for He also said, *"If anyone hears my words but does not keep them, I do not judge that person. For I did not come to judge the world, but to save the world"* (John 12:47). Aren't Christians called to be like Jesus?

Yet being judgmental comes so easily, almost like breathing. I'm sure I've made judgmental statements within this book, and I'm sorry. But like with hypocrisy, I can't rid myself of such normal human character traits, just as I can't casually brush that little devil off my shoulder.

Finally, regarding my friend's so-called Christian acquaintances who judge him for not doing God's will, by their judgment, *they* aren't doing God's will either.

Worldly

We're held captive by our worldly nature, where hypocrisy and judgment are two common elements of that nature. However, Jesus calls us to live free from this world and its influences over our nature. To His Father, Jesus prayed, *"I have given them* [His disciples] *Your word; and the world has hated them because they are not of the world, just as I am not of the world"* (John 17:14 NASB). According to Jesus, His followers are not natural citizens of this material world. As Paul said, *"For our citizenship is in heaven"* (Philippians 3:20 NASB).

Maybe our worldly experience is like a movie. It temporarily seems real while we're watching it, pulling us in, and making us feel like we're part of the story.

Yet, how will we feel once we walk out of this worldly theater and return home? The apparent reality of our earthly experience will soon fade away, like the emotions stirred by a good movie. Christians are encouraged to let go of the hold the movie has on us, and instead, focus on what waits for us at home, in heaven.

> "Since, then, you have been raised with Christ, set your hearts on things above, where Christ is, seated at the right hand of God. Set your minds on things above, not on earthly things." (Colossians 3:1-2)
>
> "So we fix our eyes not on what is seen, but on what is unseen, since what is seen is temporary, but what is unseen is eternal." (2 Corinthians 4:18)

This earthly movie is temporary; heaven is eternal.

At the beginning of this book, I used an illustration from the movie *The Matrix,* where Neo, the main character, starts out unaware he's living in a computer-generated, fake and temporary world. He soon learns the truth, a truth that sets him free.

Maybe we can become like Neo, and accept the truth of this world we live in. We, too, can live in this world, but not be of this world. I suspect that's how Jesus lived when He walked the roads of ancient Israel, immersed in the temporary material world while at the same time being fully aware of the spiritual world, and His unbroken connection to it. And as Jesus added in His prayer to God,

> "I am not asking you to take them out of the world, but I ask you to protect them from the evil one. They do not belong to the world, just as I do not belong to the world." (John 17:15-16 NRSV)

A new creation

Regarding our internal battle with a combatant on each shoulder, Paul described the conflict in more detail in his letter to the Galatians:

> "Live by the Spirit, I say, and do not gratify the desires of the flesh [i.e., sinful, worldly nature]. For what the flesh desires is

> *opposed to the Spirit, and what the Spirit desires is opposed to the flesh." (Galatians 5:16-17 NRSV)*

Yes, our worldly nature opposes our Godly nature. Paul went on to list some of the sins that result when our worldly nature wins control:

> *"Now the works of the flesh are obvious: sexual immorality, impurity, debauchery, idolatry, sorcery, enmities, strife, jealousy, anger, quarrels, dissensions, factions, envy, drunkenness, carousing, and things like these." (verses 19-21)*

Yet, by turning our back on our worldly nature, and living by the Spirit—that is, when our Godly nature wins control—we can enjoy the fruits of the Spirit, which are in stark contrast to the sins of the worldly nature:

> *"By contrast, the fruit of the Spirit is love, joy, peace, patience, kindness, generosity, faithfulness, gentleness, and self-control. There is no law against such things. And those who belong to Christ have crucified the flesh with its passions and desires." (verses 22-24)*

In living by the Spirit and enjoying the fruits of the Spirit, we can be transformed into a new creation, returning to the way humanity was in the beginning, with the original creation. As Paul said,

> *"Do not be conformed to this world, but be transformed by the renewing of your mind." (Romans 12:2 NASB)*
>
> *"Therefore if anyone is in Christ, this person is a new creation; the old things passed away; behold, new things have come." (2 Corinthians 5:17 NASB)*

The *old things* are all those self-centered and worldly character traits—like hypocrisy, judgment, and selfishness—and the resulting sins and self-inflicted wounds. The *new creation* is how God intended us to be with the original creation, when He created humanity in His image. Regarding this, here's more Bible food for you to chew on:

> "You were taught, with regard to your former way of life, to put off your old self, which is being corrupted by its deceitful desires; to be made new in the attitude of your minds; and to put on the new self, created to be like God in true righteousness and holiness." (Ephesians 4:22-24, emphasis added)
>
> "He has given us his very great and precious promises, so that through them you may participate in the divine nature, having escaped the corruption in the world caused by evil desires." (2 Peter 1:4)
>
> "And all of us, with unveiled faces, seeing the glory of the Lord as though reflected in a mirror, are being transformed into the same image from one degree of glory to another; for this comes from the Lord, the Spirit." (2 Corinthians 3:18 NRSV)

Paul also said, *"Since you are his child, God has made you also an heir"* (Galatians 4:7). Children are images of their parents. As God's created children, humanity inherited His likeness in the form of His character and nature. Then sin entered the scene—you know, Adam, Eve, Satan, and the tree—and disfigured our God-like image. Humanity was no longer the image of God He had created us to be. Yet, based on the Bible verses cited above, we can get that image back.

Be holy, because I am holy

Some believe that holiness is only for special people. However, God was speaking to all of us when He said, *"I am the Lord your God. Consecrate yourselves therefore, and be holy, because I am holy"* (Leviticus 11:44 NASB). Paul and Peter reinforced this message:

> "For God did not call us to be impure, but to live a holy life." (1 Thessalonians 4:7)

> "But just as he who called you is holy, so be holy in all you do; for it is written: 'Be holy, because I am holy.'" (1 Peter 1:15-16)

Be holy—that's the *new creation* image-of-God that Jesus offers us. Yet we're made holy not by works or effort, but rather by accepting God's truth of Jesus' sacrifice. If we believe, then by Jesus' efforts, not ours, we are holy:

> "We have been made holy through the sacrifice of the body of Jesus Christ once for all. ... for by one sacrifice he has made perfect forever those who are being made holy." (Hebrews 10:10, 14)
>
> "And so Jesus also suffered outside the city gate to make the people holy through his own blood." (Hebrews 13:12)
>
> "Once you were alienated from God and were enemies in your minds because of your evil behavior. But now he has reconciled you by Christ's physical body through death to present you holy in his sight, without blemish and free from accusation—if you continue in your faith, established and firm, and do not move from the hope held out in the gospel." (Colossians 1:21-23)

For all who believe, with Jesus' death on the cross our sin was transferred to Him, and His righteousness and holiness were transferred to us. Since Jesus took all our sins upon Himself, leaving us *without blemish and free from accusation*, in God's eyes it's as if we don't sin, and never have. Oh sure, we may still sin, but by our faith and Jesus' sacrifice, when God looks at us, He doesn't see our sin. Rather, what He sees is holiness.

Finally, Jesus' holiness comes from His Holy Spirit. You can be holy because the Holy Spirit within you is holy. As Andrew Murray said:

> "It is God who makes us holy by the Spirit of holiness who dwells within us. He works in us the very mind and attitudes of Christ." [2]

Now then, hypocrisy, judgment, selfishness, and many other worldly traits tend to hold us captive to things like fear, anger, anxiety, and depression. These traits seem like branches of a tree, branches I'd like to chop off. Yet I don't want to only deal with individual branches. I want to go for the root, the source of all sin that's lurking below the surface. Kill the root and I'll finally experience the freedom from captivity I've been looking for.

18. The Root Cause

We all suffer from the conflict between the extremes of our humanity—our prideful self on one shoulder, and our humble conscience on the other. On one extreme, we have the root cause of all suffering—pride and sin. On the other extreme, we have the cure for all suffering—humility and love. And where pride is the root of all sin, humility is the root of true love. *"That is why Scripture says: 'God opposes the proud but shows favor to the humble'"* (James 4:6).

Adam and Eve were deceived by Satan and infected by pride and selfishness. With the rest of humanity inheriting this affliction, we've all been born into captivity, as unwary prisoners held captive by pride. The stronger the pride in someone, the tighter the bonds that bind them. The more there is of pride and sin, the less there is of humility and love. More pride means we think more about ourselves and less about others. That's why God said,

> "When I fed them, they were satisfied; when they were satisfied, they became proud; then they forgot me." (Hosea 13:6, emphasis added)

In my efforts to be more humble, it's no surprise that self doesn't cooperate. For several years now, I've been fighting a battle against my prideful self—that little devil on my shoulder who's frequently screaming in my ear. But at least I have a chance, since I no longer pretend he doesn't exist.

Three faces of pride

There are many facets to our prideful human nature. I'd like to take a quick look at three of the most common, and most harmful.

Arrogance

According to a dictionary I have, arrogance is an "offensive display of superiority or self-importance; overbearing pride." Arrogance is highly visible, for all to see. Yet arrogance itself sees very little; only what it wants to see. Arrogance can't see or accept anything that doesn't fit into its self-centered set of beliefs. Therefore, truth has little or no meaning to arrogant people. To them, truth is whatever they define it to be. Also, arrogant people are likely to attack those who disagree with them, acting much like a child who's a spoiled brat.

God has warnings for these people:

> *"I hate pride and arrogance, evil behavior and perverse speech." (Proverbs 8:13)*
>
> *"The Lord detests all the proud of heart. Be sure of this: They will not go unpunished." (Proverbs 16:5)*
>
> *"The proud look of humanity will be brought low, and the arrogance of people will be humbled." (Isaiah 2:11 NASB)*

Selfishness

Selfishness is less visible than arrogance, and includes such traits as greed. Also, peel away the layers of any conflict, like in a struggling marriage, and at the core is usually selfishness. Let go of selfishness, and you'll find that understanding, forgiveness, and reconciliation come easily. Maybe that's why God finds reconciliation so desirable and easy—He's not selfish.

God has these warnings about selfishness:

> *"Do nothing from selfishness or empty conceit, but with humility consider one another as more important than yourselves" (Philippians 2:3 NASB)*
>
> *"For where jealousy and selfish ambition exist, there is disorder and every evil thing." (James 3:16 NASB)*
>
> *"Watch out! Be on your guard against all kinds of greed; life does not consist in an abundance of possessions." (Luke 12:15)*

Self-reliance

We typically consider self-reliance a positive trait, simply believing we should be able to handle our own difficulties. The problem is, self-reliance is a distraction from God, another way to forget God—as God said, "*they became proud; then they forgot me.*" Relying on self rather than God is like building your house on a foundation of sand, rather than solid rock. And …

> "Those who trust in the Lord will prosper. Those who trust in themselves are fools, but those who walk in wisdom are kept safe." (Proverbs 28:25-26)

Christian pride

Now consider this, from some Barna Group research:

> "Outsiders told us that the underlying concern of Christians often seems more about being right than about listening. There is an undercurrent of arrogance that outsiders perceive." [1]

What these outsiders perceive is normal human behavior, though evidently they expect Christians to be different—we know Jesus does. Anyway, here are other examples of pride-influenced Christian behavior that I've witnessed, some of which I've exhibited myself:

Self-righteousness and conceit

Some Christians convince themselves that by their own self-effort, they're spiritually better than others. Such self-proclaimed righteousness, though common among Christians, is also flawed in that it reflects a misunderstanding of where righteousness comes from. Regardless, whether from a sense of self-righteousness or other cause, some Christians exude an air of high-mindedness and conceit. Regarding this, Paul has the following advice:

> "Live in harmony with one another. Do not be proud, but be willing to associate with people of low position. Do not be conceited." (Romans 12:16)

Changing God's word

Some people modify the meaning of God's words and call it interpretation. I discussed this in chapter 4. This misuse of the Bible puts more value on personal opinion than God's opinion. Such pride-influenced graffiti covers up God's word with its own. And as Jesus said, *"You do not have in mind the concerns of God, but merely human concerns"* (Mark 8:33).

Wrong motives

Christian charity has healed much suffering throughout history. However, good deeds are appealing to our ego, because they're visible to others, giving us something to brag about. A.W. Tozer observed, *"Promoting self under the guise of promoting Christ is currently so common as to excite little notice."* [2] We might not notice, but Jesus would. As He said:

> "When you give to the needy, do not let your left hand know what your right hand is doing, so that your giving may be in secret. Then your Father, who sees what is done in secret, will reward you." (Matthew 6:3-4)

Making God into our image

Most of the graffiti hiding the truth of Christianity comes from seeing God, Jesus, and Christianity as images of ourselves. Instead of accepting God as He is, some Christian graffiti artists paint a picture of God as they think He should be. Hate-filled people may make a hate-filled God. Those who believe certain behaviors aren't sins may make a God who believes as they do.

I've heard it said many times that we all need to be accepting of others who are different from ourselves, which is great advice. Yet the pride of some Christians isn't willing to accept a God who is different from them. Many of us are tempted to expect God to be an image of us. However, as He said, *"You thought that I was just like you; I will rebuke you"* (Psalm 50:21 NASB).

The root of all evil

"The time has come for people of reason to say: enough is enough. Religious faith discourages independent thought, it's divisive, and it's dangerous." That statement, by well-known atheist Richard Dawkins, captures the theme of his documentary, *The Root of All Evil*. Is religious faith really the root of all evil, as Dawkins claims? Digging below the surface, I ventured to uncover the answer. I didn't have to dig far.

What motivates a mean parent to abuse their child? What motivates the evil dictator to murder their own people? Why does the religious extremist set off a car bomb in a crowded marketplace? Why does the bigot abuse their target group or race?

Though it's easy to attach religious faith to the car bomb example, that's not the root of the evil behavior. The motivation beneath each of these examples is pride. It's what makes certain people lord their power over their victims. It's what hinders others from accepting people who are different from themselves.

The cure for all evil

> "To fear the Lord is to hate evil; I hate pride and arrogance, evil behavior and perverse speech." (Proverbs 8:13)

Pride is the root of all evil, the seed of all sin. It's pride that discourages independent thought, is divisive and dangerous and damages relationships. Since pride is part of our flawed human nature, the cure needs to come from outside of ourselves. That leaves only one source.

With our faith and trust in God and Jesus, the Holy Spirit will free us from the shackles of pride, and lead us up the path to humility. Humility, empowered by the Spirit, will feed our desire to surrender ourselves to God, which is the cure for all evil.

Finally, where pride twists our gaze inward to self, the humility that comes from faith will free our gaze to look outward, to God and others. That's why …

> "God opposes the proud but shows favor to the humble." (James 4:6)

Now, with a better understanding of what holds aspiring Christian's captive, let's start to look at what freedom looks like, by revealing the truth of what it means to be Christian.

What it Means to be Christian

19. Faith

What does it mean to be a Christian? No surprise, it all begins with faith. Yet according to the 2014 PEW Research survey:

> 66% of all Protestants and 64% of Catholics are certain of the existence of God. [1]

Wondering why a third or more of Christians in the US are *not* certain about God, I glanced back at chapter 3 and the list of things that Christians believe are important priorities for being Christian. It seemed to be implied, or maybe taken for granted, that faith is a priority. However, there's no mention of nurturing your own faith, and no mention of being certain of the existence of God.

> When born-again Christians were asked to list two or three of the most important priorities for being Christian in terms of their faith:
> - 37% said being good and not sinning
> - 31% said learning about Jesus and the Bible
> - 25% said sharing their faith and helping others come to know Jesus
> - 25% said worshiping God and singing
> - 23% said loving others and making friends
> - 18% said helping the poor and serving other people
> - 4% said giving money and time to bless others
> - 1% said influencing and shaping the faith of family
> - 10% aren't sure

Someone once uttered this request to Jesus: *"I do believe; help me overcome my unbelief!"* (Mark 9:24). I've often felt that way—uncertain. Faith can be a strange concept to us worldly humans. What exactly is faith, and what does a faith-filled Christian look like?

Certainty

Up until ten years ago, I believed that Hawaii is a beautiful place, where you can relax and leave your mainland worries behind. However, my belief hadn't been strong enough to get me on a plane. My wife didn't suffer from such weak faith, so off we flew. Now that we've visited and experienced Hawaii, or at least parts of it, I'm certain that it's a great place to visit. I want to go back.

Faith in God is like my experience visiting Hawaii. It's a journey, with the first step being curiosity, leading to the beginning of belief. Yet belief needs a personal experience to grow into certainty. While praying to His Father for the disciples, Jesus said, *"They knew with certainty that I came from you, and they believed that you sent me"* (John 17:8). The disciples knew with certainty because they'd experienced Jesus. So can we, via His Spirit living within us.

Obstacles on the journey

I've stumbled against many obstacles in my journey on the road to faith. What follows are a few examples I've either run into myself, or heard of from fellow faith road travelers.

God is missing

Recall the Barna Group survey results showing that 20% of de-churched Christians said God was missing from their experience of church, and the majority of the de-churched left church without finding a connection with God. My friend Dave eventually gave up on God and faith, complaining that he never felt a connection while attending church. He never felt any evidence of God's presence. And where God is missing, so is faith, because the faith of certainty requires an experience of the presence of God.

His word is missing

Along with the presence of God, faith requires the word of God. As Paul said,

> "Consequently, faith comes from hearing the message, and the message is heard through the word about Christ." (Romans 10:17)

But what if the message is filled with manmade ideas, false doctrine, and worldly distractions, rather than God's word? As I cited in chapter three, 23% of de-churched people said the Bible isn't taught clearly or often enough. This is one reason so many Christians aren't certain about the existence of God, because God and His word about Christ are missing from their church experience.

Yet, even if God's word is present, you still need to be willing to take His word seriously. In chapter four I cited PEW Research statistics showing that most Christians believe the Bible should *not* be taken literally—the Bible that defines Christianity and what it means to be Christian. Such Christians are guaranteed to live by a false manmade Christianity, with a weak uncertain faith.

Rationalism

Maybe not understanding the real reason for his lack of faith, my friend Dave once told me he doesn't believe in God because he's a rational person, and he thinks it's irrational to believe in things you can't see. I was once like that. However, believing in such things isn't irrational.

Take electrons for example. Most people believe in electrons, even though you can't see them. Oh sure, maybe scientists can with advanced equipment, but before they had access to such equipment scientists knew electrons existed because of their influence upon their surroundings. Just flip on the light switch and you'll see the influence of electrons on the light bulb.

As another example, you can't see wind, yet you can see, hear, and feel the influence of winds presence. Electrons, wind, and God have that much in common. Just because we can't see them doesn't mean they aren't real.

Pride

Pride is perhaps the biggest obstacle on our road to faith. Our prideful nature is hungry, though it has a picky appetite. It'll turn up its nose at the unfamiliar, refuse to believe what it can't see, and won't accept ideas it doesn't understand.

Since most children haven't developed the pride of adulthood, a child's lack of understanding doesn't hinder them from believing. They humbly accept what we tell them as fact. Therefore, Santa Claus exists. With such children in mind, Jesus said,

> *"Truly I say to you, unless you change and become like children, you will not enter the kingdom of heaven."*
> *(Matthew 18:3 NASB)*

He was talking about having the faith of a child, a faith that comes from humility, a humility that accepts God as He is and trusts Him, without the need to understand.

A Faith that sets you apart

Is believing in God and Jesus with certainty all there is to faith? According to Jesus' brother James, the answer's no. Imagine the sarcasm in his voice when he said, *"You believe that there is one God. Good! Even the demons believe that—and shudder"* (James 2:19). Satan believes in God, with certainty. Satan has experienced God and has a relationship with Him, poor as it is. So, what is the faith that sets us apart from demons?

Love is the first element of faith that sets us apart, as love is clearly not something that Satan shares. Paul and Peter said:

> "The only thing that counts is faith expressing itself through love." (Galatians 5:6)
>
> "Although you have not seen him, you love him; and even though you do not see him now, you believe in him and rejoice with an indescribable and glorious joy." (1 Peter 1:8 NRSV)

Another aspect of a faith that sets you apart is trust, which requires humility and the willingness to rely on someone else. Trusting God is also letting go of our need to understand. Such is the trust of a child for their parents. How much trust does God desire from His children?

> "Trust in the Lord with <u>all</u> your heart and do not lean on your own understanding." (Proverbs 3:5 NASB, emphasis added)

James brings us the third aspect of faith, which he mentioned right before he declared that even demons believe.

> "Faith by itself, if it is not accompanied by action, is dead." (James 2:17)

However, some Christians take action that's motivated by pride—the action gives them something to brag about. Others take action out of a sense of obligation. Some put too much focus on action, like those who believe salvation comes from hard work. Neither pride, compulsion, nor fear of hell are proper motives for action. Action that breathes life into our faith is action motivated by love. As John and Paul said,

> "Dear children, let us not love with words or speech but with actions and in truth." (1 John 3:18)
>
> "We remember before our God and Father your work produced by faith, your labor prompted by love." (1 Thessalonians 1:3)

Action without love, trust, humility, and faith can't help but be polluted by our prideful worldly nature, and therefore produce weak worldly results. In contrast, action prompted by love for God will produce strong spiritual results. Yet, for us to have a faith that truly sets us apart, we'll need help.

By the Spirits power

Help is just what God provides. The apostle Paul said,

> "My message and my preaching were not with wise and persuasive words, but with a demonstration of the Spirit's power, so that your faith might not rest on men's wisdom, but on God's power." (1 Corinthians 2:4-5)
>
> "I pray that out of his glorious riches he may strengthen you with power through his Spirit in your inner being, so that Christ may dwell in your hearts through faith." (Ephesians 3:16-17)

And action prompted by faith and love and powered by the Holy Spirit will produce the fruits of the Spirit—the love, joy, peace, patience, kindness, generosity, faithfulness, gentleness, and self-control.

William Law also talked about Jesus' presence being the power behind our faith:

> "Faith is not in us by reason of this or that opinion, assent or consent, but it is Christ, or the divine nature in us; or its operations could not be righteousness, peace, and joy in the Holy Ghost. ... For faith is nothing else but so much of the nature, and Spirit of Christ, born and living in us." [2]

True faith doesn't come from study, or a prayer where you recite some magic words. A living faith—the faith of love, trust, humility, and action—can only come from the Spirit of Christ born and living within you.

So, action shouldn't be our goal; it's not our responsibility, it's God's. Like Paul said,

> "It is God who is at work in you, enabling you both to will and to work for his good pleasure." (Philippians 2:13 NRSV)

As in all aspects of our Christian life, our singular goal should be the presence of the Holy Spirit. When it comes to nurturing the growth of our faith and breathing power into our faith, I believe all we can contribute is humility, desire, and a bit of belief. The Holy Spirit will do the rest. It's like that man who humbly showed his desire when he said to Jesus, *"I do believe; help me overcome my unbelief!"*

More than a ticket to heaven

"I can't relate to heaven; I can't imagine it. So offering me heaven does nothing for me. Anyway, I don't care what happens after I die." Many years ago, those were my words. What didn't help was that I knew many Christians who, though "saved," were miserable. They were depressed, stressed, afraid, angry, addicted to bad habits, you name it. Or, they were just jerks. The image they painted of faith was that it gave you a ticket to heaven and nothing else. For many of those people, faith boiled down to this promise from Jesus:

> "For God so loved the world, that He gave His only Son, so that everyone who believes in Him will not perish, but have eternal life." (John 3:16 NASB)

This is a cornerstone of Christianity. It's so huge that some people can't see past it. Yet, in response to our faith and trust, Jesus offers us more than a ticket to heaven:

> "May the God of hope fill you with all joy and peace as you trust in him, so that you may overflow with hope by the power of the Holy Spirit." (Romans 15:13)
>
> "For you are all sons and daughters of God through faith in Christ Jesus." (Galatians 3:26 NASB)
>
> "Who is it that overcomes the world? Only the one who believes that Jesus is the Son of God." (1 John 5:5)

Overcome the world? Seriously? Look, I don't know how this world appears to you, but to me it's a political mess choked by conspiracy theories and lies, rattled by wars and the threat of wars, where the climate is out of control, and truth, integrity, humility, and honor seem to have no value. But according to the Apostle John, with faith we can overcome the stress, depression, fear, and anxiety of this broken world. Such is the freedom from the world that begins with faith.

This is faith: certainty based on experience and filled with desire, love, trust, action, and humility, all by the inspiration and power of the Holy Spirit. Faith is one of the primary elements of the image depicting what it means to be Christian. And it will take at least a small chunk of humility-filled faith to have an open mind in order to see the rest of the image, much of which still lies hidden beneath the manmade graffiti.

20. Righteousness and Obedience

"Anti-gay church to picket funeral." Many years ago, that was the front-page headline in my local newspaper. The quote in the article that stood out for me was from a daughter of the founder of that church. "You can sum up the Bible in three words," she said, "Obey, Obey, Obey."

This church isn't alone in prioritizing the obedience theme. The Barna Group survey of born-again Christians revealed that 37% of them see "being good and not sinning" (i.e., being righteous and obedient) as one of the top priorities for being Christian.[1] Almost 70% of all churchgoers said, "Rigid rules and strict standards are an important part of the life and teaching of my church." [2] This form of religion is built on the belief that righteousness—being right with God—comes from obedience to rigid rules by personal effort.

For such rule-worshippers, it looks like Jesus died for nothing, for as Paul said in his letter to the Galatians,

> *"I do not set aside the grace of God, for if righteousness could be gained through the law* [via obedience to that law], *Christ died for nothing! ... You who are trying to be justified by law have been alienated from Christ; you have fallen away from grace." (Galatians 2:21, 5:4)*

Then there's the recent survey data showing the continuing decline in church membership and the increasing number of church closures. Could it be that churches who preach righteousness by obedience to rigid rules—those who act as if Jesus died for nothing—are themselves dying?

Righteousness and obedience by self-effort—sometimes crossing the line into smug self-righteousness—is another splotch of ugly graffiti obscuring the truth of what it means to be Christian. And the truth is, righteousness and obedience don't come by self-effort. Neither are they natural traits of our human nature—sin is:

> *"Indeed, there is not a righteous person on earth who always does good and does not ever sin." (Ecclesiastes 7:20 NASB)*

> *"If we say that we have no sin, we are deceiving ourselves and the truth is not in us. ... If we say that we have not sinned, we make Him* [Jesus] *a liar and His word is not in us."* *(1 John 1:8, 10 NASB)*

Yet righteousness and obedience are still worthy goals for anyone who wants to be Christian, as long as we accept that self-effort is not part of the power that will get us to those goals. So, how can we become righteous, and what role does obedience play? Let's now uncover God's truth about righteousness, obedience, and their relationship to each other.

The law and faith

First, what about all the rules? If righteousness isn't about our efforts to obey those rules, why's there so much focus in the Bible on the law? Well, as Paul said,

> *"Therefore no one will be declared righteous in God's sight by the works of the law; rather, through the law we become conscious of our sin."* *(Romans 3:20)*

Only after I started reading about God's laws in the Bible did I see the nature and magnitude of my own sins. My sins felt like a burden pushing me to my knees, and I knew it'd be futile trying to throw them off on my own. When we find ourselves in this helpless place, we'll have reached a sacred crossroads. At this crossroads we have two paths to choose from: the path of self-effort, or the path of relying on Jesus; the path of obey, obey, obey, or the path of faith, trust, and humility.

God's laws show us our sins, and if we're humble enough to admit our helplessness, we can then put our faith and trust in Jesus as the only way to overcome those sins. Once we turn to Jesus, the law has completed its job, for Jesus will take it from there. As Paul also said,

> *"Therefore the Law has become our guardian to lead us to Christ, so that we may be justified* [made righteous] *by faith. But now that faith has come, we are no longer under a guardian* [the law]*."* *(Galatians 3:24-25 NASB)*

The law is like a guide leading us up a path that ends at the sacred crossroads, where we come face-to-face with Christ. When you come to the crossroads and choose the path of faith, trust, and humility, you can leave the law behind you. Jesus will then take your hand and lead you the rest of the way … to righteousness.

Faith and righteousness

Jack had been a member of one of those all-rules-and-obedience churches. He followed their rules for a long time, but never found the spiritual feeling he was looking for. Sometime after leaving that church, Jack shifted from reliance on rules to reliance on Jesus, from following rules to following Jesus. That's when Jack's faith grew to a new level, and for the first time in his life, he felt the presence of God. The fear and guilt he felt in the past were gone.

As Jack learned and as Paul preached, righteousness with God comes from faith, not obedience:

> *"This righteousness is given through faith in Jesus Christ to all who believe. There is no difference between Jew and Gentile, for all have sinned and fall short of the glory of God, and all are justified freely by his grace through the redemption that came by Christ Jesus."* (Romans 3:22-24)
>
> *"A person is not justified* [made righteous] *by works of the Law but through faith in Christ Jesus."* (Galatians 2:16 NASB)
>
> *"Christ is the culmination of the law so that there may be righteousness for everyone who believes."* (Romans 10:4)
>
> *"For in the gospel the righteousness of God is revealed—a righteousness that is by faith from first to last, just as it is written: 'The righteous will live by faith.'"* (Romans 1:17)

Yet, chasing righteousness by obedience and personal effort has always been a temptation for Christians. As with all our manmade problems, the reason is our pride and ego. Our ego needs something to be proud of, something to boast about. However, as Paul also said:

> *"Where then is boasting? It has been excluded. By what kind of law? Of works? No, but by a law of faith. For we maintain that a person is justified by faith apart from works of the Law." (Romans 3:27-28 NASB)*

Pursuing righteousness and obedience by self-effort relies on ourselves. Faith relies on God and Jesus. So which word do you think better sums up God's messages in the Bible, obedience, or faith?

Yet faith is only the beginning. Faith leads us to Jesus, placing our hand in His. Jesus then leads us to the cross, where He died and our righteousness was born. Righteousness can only come from Jesus, because when He died on the cross, He exchanged His righteousness for our sins. As Paul and Peter said,

> *"God made him who had no sin to be sin for us, so that in him we might become the righteousness of God." (2 Corinthians 5:21)*
>
> *"He himself bore our sins in his body on the cross, so that, free from sins, we might live for righteousness; by his wounds you have been healed." (1 Peter 2:24 NRSV)*

As I've mentioned before, we're not credited with that exchange until we have the faith to believe in it, then reach out and accept it. And as Jesus said, *"Blessed are those who hunger and thirst for righteousness, for they will be filled"* (Matthew 5:6 NRSV).

Faith, love, and obedience

So where does obedience come in? I mean, it's all over the Bible; we just can't ignore it. To work my way to an answer, first consider this: along with the word *faith*, how else might Jesus sum up the Bible? Someone once asked Him a related question, which was, *"Teacher, which is the greatest commandment in the Law?"* (Matthew 22:36). Jesus replied:

> *"Love the Lord your God with all your heart and with all your soul and with all your mind. This is the first and*

> *greatest commandment. And the second is like it: Love your neighbor as yourself." (Matthew 22:37-39)*

Now consider something Paul said:

> *"The only thing that counts is faith expressing itself through love." (Galatians 5:6)*

Love is an expression of faith, a result of faith. Faith in God leads us to love for God. But where does love lead us?

When I was a careless teenager, I tried to obey my mom and stepfather because of my love for them—I didn't want to hurt or disappoint them, though I sometimes did. My desire to obey was a result of my love, not compulsion. For there to be obedience—I mean Christ-like obedience—there must first be love. As Jesus said:

> *"If you love Me, you will keep My commandments." (John 14:15 NASB)*
>
> *"Anyone who loves me will obey my teaching." (John 14:23)*

Faith leads to love, which then leads to obedience. That's why Jesus stressed faith and love, rather than obeying rules. He knows that where there's love, obedience will naturally follow. And as Paul emphasized:

> *"Therefore love is the fulfillment of the law." (Romans 13:10)*

Notice that he didn't say "obedience is the fulfillment of the law."

Our Rescuer

The problem with prioritizing obedience by self-effort is that when Christians come to the crossroads, they choose the path of self-reliance. I know Christians who kept choosing that path, each time hitting the wall of futility and eventually giving up on themselves, and Christianity. Since God is often missing from people's experience of church—as the survey data shows—many Christians don't realize there's another path to choose, the path of relying on God.

The apostle Paul struggled with his own efforts of self-reliance. As he said in his letter to those in Rome, *"For I have the desire to do what is good, but I cannot carry it out. For I do not do the good I want to do, but the evil I do not want to do—this I keep on doing"* (Romans 7:18-19). Reading further, picture Paul on his knees, weighed down by his sins, fists clinched, tears streaming down his face as he agonizingly exclaims: *"What a wretched man I am! Who will rescue me from this body that is subject to death?"* (verse 24). At the end of chapter 7 of Romans, Paul was at the crossroads.

Even as Paul asked the question, he knew the answer:

> "Therefore, there is now no condemnation for those who are in Christ Jesus, because through Christ Jesus the law of <u>the Spirit who gives life has set you free from the law of sin and death</u>. ... The mind governed by the flesh [i.e., self and our sins] is death, but the mind governed by the Spirit is life and peace. ... You, however, are not in the realm of the flesh but are in the realm of the Spirit, if indeed the Spirit of God lives in you." (Romans 8:1-2, 6, 9 emphasis added)

As I'd seen many times on this journey, the Spirit of God is our rescuer, freeing us from captivity to our self, our sins, and the disobedience they produce. And regarding obedience, where love provides the motivation to obey, the Holy Spirit provides the power. As God said:

> "And I will put my Spirit in you and <u>move</u> you to follow my decrees and be careful to keep my laws." (Ezekiel 36:27, NIV emphasis added)

By His sacrifice, Jesus saves us from an eternity in Hell. By His presence, the Holy Spirit saves us from our worldly, sinful, and disobedient selves. So, righteousness and obedience should not have a place on the surveyed list of priorities for being Christian, which may sound strange. Rather, all our efforts should be focused on our faith in Jesus and the presence of His Spirit in our lives.

> "So I say, walk by the Spirit, and you will not gratify the desires of the flesh." (Galatians 5:16)

"For through the Spirit we eagerly await by faith the righteousness for which we hope. ... The only thing that counts is faith expressing itself through love." (Galatians 5:5-6)

21. Salvation

For much of my ABC life—after becoming Christian—I feared for my own salvation, suffering from the guilt of my own sins, feeling like I hadn't earned my ticket to heaven. I was once in a Bible study group where eight out of the ten of us shared those feelings. Our doubts came from our painful memories of bad behavior. In our minds, our past was full of unforgivable sins. It felt like Paul was talking to us when he said, *"Once you were alienated from God and were enemies in your minds because of your evil behavior"* (Colossians 1:21).

Where salvation is commonly seen as living eternally with God in a loving relationship, the opposite of salvation is divorce from God. As most people who've gone through it know, divorce is hell. Unlike people however, God doesn't hold onto memories of our evil behavior, and because of His unshakable love and humility, God doesn't want a divorce, preferring reconciliation instead.

After making the statement above, Paul then said:

> "But now he [God] has reconciled you by Christ's physical body through death to present you holy in his sight, without blemish and free from accusation—if you continue in your faith, established and firm, and do not move from the hope held out in the gospel." (Colossians 1:22-23)

Where sin causes separation from God, the salvation offered by Jesus' sacrifice brings us and God back together, as it was in the beginning. Salvation *is* reconciliation. Paul also proclaimed:

> "Now all these things are from God, who reconciled us to Himself through Christ and gave us the ministry of reconciliation, namely, that God was in Christ reconciling the world to Himself, not counting their wrongdoings against them. ... We beg you on behalf of Christ, be reconciled to God. He made Him who knew no sin to be sin in our behalf, so that we might become the righteousness of God in Him." (2 Corinthians 5:18-21 NASB)

Apparently ignoring what Paul said, some churches preach grueling heaven entrance requirements, where you won't know if you'll get your admission ticket until you face your personal judgment day. Other Christian's swing the threat of hell like a club, as if salvation depended upon intimidation, fear, and guilt. That's all just more graffiti of manmade Christianity. Let's scrape off that graffiti, and reveal the truth of salvation hidden beneath.

Crooked path to heaven

Among Christians, there are many misguided ideas about what the path to heaven looks like. Before revealing the path laid out by God, let's explore a few manmade paths. I'll begin with the most difficult.

Obedience

The steepest and most slippery path is salvation by obedience to rigid rules and strict standards. Though I've already challenged this with the Bible verses I cited in the last chapter, I'd like to add the following story: With Moses as His representative, God freed the Hebrew slaves from Egypt. After God led them along the path to freedom, He then gave them His laws and instructed them to obey His laws. End of story.

Notice that God didn't first require obedience as a condition for freedom. Freedom came first. All the Hebrews had to do was have the faith to follow God. Only later, once they were safe and truly free, did God ask them to obey His laws.

Like with the Hebrews, God first offers us freedom, that is, salvation. Then, once we have the faith to accept and follow Jesus, obedience will result, just as we saw in the last chapter. All we need is the faith and desire to follow. Yet those who preach salvation via obedience by personal effort would rather lead themselves to freedom, than follow Jesus.

Work

A slightly easier, though rocky path to heaven may not rely on complete obedience, yet there is work involved. Referring to people who pursued righteousness and salvation by works, Paul said, "[They] *have not attained their goal. Why not? Because they pursued it not by faith but as if it were by works. They stumbled over the stumbling stone*" (Romans 9:31-32). This crowded path is littered with the same stumbling stones as that of pursuing salvation by obedience, the hazards of pride and ego. Our accomplishments give us something to brag about.

Jesus was once asked about this idea of works:

> *"Therefore they said to Him, 'What are we to do, so that we may accomplish the works of God?' Jesus answered and said to them, 'This is the work of God, that you believe in Him whom He has sent.'" (John 6:28-29 NASB)*

I love the way Jesus redirects their question to what's truly important. Don't think about work; just believe. And as you saw in chapter 20, with faith, love, and the help of the Holy Spirit, the works of God will naturally follow.

Goodness

Here's a popular path to salvation: be good, whatever that means. It's just another way of pursuing salvation by personal effort. According to the survey results I cited at the end of chapter three, 37% of born-again Christians say being good is a top priority for being Christian.

Someone once called Jesus good, to which He replied, *"Why do you call Me good? No one is good except God alone"* (Mark 10:18 NASB). Sounds like pursuing salvation by goodness is as futile as any other path that relies on self-effort. Yet regarding a desire to be good, consider this from William Law:

> *"When man was first created, all the good that he had in him was from God alone. Mark well, this must be the state of man forever. Yet, our first created goodness is lost, because our first father* [Adam] *departed from a full, absolute dependence upon God. Our lost goodness can never come again till by a power from Christ living in us, we are brought out of ourselves and all selfish truths, into that full and blessed dependence upon God in which our first father should have lived."* [1]

Label

How many people live under a label of "Catholic," or "Lutheran," or "Christian," or whatever, where they believe they're saved by virtue of their label? You've already seen these words of Jesus, and they're worth repeating: *"Not everyone who says to me, 'Lord, Lord,' will enter the kingdom of heaven, but only the one who does the will of my Father who is in heaven. Many will say to me on that day, 'Lord, Lord, did we not prophesy in your name and in your name drive out demons and perform many miracles?' Then I will tell them plainly, 'I never knew you. Away from me, you evildoers!'"* (Matthew 7:21-23, emphasis added).

Jesus also said while praying to God:

> "And this is eternal life, that they may know You, the only true God, and Jesus Christ whom You have sent." (John 17:3 NASB, emphasis added)

Doing things in Jesus' name and calling yourself Christian won't save you. Any other label won't save you. Only *knowing* God and Jesus can do that.

Attendance

I used to sit next to them in the pews, when I was still a churchgoer. Now, some of them believe I won't go to heaven, because I no longer attend church. There are others who believe I won't go to heaven unless I attend *their* church. That's salvation by attendance record—as if salvation depends upon our relationship with a church, and perhaps their label, rather than our relationship with God.

Bible knowledge

Many people have done a thorough study of the Bible, hoping to know God and Jesus within those pages, and by that knowledge, hoping to receive salvation. To these people Jesus might say, *"You study the Scriptures diligently because you think that in them you have eternal life. These are the very Scriptures that testify about me, yet you refuse to come to me to have life"* (John 5:39-40).

Salvation isn't found in a relationship with the Bible, but rather, salvation comes from a relationship with Jesus.

Free for all

When the time comes, how can I be happy in heaven if people I love aren't there with me? My friend Gil feels the same way, and Gil's lack of understanding has driven him to believe that *everyone* will go to heaven, no matter what they believe. Though I like this idea, that's not the way it works. Salvation isn't free for all. But, it's also not expensive.

Finally, and most importantly, all of these misguided paths to heaven seem to say the same thing about the people who believe in them. Whether it's salvation by obeying rules, doing good deeds, being good, attending the right church, having

Bible knowledge, or it's just free to everyone, to these people Jesus doesn't factor into their salvation. To these people, Jesus died for nothing.

The straight and level path

Just like the Hebrews found freedom when they had the faith to follow God out of Egypt, our salvation comes from believing and following Jesus, all the way to heaven. But like many people today, even Jesus' original disciples thought the path to heaven was something they had to travel alone, by their own effort. To this, Jesus responded, *"With people this is impossible, but with God all things are possible"* (Matthew 19:26 NASB). Let's now look at how God makes this seemingly impossible journey possible.

First, consider this, from Paul:

> "For by grace you have been saved through faith, and this is not your own doing; it is the gift of God." (Ephesians 2:8 NRSV)

If salvation were a response to our behavior, it wouldn't be a gift, but a reward. We're saved because of God's grace, an un-earned gift. However, only after we believe in a gift, can we accept it. Yet, God doesn't offer the gift because of our faith. Rather, we accept the offered gift because of our faith. The offer is always there.

Also, Jesus said:

> "Very truly I tell you, whoever hears my word and believes him who sent me has eternal life and will not be judged but has crossed over from death to life." (John 5:24)

God has built a bridge between us and Him—from death to life. This bridge is open to all, though only those who believe the bridge is real will cross to the other side. In the movie *Indiana Jones and the Last Crusade*, an invisible bridge stood between Indy and his goal—salvation, in a way. To reach his goal, he needed to believe in a bridge he couldn't see, and have the faith to take that first step. So it is with us.

But humans can't seem to resist making the ways of God complicated. For example, some Christians believe that God personally selects only special people for salvation, and that He made His choices long ago. The implication here is that Jesus died only for these special people. I admit, in his letters to the Ephesians and Romans, Paul does give this impression. Yet, as Jesus declared and Paul reinforced:

> "And I, when I am lifted up from the earth, will draw all people to myself." (John 12:32 NRSV)
>
> "For there is one God and one mediator between God and human beings, Christ Jesus, himself human, who gave himself as a ransom for all people." (1 Timothy 2:5-6)

Jesus died for *all* people, not just a select few, because:

> "For my Father's will is that everyone who looks to the Son and believes in him shall have eternal life." (John 6:40)
>
> "God our Savior, who wants all people to be saved and to come to a knowledge of the truth." (1 Timothy 2:3-4)
>
> "The Lord is not slow about His promise, as some count slowness, but is patient toward you, not willing for any to perish, but for all to come to repentance." (2 Peter 3:9 NASB)

I know some Christians who live with anxious anticipation of their personal judgment day. They believe that only after we die will we find out if we go to heaven or hell. Do we really have to wait to find out? Not according to Jesus:

> "Very truly, I tell you, whoever believes has eternal life." (John 6:47 NRSV, emphasis added)
>
> "Truly, truly, I say to you, the one who hears My word, and believes Him who sent Me, has eternal life, and does not come into judgment, but has passed out of death into life." (John 5:24 NASB, emphasis added)

If you believe, then you *have* eternal life, now. Think for a moment what life can be like, knowing that your eternal future is guaranteed.

The Promise and the Way

> *"For God so loved the world, that He gave His only Son, so that everyone who believes in Him will not perish, but have eternal life." (John 3:16 NASB)*

As I was working my way through this chapter, I found myself wondering; when Jesus stated His promise of eternal life, what exactly did He expect us to believe? What does it mean to believe in Jesus? I'd always assumed the answer was limited to the obvious one. Yet given what's at stake, I think it's important to make sure I haven't been missing something.

So, I pushed away from my computer, closed my eyes, concentrated on the presence of Jesus' Spirit within me, listened, and waited. I ended up compiling a decent looking list, making sure I also included everything mentioned in a couple of well-known Christian creeds, that is, declarations of what Christians believe.

I was about to copy the list here when I realized there's no value in that. My list has no real value, other than how it completely convinced me that there's no way I can believe all those things on my own. I need help. To realize the promise of eternal life, I need help from the promised presence of the Holy Spirit within me. The Spirit of Jesus will help me in my unbelief; the Spirit will guide me into all truth.

Also, Jesus said:

> *"I am the way, and the truth, and the life. No one comes to the Father except through me." (John 14:6 NRSV)*

I've known Christians, like my friend Gil, who feel uneasy with these words. They're uncomfortable with Jesus being the only way to heaven. They want other options for other people. I get it. I used to feel the same way. Though I now accept Jesus' words, I also see something more within them. When Jesus bore the punishment for our sins, He was paying for our ticket to heaven. However, He didn't stop there. Jesus also wants to take our hand and show us the way.

At the beginning of this chapter, I referred to the Bible story of how God freed the Hebrew slaves from Egypt. With encouragement from Moses, all the Hebrews had to do was have faith, desire, and willingness to follow God to freedom. God sent Jesus with the same mission—to lead God's children to freedom. Many times Jesus said, *come, follow me*. When it comes to our salvation, all we have to do is have the faith, desire, and willingness to follow the Spirit of Jesus, all the way to heaven.

The outcome of your faith

As Jesus was hanging on the cross waiting for death, a thief crucified next to Him said, *"Jesus, remember me when you come into your kingdom"* (Luke 23:42). This thief certainly wasn't a good person. There was no obedience in him, no time for obedience, or anything else. All he had in his final moments of life was the faith to believe Jesus was who He claimed to be. Now that might have been difficult, given that Jesus certainly didn't look like the Son of God as He hung there on a cross. But the thief did believe, and Jesus responded to the thief's expression of faith with, *"Truly I tell you, today you will be with me in paradise"* (v. 43).

I know that sometimes it sounds like salvation requires more than faith. Not according to the story of the thief. Besides, those other things we might suspect are requirements for salvation are just natural outcomes of faith. We are saved by faith alone, not the impact faith has on our behavior. Faith comes first, a faith that's more than believing in God and Jesus; it's also *knowing* them. As Jesus said in His prayer to God,

> "And this is eternal life, that they may know You, the only true God, and Jesus Christ whom You have sent." (John 17:3 NASB)

When it comes to our salvation, we just need to trust God, Jesus, and the Holy Spirit with where our eternal home will be, and believe that someday, we, too, will be with them in paradise.

Finally, as Peter said,

> "You are receiving the outcome of your faith, the salvation of your souls." (1 Peter 1:9 NRSV)

22. Evangelism

On Sunday mornings long ago and far away, you'd find me in front of the TV, my little hand on the channel selector knob, searching for cartoons. Sometimes I'd land on a channel with a fiery preacher yelling at me to accept *Geeezus* into my heart … or, I'd go to hell. I grew up with that image of evangelism. Not helpful.

However, I can't ignore evangelism, as it's a key element of what it means to be Christian. Besides, Jesus told us to …

> "Therefore go and make disciples of all nations, baptizing them in the name of the Father and of the Son and of the Holy Spirit, and teaching them to obey everything I have commanded you." (Matthew 28:19-20)

But, what's the truth about *how* we should go about making disciples of all nations? As I began looking beneath the graffiti of manmade methods of evangelism—like that over-zealous, hell-threatening preacher—in addition to finding Christ-like evangelism, I found the best evangelist.

Manmade evangelism

Here are three examples of common manmade methods of evangelism that I've experienced:

Fear-inducing evangelism: Like that TV evangelist, some Christians try to make disciples by beating people over the head with the Bible. Their strategy seems to be to frighten people into believing by showing them how screwed up they are. If you're a homosexual, God hates you. If you're not baptized, you'll go to hell. You know the rest. People are sometimes bludgeoned with such lies by so-called Christians. Even if the evangelists stick to the truth, I suspect preaching fear doesn't win many converts. It never worked on me.

Judgmental evangelism: My Christian friend Tim is afraid that family members who don't share his beliefs will end up in hell. So, being careful to stick to the truth, Tim tells them what will happen if they don't believe in Jesus. Yet, as often as he tries to convince his family of the seriousness of what's at stake, he never gets the reaction he hopes for, and he doesn't understand why.

What Tim doesn't understand is the role he's trying to take in this evangelism play. Like a calmer version of the TV evangelist, Tim has taken on the role of judge, as he declares the verdict and sentence to his unreceptive family. Perhaps it's behavior like Tim's that adds to the perception outsiders have of Christians being judgmental.

Trial lawyer evangelism: Linda is a friend who has a passion for "bringing people to Jesus." Her motives are honest, humble, and completely centered on the well-being of the other person. Though she's not frightening or judgmental, she comes across as pushy, sometimes too pushy. If you ask her about it, she'll say it's because she cares a lot. She cares so much that Linda has taken on the role of an overly passionate trial lawyer, trying to convince the jury of the truth of Jesus. But is this the part Jesus wants Linda to play?

Christ-like evangelism

In Jesus' call to make disciples of all nations, Christians are to be neither judge nor trial lawyer. The role Jesus gives us in this evangelism play is the witness. It's a simple part—just testify to His truth. And it should be no surprise by now that our ability to be a good witness comes from the Holy Spirit living within us. As Jesus said:

> "You will receive power when the Holy Spirit has come upon you; and you will be my witnesses in Jerusalem, in all Judea and Samaria, and to the ends of the earth." (Acts 1:8 NRSV)
>
> "When the Advocate comes, whom I will send to you from the Father, the Spirit of truth who comes from the Father, he will testify on my behalf. You also are to testify because you have been with me from the beginning." (John 15:26-27 NRSV)
>
> "You are my witnesses," declares the LORD, "that I am God." (Isaiah 43:12)

In a complex court trial, it's rarely the testimony of one witness that convinces the jury. It's the testimony of all the witnesses, paraded past the jury by a skilled attorney. In her efforts to evangelize and "bring people to Jesus," Linda should be content with her role as one in a potentially long line of witnesses, and accept God as the skilled attorney. Likewise, Tim needs to step down from the bench, accept his role as a witness, and accept God in His dual role as both attorney and judge.

Also, Christ-like evangelism is all about the needs of the audience, rather than the desires of the evangelist. As Peter and Paul advised:

> "Always be prepared to give an answer to everyone who asks you to give the reason for the hope that you have. But do this with gentleness and respect." (1 Peter 3:15)
>
> "Do not let any unwholesome talk come out of your mouths, but only what is helpful for building others up according to their needs, that it may benefit those who listen." (Ephesians 4:29, emphasis added)

Yet when trying to be a good witness, the right words don't always come to me, and sometimes the words that do pop out are more lame than helpful. James and Peter give me this advice:

> "My dear brothers and sisters, take note of this: Everyone should be quick to listen, slow to speak and slow to become angry. ... Those who consider themselves religious and yet do not keep a tight rein on their tongues deceive themselves, and their religion is worthless." (James 1:19, 26)
>
> "If any of them do not believe the word, they may be won over without words by [your] behavior." (1 Peter 3:1)

Therefore, sometimes the best way to evangelize is to rely on listening and doing, rather than talking. Maybe that's why Saint Francis of Assisi said, "*Preach the Gospel at all times, using words only when necessary.*"

When words *are* necessary, the best words are those of God. As Peter said, *"Whoever speaks must do so as one speaking the very words of God"* (1 Peter 4:11 NRSV). Maybe Peter advised it, because Jesus did it. As Jesus said, *"For I did not speak on my own, but the Father who sent me commanded me to say all that I have spoken. I know that his command leads to eternal life. So whatever I say is just what the Father has told me to say"* (John 12:49-50).

Any of us can be God's spokesperson, His witness, His ambassador. As Paul said:

> "We are therefore Christ's ambassadors, as though God were making his appeal through us." (2 Corinthians 5:20)

Imagine how effective evangelism can be if it's God making the appeal, not us.

The best evangelist

What would outsiders think if they saw Christians loving their enemies and in all other ways doing as Jesus would do? What would outsiders think if, when looking at Christians, instead of seeing hypocrisy, judgment, bigotry, and an absence of love, they saw the fruits of the presence of the Holy Spirit—the love, joy, peace, patience, kindness, generosity, faithfulness, gentleness, and self-control? Now *that's* powerful and compelling evangelism.

And that's the power Jesus promised when He said the Holy Spirit would make us witnesses, witnesses to what Christianity and Christian life is all about. The presence of the Spirit of Jesus within Christians does the most to help make disciples of all nations. As D.L. Moody once said, *"There is no better evangelist in the world than the Holy Spirit."* Paul knew this as well:

> "My message and my preaching were not with wise and persuasive words, but with a demonstration of the Spirit's power, so that your faith might not rest on men's wisdom, but on God's power." (1 Corinthians 2:4-5)

So I hope it is with me and what I write in this book.

23. Prayer

In addition to the dinner table and church, I've seen people praying on street corners, in parking lots, restaurants, and football field end zones—just about anywhere. Some prayers are scripted, others improvised. Many prayers have felt overused, meaningless, or confusing. Some prayers have felt good; others uncomfortable.

In my search for the truth of Christianity and what it means to be Christian, when I paused to think about prayer, my mind filled with questions. For example, what *is* prayer, from God's perspective? Where should we pray, and how often? Why do so many of my prayers seem to go unheard? Is there something wrong with how I'm praying?

Like Jesus' first disciples, I wanted Him to teach me how to pray: *"One day Jesus was praying in a certain place. When he finished, one of his disciples said to him, 'Lord, teach us to pray'"* (Luke 11:1). Jesus talked a lot about prayer, like when He said:

> "When you pray, go into your room, close the door and pray to your Father, who is unseen. Then your Father, who sees what is done in secret, will reward you. And when you pray, do not keep on babbling like pagans, for they think they will be heard because of their many words. Do not be like them, for your Father knows what you need before you ask him." (Matthew 6:6-8)

Because of prayers I've experienced, both in church and outside of church, Jesus' advice brings up other questions. It's time to get some answers.

What is prayer?

Voicing concerns and asking for favors—that's what prayer has always meant to me. For most of my life as a Christian, I've done all the talking, expecting God to do all the listening. After all, God said He's happy to listen:

> *"I know the plans I have for you," declares the Lord, "plans to prosper you and not to harm you, plans to give you hope and a future. Then you will call on me and come and pray to me, and I will listen to you." (Jeremiah 29:11-12, emphasis added)*

However, God and Jesus also want their chance to talk:

> *"While he* [Jesus] *was still speaking, a bright cloud covered them, and a voice from the cloud said, 'This is my Son, whom I love; with him I am well pleased. Listen to him!'" (Matthew 17:5, emphasis added)*

As in any healthy relationship, we need to be willing to stop talking and quietly listen, and the more we listen, the more we'll understand. Jesus said so: *"Jesus called the crowd to him and said, 'Listen and understand'"* (Matthew 15:10). In order to listen, we need quiet, which is why Jesus tells us to go into our room and close the door, leaving the noise of life outside.

Speaking of noise, I spent three years helping lead the junior high youth group at church. The erratic energy and short attention spans were a chaotic mix. Early on, when I was a rookie, I learned a trick from a battle-tested fellow leader. At first, I attempted to get the kids attention by trying to be louder than they were. You can guess who won that contest. The trick I learned was to be quiet and soft-spoken. For some weird reason, the kids would quiet down so they could hear. Maybe they thought I was saying something worth listening to. Hey, it could happen.

I think this helps illustrate why God is often hard to hear—He doesn't speak in thunderclaps. Maybe He's quiet because that's His way of urging me to become quiet myself. To hear God, I need to first silence the random pinball thoughts that ricochet around my mind. I need noise cancelling headphones for my brain. Plus, as Andrew Murray said:

> *"Who would dispute that* [while praying]*, that which God has to say must have infinitely more worth than what that person has to say?"* [1]

I certainly can't dispute it.

When I was in college, long before cell phones existed, often I'd feel homesick and lonely enough to spend the money to call my mom long-distance. It felt good to hear her voice—I missed her, a lot. She'd eagerly listen to whatever I had to say, and then she'd tell me what was going on back home. Those calls helped me feel connected to home, and less lonely.

Jesus frequently went off alone to pray, and maybe some of His quiet times with God were like those phone calls. Perhaps Jesus wanted to hear His Father's voice without the noise of the world breaking in on their conversation. Jesus was dealing with stressful stuff, and He might have wanted to privately talk to the only person who could understand. Also, maybe Jesus was feeling homesick and lonely.

When we're feeling uneasy, afraid, stressed, or lonely, prayer is our way to talk to the only person who can truly sympathize and understand. Prayer is more than a conversation with God. Prayer can be our phone call back home.

Come as you are

One evening, Jesus was having dinner at the house of a religious elitist. Shortly after they sat down at the table, something unusual happened: *"There was a woman in the city who was a sinner; and when she learned that He* [Jesus] *was reclining at the table in the Pharisee's house, she brought an alabaster vial of perfume, and standing behind Him at His feet, weeping, she began to wet His feet with her tears, and she wiped them with the hair of her head, and began kissing His feet and anointing them with the perfume"* (Luke 7:37-38 NASB).

This woman was a sinner—by scholarly accounts, likely a prostitute. The elitist host reacted by aiming his scorn at Jesus, who should have known better than to let such a filthy woman touch him. Yet Jesus didn't respond as predicted. Instead, He said, *"Do you see this woman? I entered your house; you gave Me no water for My feet, but she has wet My feet with her tears and wiped them with her hair. You gave Me no kiss; but she has not stopped kissing My feet since the time I came in. You did not anoint My head with oil, but she anointed My feet with perfume. For this reason I say to you, her sins, which are many, have been forgiven, for she loved much"* (verses 44-47).

What's this have to do with prayer? Well, the woman doesn't first take on what might be considered appropriate behavior, dress, or attitude before approaching Jesus. She comes to Him just as she is, sins and all. And Jesus accepted the woman that way, without the need for religious correctness or some manmade standard of acceptability.

With prayer, Jesus doesn't expect us to adopt churchy language or special behavior. After all, our words don't matter, nor how we say them. What matters is where our heart is, like with that woman at Jesus' feet.

Faith and prayer

Back in my churchgoing days, I once received an email from the church prayer chain coordinator, requesting prayers for a young woman who was very ill. The request was to, "Pray for correct diagnosis and treatment as indicated. Healing would be nice." Hmm. Well, doctors with no help from God could likely handle the first part of the prayer. But it struck me; if Jesus were to email out a prayer request, would He say, "Healing would be nice," tacked on as if it were a hesitant afterthought?

Such weak prayers reflect a weak faith, and maybe a belief in a weak God. But Jesus said that with God, "*all things are possible*." So why do some people ask for so little? Based on how often Jesus encourages us to ask, He doesn't expect us to be timid or economical about it:

> "Ask, and it will be given to you." (Matthew 7:7 NRSV)
>
> "If you believe, you will receive whatever you ask for in prayer." (Matthew 21:22)
>
> "I will do whatever you ask in my name, so that the Father may be glorified in the Son. If in my name you ask me for anything, I will do it." (John 14:13-14 NRSV)
>
> "If you remain in me and my words remain in you, ask whatever you wish, and it will be given you." (John 15:7)
>
> "Truly, truly I say to you, if you ask the Father for anything in My name, He will give it to you." (John 16:23 NASB)

I went through the Gospels and found all the verses where Jesus talked about prayer—28, according to my count. Of these 28, thirteen verses say the same thing—ask and you *will* receive. And what will we receive? *Whatever you ask … whatever you wish … anything*. However …

"When you ask, you must believe and not doubt." (James 1:6)

When I ask God to heal my friend of cancer, do I believe He'll do it? I know He's capable. Yet sometimes when I ask for such things, I don't fully expect God to respond. It's like when my son was a pre-teen, and he came to my wife and me at 9:30 one summer evening and said, "You wouldn't be willing to let me spend tonight at Peter's, would you?" He asked for what he wanted, and he knew we were capable of granting his request, but he didn't believe we'd give it to him (and he was right).

Is that me with some of my requests to God? Do I suffer from such doubt? What I need—what we all need—is the faith of a child, the faith to believe without doubt or hesitation, free from the skepticism of adulthood.

Now think about how it would feel to ask God for something and *know* that He'd give it to you. As Jesus said, *"If you believe, you <u>will</u> receive whatever you ask for in prayer."* If we believe God will give it, He will give it. Jesus said it, and I accept it, though do I really believe it? I can't deny that sometimes my faith feels weak. I need help, and as with everything else in life, the help I need can only come from the Holy Spirit.

In Jesus name I pray, amen

Jesus said, *"I will do whatever you ask in my name"* (John 14:13 NRSV). By now, I know this means more than tacking on "in Jesus' name I pray, amen," to the end of my prayers. In my search for a better understanding of what Jesus meant by "in my name," I found this from Andrew Murray:

> "Abiding in Christ, and having His words abiding in us, teaches us to pray in accordance with the will of God. ... Abiding in Christ, we can fully avail ourselves of the name of Christ. Asking in the name of another means that the other person authorized me and sent me to ask, and wants to be considered as asking himself: he wants the favor done for his sake." [2]

Abiding in Christ, our requests rise to God as if coming directly from Jesus. Murray went on to say:

> "It is in real spiritual unity with Christ that we are accepted and heard. Our union with the Son of God is a life-union: we are in very deed one with Him. And so our prayer ascends as His prayer. It is because we abide in Him that we can ask what we will and it is given to us!" [3]

As I've mentioned several times already, Jesus often promised and prayed that He and each believer would be united as one, just as He and His Father are one. In this state of unity, our prayers ascend to God as Jesus' prayers, and as Jesus said,

> "If you remain in me and my words remain in you, ask whatever you wish, and it will be given you." (John 15:7)

Now then, if I'm in Jesus and He's in me, and He's the greater portion of this mixture of the two of us, then it's only right that this mixture takes His name. I don't know if I'm clearly expressing the image in my mind, but maybe something else Andrew Murray said will help:

> "If the name of Christ is to be wholly at my disposal, so that I may have full command of it for all I will, it must be because I first put myself wholly at His disposal, so that He has free and full command of me! It is the abiding in Christ that gives the right and power to use His name with confidence. To Christ the Father refuses nothing. Abiding in Christ, I come to the Father as one with Him. His righteousness is in me, His Spirit is in me; the Father sees the Son in me, and gives me my petition." [4]

I know this appears to be asking a lot—putting ourselves completely at Jesus' disposal so He can have free and full command of our lives. But I no longer consider this as giving up anything. For look at what I gain: "ask whatever you wish, and it will be given you."

Here's another thought regarding praying in Jesus' name:

> "In all prayer, the one essential condition is that we are able to offer it in the name of Jesus, as according to His desire for

> *us, according to the Father's will, according to the Spirit's teaching. And thus praying in Christ's name is impossible without self-examination, without reflection, without self-denial; in short, without the aid of the Spirit."* [5]

Denying myself and my name with the aid of the Holy Spirit—it's the one essential prerequisite to taking Jesus' name. That's part of the reason why, as Jesus was about to return to heaven, He instructed His disciples to *wait* for the arrival of the Holy Spirit: *"... wait for the gift my Father promised, which you have heard me speak about"* (Acts 1:4). Once we receive the gift of the Holy Spirit, we can then pray as Paul instructs us to pray:

> *"And pray in the Spirit on all occasions with all kinds of prayers and requests." (Ephesians 6:18)*
>
> *"But you, beloved, build yourselves up on your most holy faith; pray in the Holy Spirit." (Jude 1:20 NRSV)*

Praying in the Holy Spirit—this is the abiding in Christ that Andrew Murray was talking about. This is you in Jesus, and He in you. This is self-denial, relying on the Holy Spirit rather than yourself, and giving the Spirit free and full command of your life.

Yet, even in my strongest moments of faith, self-denial, and intimacy with the Holy Spirit, sometimes God says no, or so it seems. Parents occasionally say no, because the parent is wiser than the child. But I try not to let a negative response hinder my reliance upon God, because I trust Him more than I trust myself.

For the glory of God

Paul said, *"Whatever you do, do it all for the glory of God"* (1 Corinthians 10:31). And Jesus calls us to pray, *"so that the Father may be glorified."* Umm, I know this is a bit off topic, but before I talk about glorifying God with our prayers, I want to point out that, regarding the Barna Group survey results at the end of chapter 3 and the list of priorities for being Christian, glorifying God is not on that list.

Anyway, in chapter 10, I told the story about the time I gave my testimony at church. While praying before heading to church that morning, I decided to trust

God and leave my testimony notes at home. God then granted my prayer as He led me, and even seemed to speak through me, while I spoke to the congregation. What was my prayer before I left home? I prayed that by telling my story, with God's help I'd glorify Him. And God granted my request.

Now then, regarding praying for the glory of God, Andrew Murray said,

> "To such a life, with God's glory our only aim, we cannot attain by any effort of our own. ... It is Jesus Himself coming in, who can cast out all self-glorifying, and give us instead His own God-glorifying life and Spirit. It is Jesus, who longs to glorify the Father in hearing our prayers, who will teach us to live and to pray to the glory of God." [6]

Here again, the Holy Spirit helps us to pray in Jesus' name, all for the glory of God.

Here's another thought regarding prayers that glorify God. In the salvation chapter I mentioned how God answered the Hebrew's prayers and freed them from Egypt. Only after they were free did He expect them to follow His laws. Jesus did the same thing. From the stories in the Bible, first He'd grant a request and heal someone of a disease or deformity. Only after He healed them did He then say something like, "Go, and sin no more." I believe the same applies to prayer requests today. Jesus doesn't first require someone to be sin-free, or even a follower of His, as a condition for healing. Rather, He hopes they'll become a devoted follower *because* of a healing. Praying that God be thus glorified in the lives of others—now that seems like the type of prayer Jesus would pray.

Location, location, location

My son was playing saxophone in a junior high school band concert in the parking lot of a shopping center. Off to the side was a table with signs advertising a local church. I walked over to check it out. The people behind the table soon offered to join hands, bow our heads, and pray together in the midst of hundreds of people and the noise of the band.

Why do some Christians insist on praying in highly visible public places? If they really feel the need to speak with God, can't they do that without making their praying obvious to those around them? Could they be trying to display their (self) righteousness? Are they looking to glorify God, or themselves? And how can they truly listen and feel the presence of the Holy Spirit while being pummeled by the distractions of the material world?

Parking lots, street corners, restaurants, football field endzones—are these really the types of places where God wants us to pray? After all, Jesus said:

> "When you pray, do not be like the hypocrites, for they love to pray standing in the synagogues and on the street corners to be seen by others. ... But when you pray, go into your room, close the door and pray to your Father." (Matthew 6:5-6)

Does praying in public, to be seen by others, glorify God or just make Christians look weird to outsiders? Regarding location, Jesus showed us how to pray in His own times of prayer:

> "Jesus often withdrew to lonely places and prayed." (Luke 5:16)
>
> "And after he had dismissed the crowds, he went up the mountain by himself to pray. When evening came, he was there alone." (Matthew 14:23 NRSV)
>
> "Very early in the morning, while it was still dark, Jesus got up, left the house and went off to a solitary place, where he prayed." (Mark 1:35)
>
> "One of those days Jesus went out to a mountainside to pray, and spent the night praying to God." (Luke 6:12)

Look, prayer can be anywhere, as long as we're alone with God and free from the distractions of the world.

The wonderful power of prayer

Prayer is a privilege that many consider an obligatory—

Wait! Hold on a minute. Sorry about this, but looking back to chapter 3 again, to that list of things Christians believe are important priorities for being Christian, is it there? Hmm, not again? Yes, again. Not only is glorifying God missing from the list, but Prayer is also missing. Yet from what I've learned on this journey, prayer should be one of the *most* important priorities for being Christian. Andrew Murray agreed:

> When born-again Christians were asked to list two or three of the most important priorities for being Christian in terms of their faith:
> - 37% said being good and not sinning
> - 31% said learning about Jesus and the Bible
> - 25% said sharing their faith and helping others come to know Jesus
> - 25% said worshiping God and singing
> - 23% said loving others and making friends
> - 18% said helping the poor and serving other people
> - 4% said giving money and time to bless others
> - 1% said influencing and shaping the faith of family
> - 10% aren't sure

> "If there is one thought with regard to the church of Christ that at times comes to me with overwhelming sorrow; if there is one thought in regard to my own life of which I am ashamed; if there is one thought of which I feel that the church of Christ has not accepted and not grasped; ... it is the wonderful power that prayer is meant to have in the kingdom. We have so little availed ourselves of it. ... We believe more in speaking to men than we believe in speaking to God." [7]

Prayer is how we grow closer to God, for prayer is where we meet Him. Prayer is where we find Jesus' Spirit living within us—*you in me and I in you*. Prayer is where we are one with Jesus, as He is one with the Father. Prayer opens up our souls, so Jesus can pour the fruits of His Spirit into and through us, to be shared with the world around us, all for the glory of God. In referring to Jesus' purpose for prayer, Andrew Murray said,

> "He considers it as one of the chief channels of influence by which, through us, as fellow-workers with God, the blessings of Christ's redemption are to be dispensed to the world." [3]

And prayer does more than glorify God and bless those we pray for. As Paul said,

> *"Do not be anxious about anything, but in every situation, by prayer and petition, with thanksgiving, present your requests to God. And the peace of God, which transcends all understanding, will guard your hearts and your minds in Christ Jesus."* (Philippians 4:6–7)

Since prayer is the presence of God, prayer brings the peace of God. So my advice to you is to pray, as best you can, as often as you can. Then in your prayers, ask Jesus, "Lord, teach me to pray."

Lord, teach me to pray

When the apostles made this request, Jesus replied, *"This, then, is how you should pray: 'Our Father in heaven, hallowed be your name, your kingdom come, your will be done, on earth as it is in heaven. Give us today our daily bread. Forgive us our debts, as we also have forgiven our debtors'"* (Matthew 6:9-12). Notice that our prayers should start as prayers for God, His kingdom, and His will. The priority is for God's glory.

Now, as there's no better evangelist than the Holy Spirit, there is also no better teacher of prayer. As Andrew Murray said, *"But let us look to Jesus* [i.e., His Spirit within us] *to teach us as none but He can teach."* [8] I find it interesting that Murray also said, *"Jesus never taught His disciples how to preach, only how to pray."* [9] Think about that for a moment.

As I mentioned earlier, while going through the Gospels I found 28 verses where Jesus talked about prayer, many of which I've quoted in this chapter. Here's a summary of Jesus' instructions, with a fair amount of paraphrasing: "Pray that you will not fall into temptation. Pray for those who persecute or mistreat you. Pray to God in private, with the Holy Spirit. Pray for God's glory, kingdom, and will, on earth as it is in heaven. Keep it concise and to the point—it's not the words that matter, rather where your heart is. If you remain in Jesus and His words remain in you, and you truly believe and pray in His name, God will give you whatever you ask for. So keep praying, don't give up. And don't forget to listen."

Prayer is living in the presence of the Holy Spirit, leaving the world behind to be alone with God and Jesus. Prayer is expressing our love for God and Jesus. Prayer is trust. Prayer is worship. Yet regarding those favor requests, as Jesus said,

> "Therefore I tell you, whatever you ask for in prayer, believe that you have received it, and it will be yours." (Mark 11:24)

Finally, I want to return to the topic of listening in prayer, since what God has to say most certainly has more worth than what I have to say. In chapter 4, I said one reason I trust the Bible is because God inspired men to write His words, men who had the self-denial and humility to respect God's truth and not distort it or spin it to their own advantage. God spoke to those who were willing to humbly wait, listen, and honor His words. I think the same goes for prayer. I believe God speaks most clearly to those who have the humility to deny themselves, their own thoughts, and their name, and quietly wait and listen.

24. Humility

While humility is an element of our human nature, it's not always the dominant element. Our prideful self is also present, fighting for attention and control, and often winning the battle. Yet, where pride can blind us to the truth of God, Jesus, and Christianity, it takes humility to see them as they really are. And Andrew Murray said,

> "It is indeed pride which makes faith impossible. ... The highest lesson a believer has to learn is humility. ... Humility, the place of entire dependence on God, is, from the very nature of things, the first duty and the highest virtue of man. It is the root of every virtue. ... The first and chief mark of the relationship of man with God, the secret of his blessedness, is the humility and nothingness which leaves God free to be all." [1]
>
> "In the life of faith, humility has a far greater place than we think. It leads us to know our absolute and entire impotence to do any good in our own strength. Humility leads us to Jesus Christ." [2]

Where pride leads us to sin, humility leads us to Jesus Christ. Where pride depends on self, humility depends entirely upon God. Where pride reflects weakness, it takes strength to be humble. Where pride hurts relationships, humility heals relationships. Where pride causes stress and anxiety, humility brings peace. Where pride is captivity, humility is freedom.

By the way, I suspected it wouldn't be there, and sure enough it's not—in the survey results in chapter 3. The surveyed born-again Christians don't consider humility a priority for being Christian. However, as Andrew Murray said, and the Bible reinforces, humility is "the highest lesson a believer has to learn."

Yet unlike pride, humility doesn't come easily, or naturally. While humility leads us to Jesus, we first need the Holy Spirit to lead us to humility.

Humility, noun: freedom from pride or arrogance (merriam-webster.com)

It looks like Merriam-Webster and I share the same opinion—humility is freedom. Wanting a more utilitarian definition that might help us experience that freedom, I found this from C. S. Lewis: *"Humility is not thinking less of yourself; it's thinking of yourself less."* By thinking of ourselves less, we have room to think of others more. As Paul advised,

> *"Do nothing from selfishness or empty conceit, but with humility consider one another as more important than yourselves; do not merely look out for your own personal interests, but also for the interests of others." (Philippians 2:3-4 NASB)*
>
> *"Be devoted to one another in love. Honor one another above yourselves." (Romans 12:10)*

Humility is more than how we relate to other people. As Murray said, humility is entire dependence upon God. When we humbly accept that we can't trust ourselves, we'll then be able to trust God. Yet our do-it-yourself society doesn't seem to value trusting others. Pride deceives us into believing in the power of personal effort. As the old saying goes, "God helps those who help themselves." Though this isn't from the Bible, scripture does say that God helps those who trust Him:

> *"He answered their prayers because they trusted in him." (1 Chronicles 5:20 NASB)*
>
> *"Blessed is the one who trusts in the Lord, who does not look to the proud." (Psalm 40:4)*

Finally, in his book aptly titled *Humility*, Murray said,

> *"It* [humility] *is the being and doing nothing by ourselves so that God may be all. ... It is the displacement of self by the enthronement of God. Where God is all, self is nothing."* [3]

Humility in action

Here are a few examples of what humility can look like:

Jamie

As I came out of the restaurant Jamie was walking by, pulling a small cart carrying all his belongings. He paused and said something I couldn't ignore. We ended up spending the afternoon together.

Jamie is homeless and an alcoholic. He's 50 years old and he's been drinking for 38 years. He told me about waking up that morning in some weeds behind a church, covered in dirt, leaves, vomit, with urine-soaked pants. The end of a 3-day drunk. By the time we met, he'd been to the mission where he'd gotten cleaned up and was given a new set of clothes.

Jamie then told me about his love for Jesus. We talked a lot about Jesus and God. Jamie's knowledge of scripture was amazing. And he kept giving God credit for the blessings in his life, like waking up alive that morning. Before I left Jamie, we prayed together. He asked for forgiveness of his selfishness. He said selfishness hinders him from relying on God to keep him sober.

Jamie knew something I hadn't yet learned, that within himself, even though he appeared incredibly humble, God was not all and his self was not nothing. Jamie knew that his self still held potent influence over him. Yet he had enough humility to see that truth, a truth unseen by pride.

John the Baptist

Jesus' cousin John went from the spotlight to the shadows. He went from having swarms of people following him, to being forgotten in prison. However, I suspect his loss of fame didn't bother him. As John said while still in the spotlight, *"I baptize you with water; but He* [Jesus] *is coming who is mightier than I, and I am not fit to untie the straps of His sandals"* (Luke 3:16 NASB). John didn't take pride in his fame. Rather, he wanted the spotlight to leave him and shine on Jesus. As John also said in referring to Jesus, *"He must become greater; I must become less"* (John 3:30). That's humility.

Jesus

Our greatest example of humility is Jesus Christ, the Son of the creator of all that exists, who was willing to serve and consider the needs of others above His own. In referring to Himself, Jesus said, *"For even the Son of Man did not come to be served, but to serve, and to give his life as a ransom for many"* (Mark 10:45 NASB).

Jesus could have flaunted His divinity and bragged about being the Son of God. Instead, Jesus stressed His human roots, calling Himself *the Son of Man*. Paul described Jesus and His humility this way:

> "In your relationships with one another, have the same mindset as Christ Jesus: Who, being in very nature God, did not consider equality with God something to be used to his own advantage; rather, he made himself nothing by taking the very nature of a servant, being made in human likeness. And being found in appearance as a man, he humbled himself by becoming obedient to death—even death on a cross!" (Philippians 2:5-8)

Andrew Murray said, *"Christ is the humility of God embodied in human nature."* [4] To see the humility of God, look to Jesus. God's humility became Jesus' humility. Maybe Jesus' humility can become our humility.

Encouragement

From beginning to end, the Bible is full of God's encouragement to let go of our natural pride and seek humility. Here are more examples:

> "Seek the Lord, all you humble of the land, you who do what he commands. Seek righteousness, seek humility." (Zephaniah 2:3)
>
> "And what does the Lord require of you? To act justly and to love mercy and to walk humbly with your God." (Micah 6:8)
>
> "Be completely humble and gentle; be patient, bearing with one another in love." (Ephesians 4:2)
>
> "All of you, clothe yourselves with humility toward one another, because, 'God opposes the proud but shows favor to the humble.'" (1 Peter 5:5)
>
> "He [God] guides the humble in what is right and teaches them his way." (Psalm 25:9)

> *"When pride comes, then comes disgrace, but with humility comes wisdom." (Proverbs 11:2)*
>
> *"Finally, all of you, be like-minded, be sympathetic, love one another, be compassionate and humble." (1 Peter 3:8)*

With pride comes disgrace, like yesterday morning when I fell into my pit of pride. It's where I fall whenever I'm so focused on myself and my problems, that I have a hard time thinking about anyone else. The walls of this pit are steep and slippery, and the muck at the bottom grabs hold and sucks the strength right out of me. I've sometimes spent weeks captive in that pit.

But with humility comes wisdom, the wisdom to trust God to lift you up from the grip of pride. It's the wisdom to desire nothing, so that God can be all. James and Peter said:

> *"Humble yourselves before the Lord, and he will lift you up." (James 4:10)*
>
> *"Humble yourselves therefore under the mighty hand of God, so that he may exalt you in due time. Cast all your anxiety on him, because he cares for you." (1 Peter 5:6-7 NRSV)*

Now picture your life as a journey on a bicycle-built-for-two, with you in the front seat. You have a white-knuckle grip on the handlebars while you try to dodge the deep holes that line your path, the holes that represent things like fear, anxiety, stress, depression, pride, selfishness, and other burdens. For many people, the backseat is empty; they're facing life's problems alone. For others, the Holy Spirit is sitting back there. He even peddles if you ask Him to. However, if you have the humility to trade places and give the Holy Spirit the front seat, your life will have direction, purpose, and power—the power of God.

Yet, in surrendering control to God, you don't lose your freedom. That's when you finally gain your freedom, freedom from pride and the burdens of life. Though the burdens don't go away, by your surrender to God the burdens lose their power to control you. Such is the freedom of humility. As Andrew Murray said, *"We will find that the deepest humility is the secret of the truest happiness, of a joy that nothing can destroy."* [5]

Jesus' humility

We can crave humility. We can think more about others and God, and less about ourselves. We can try to trust God more. But in the war for control, pride and self will sabotage our efforts. Self has ruled for a long time, and it won't step aside just because we want it to. So the humility we seek needs to come from outside of ourselves. To this, Andrew Murray said,

> *"It is only by the indwelling of Christ in His divine humility that we become truly humble. ... The humility of Jesus is our salvation. Jesus Himself is our humility. Our humility is His care and His work. ... It is in the death to self that humility is perfected."* [6]

So our goal shouldn't be humility. As I've seen many times on this journey, our goal should be the presence of Jesus' Spirit within us. With His Spirit inside you, His perfect humility will become your humility. And Jesus' humility is more powerful than our prideful self.

25. Forgiveness

He didn't break any rules, though he sure made enemies. He forced his opinion into unwelcomed places, sometimes overruling the decisions of others. And not surprisingly, church committees don't like their decisions overruled, even by the pastor.

Complaints spewed forth like projectile vomit. Something must be done! So, the elders formed another committee, conducted an investigation, and chastised the pastor. He admitted his wrongs, sincerely repented, promised to change, even agreed to get some counseling. Also, he asked for forgiveness. However, for many in the congregation, forgiveness was a language they didn't speak. The pastor endured their scorn for a while and then resigned. I stayed with that church until I couldn't take the hypocrisy and judgment any longer. Then I also quit, feeling that Christianity had to be better than that, more forgiving than that.

The memory of that episode returned as I pondered this chapter. On my journey to find the truth of Christianity, I wanted to see the truth of Christ-like forgiveness, a kind of forgiveness I felt I hadn't experienced in church. Otherwise, how could I hope to forgive as God forgives me?

> "As God's chosen ones, holy and beloved, clothe yourselves with compassion, kindness, humility, meekness, and patience. Bear with one another and, if anyone has a complaint against another, forgive each other; <u>just as the Lord has forgiven you, so you also must forgive</u>." (Colossians 3:12-13 NRSV, emphasis added)

As God forgives

Running late for my morning class at the junior college, I jumped into my '67 Camaro and sped off. No problems on the country roads, but I didn't slow down while flying into the outskirts of the city. As I pulled to the side of the road with the police car on my bumper, I thought of my mom just minutes behind me, coming to town to do some shopping. Sure enough, while the officer stood by my door writing the speeding ticket, my mom drove by in the pickup truck, looking right at me as she did.

I drove much slower on the way home, dreading what likely waited for me there. My mom came out the front door as I was getting out of my car. But when she stepped off the porch, she wrapped her arms around me in a big hug. She didn't even wait for an apology.

My mom's response reminds me of the story Jesus told of the Prodigal son, where the father in the story represents God. The runaway rebellious son finally, and reluctantly, decided to return home. *"But while he was still a long way off, his father saw him and was filled with compassion for him; he ran to his son, threw his arms around him and kissed him"* (Luke 15:20). My mom's forgiveness is like God's forgiveness—immediate and unconditional.

Here's what else this journey has shown me about God's forgiveness:

All sins

My friend Mary once asked me, "God doesn't forgive all sins … right?" At the time, I didn't know the answer. Yet, Jesus might have responded with,

> "Therefore I tell you, people will be forgiven for every sin and blasphemy, … Whoever speaks a word against the Son of Man [Jesus] will be forgiven." (Matthew 12:31-32 NRSV)

Another friend once said to me, "This idea that a terribly evil person can magically be forgiven of their sins is one part of the Christian faith I can't handle." My friend is assuming that God's forgiveness is selective and conditional, like human forgiveness. However, God's ways are not our ways. Also,

> "He [God] does not treat us as our sins deserve or repay us according to our iniquities. For as high as the heavens are above the earth, so great is his love for those who fear him; as far as the east is from the west, so far has he removed our transgressions from us." (Psalm 103:10-12)

Shocking? Sure. Yet again, God's not an image of unforgiving humans—we're a distorted image of Him.

Forgive and forget

> "If you, Lord, kept a record of sins, Lord, who could stand? But with you there is forgiveness." (Psalm 130:3-4)

Consider all your sins as a shadow clinging to you. As you go through life and your collection of sins grows, so grows your shadow, becoming darker and larger. I've felt the weight of my own shadow, as if my sins were dragging me down. However, God's forgiveness is like a brilliant light shining upon us from all directions. Within God's light, there is no shadow. It's as if our sins never existed.

> "For I will forgive their wickedness and will remember their sins no more." (Jeremiah 31:34)
>
> "Their sins and lawless acts I will remember no more." (Hebrews 10:17)

Though we may hold onto the memory of past sins, God doesn't. Forgive and forget; it's the way of God.

God never gives up

"I used to believe; I used to go to church," a friend confided. "But no more. I'm lost for good now. God can't forgive me. God won't take me back." My friend believes that once you turn your back on God, He'll turn His back on you. But look again at the story of the Prodigal son. Not only did the father in the story take the lost son back, he anxiously waited for his son to return. Quitting on God doesn't mean He'll quit on us. God never gives up.

Even enemies

Do God and Jesus forgive their enemies? I mean, why should they? Check this out, from Jesus:

> "To you who are listening I say: Love your enemies, ... If someone slaps you on one cheek, turn to them the other also." (Luke 6:27, 29)

Jesus didn't just say it—He did it. Shortly after they nailed Him to the cross, Jesus looked down upon His enemies. There were the religious leaders who had falsely accused Him and pressured Pilate for the death penalty, along with the Roman soldiers who carried it out. In whatever pain He must have been enduring, Jesus had the strength to pray, *"Father, forgive them, for they do not know what they are doing"* (Luke 23:34). Jesus forgave His enemies. So does God.

God offers His forgiveness to everyone, though this gift only becomes real for those who have the faith to accept it.

It's our turn

What we most often experience in life is worldly forgiveness, a forgiveness that must be earned, and even if it is earned, it's not always given. Yet, Jesus calls us to forgive as God forgives—*just as the Lord has forgiven you, so you also must forgive*—with a forgiveness which is unearned, unconditional, always given, and just waiting to be accepted.

People have trouble forgiving because their natural focus is on themselves rather than others. To our prideful self, forgiving feels like we've lost a battle, and pride hates losing. That's why forgiveness requires humility. God's forgiveness comes from God's humility, and God's humility is why forgiveness is so easy for Him. With true humility—where God is all and self is nothing—forgiveness can be easy for us too.

Okay, I'm sorry, but the survey data showing priorities for being Christian is again beckoning to me. So are Jesus' instructions for how we should pray: *"Our Father in heaven ... Forgive us our sins, for we also forgive everyone who sins against us"* (Luke 11:4). Even though it's in the prayer Jesus taught us to pray, forgiving others isn't on the list of priorities.

Some Christians act as if forgiveness is God's business, not theirs. Let God do the forgiving while they'd rather hold a grudge. This helps fuel the perception of Christians as hypocritical and judgmental—that is, a lot like everyone else. But Jesus calls us to be different:

> "If your brother or sister sins against you, rebuke them; and if they repent [i.e., apologize], forgive them. Even if they sin against you seven times in a day and seven times come back to you saying 'I repent,' you must forgive them." (Luke 17:3-4)
>
> "And whenever you stand praying, forgive, if you have anything against anyone, so that your Father who is in heaven will also forgive you for your offenses." (Mark 11:25 NASB)

And Paul advises:

> *"Be kind to one another, compassionate, forgiving each other, just as God in Christ also has forgiven you." (Ephesians 4:32 NASB)*

Forgive others as God has forgiven you. Yet, maybe a reason we see so little humility and forgiveness in some churches is because God isn't there either—God is missing, as the survey data shows. So yes, forgiveness shouldn't be our goal; the Holy Spirit should. With the Spirit of God within you—when God is no longer missing in your life, and where He is all and self is nothing—His humility and forgiveness can become yours.

Finally, where there's humility, there is love, and in his definition of love, Paul declared: *"It is not self-seeking, it is not easily angered, <u>it keeps no record of wrongs</u>"* (1 Corinthians 13:5, emphasis added). True love forgives and forgets. And with that, it's time to scrape off the graffiti that obscures the last truth, the greatest truth.

> *"And now these three remain: faith, hope and love. <u>But the greatest of these is love</u>." (1 Corinthians 13:13, emphasis added)*

26. Love

Miracle Max: *"Hey! Hello in there! Hey! What's so important? What you got here that's worth living for?"*
Westley: *"T-r-u-e l-o-v-e."*
Inigo: *"'True Love,' you heard him? You could not ask for a more noble cause than that."*
Miracle Max: *"Sonny, true love is the greatest thing in the world."* [1]

Hey, what's so important? What's Christianity have that's worth living for? In my search for the truth of what it means to be Christian, I started with the foundation, faith. I'll now finish with the mortar that holds it all together, love.

It's often stated, though not always seen, that love is what Christianity is all about. However, according to survey results I cited in chapters two and three, when outsiders and the de-churched look at Christians and churches, they see judgment, hypocrisy, bigotry, barriers, and rules. What they apparently don't see is love. According to the Barna Group survey that asked people if they see Christian churches as unconditionally loving regardless of how people look or what they do, of those outside the church, 80% said no. Perhaps surprisingly, 59% of those inside the church also said no. [2]

Yes, love and God seem to be missing from many factions of modern Christianity. Let's now look at the love that's hidden beneath that graffiti, true God-like love, a love that's the greatest thing in the world.

From conditional to True Love

For most of my life, I reserved my love for my family and closest friends. My love was a gift I gave only to those who earned it. We give such love to people who are kind, funny, sincere, compassionate, responsive to our actions and feelings, a good listener, or a good provider of our needs. Most love we experience is like that; it's a result of someone being lovable. That's conditional love.

Conditional love is self-centered, being all about how the other person makes us feel. In most relationships, this is how love starts. It's a shallow love with shallow roots, and it'll eventually wither and die if it doesn't grow out of the conditional, self-centered phase.

As an example, when my friend Mike began dating the woman who later became his wife, his feelings for her seemed out of control. While his job at the hardware store consumed his time, she consumed his thoughts. Where work kept his hands busy, those thoughts kept a goofy smile on his face. He was smitten, in love.

In those early weeks, his blossoming love sometimes overwhelmed him and filled him with a thrill he still remembers. Back then, his love for her was young and fresh and full of passion. If anyone asked him why he loved her, he'd answer with all the things about her that captivated him and made him smile. Although he wouldn't believe it at the time, his love for her was far from true love.

They've now been married over twenty years. As those years passed, his love kept growing and maturing, though he didn't always see it. Then one day, when she was feeling a bit feisty and silly and began teasing him, she asked, "Why do you love me, anyway?"

The question caught him off guard and groping for an answer. Why indeed? He wanted to give an honest answer, nothing cliché or corny. Yet he had to admit that he had no reason for his love. His love for her lost the need for a reason many years ago.

Mike now sees that his love for her is unconditional—no reason required. And he understands that what he finally feels is true love. Not storybook love, not *Princess Bride* love, but the real thing, a love that's permanent and undiminished by events or the passing of years.

A love that never fails

Paul defined true love this way:

> "Love is patient, love is kind. It does not envy, it does not boast, it is not proud. It does not dishonor others, it is not self-seeking, it is not easily angered, it keeps no record of wrongs. Love does not delight in evil but rejoices with the truth. It always protects, always trusts, always hopes, always perseveres. Love never fails." (1 Corinthians 13:4-8)

"Love is not proud ... it is not self-seeking." Where there's humility, there is love. Picture a marriage where each person lives for the emotional wellbeing of the

other person, without regard for self. In this way, they take care of each other. Such humble love feeds itself, with each person giving, rather than taking.

"Love never fails." Really? What about failed marriages? Well, as a friend going through a divorce once confided in me, "My needs are no longer being met by my spouse." I wonder how the spouse felt. Look at any failing relationship—chances are, selfishness is the cause. However, true love, unconditional love, humble and selfless love that gives rather than takes, God's love—this love never fails.

God's love

My wife and I were babysitting our one-year-old grandson. It was time for him to take a nap, and it was my turn to try to settle him down and get him to sleep. With a fresh diaper installed and my grandson snug in his sleeping bag thing, I sat on the bed with him on my lap and read to him a couple of books, followed by my set of four songs. Before I finished, his eyes had closed and his breathing had deepened. I carefully laid him in the crib amongst his stuffed-animal friends. Then, as I crept toward the bedroom door, he stood and started shaking the crib.

So, I scooped him up, laid down on the nearby bed with him on my chest, and began softly singing again. By the time the first song was over, he was gently snoring, in that oh-so-cute-tiny-nose-snore of his. In that moment, with my arms wrapped around him while he rose and fell as I breathed, my love for him felt … well … I can't define something that feels too big to be defined. My thesaurus doesn't have a word that's worthy to describe it. Yet I believe that my love for my grandson—a love that I've always felt for my sons—is an image of God's love for His children, admittedly a faded image.

As God is not an image of us, neither is His love an image of our love. God's love doesn't suffer from human weaknesses, and God's love is unaffected by things *in* this world or *out* of this world. As Paul proclaimed:

> "For I am convinced that neither death nor life, neither angels nor demons, neither the present nor the future, nor any powers, neither height nor depth, nor anything else in all creation, will be able to separate us from the love of God that is in Christ Jesus our Lord." (Romans 8:38-39)

Not even our sins can separate us from the love of God, for as Paul also said: *"God demonstrates his own love for us in this: While we were still sinners, Christ died for us"* (Romans 5:8). Also, Jesus and John said:

> *"For God so loved the world, that He gave His only Son, so that everyone who believes in Him will not perish, but have eternal life." (John 3:16 NASB)*
>
> *"This is how God showed his love among us: He sent his one and only Son into the world that we might live through him. This is love: not that we loved God, but that he loved us and sent his Son as an atoning sacrifice for our sins." (1 John 4:9-10)*

Regarding the oft-quoted John 3:16, maybe the last half of that verse draws all the attention, while the first half is quickly passed over. *The world* includes everyone. Also, where our eternal life requires the condition of faith, God's love requires no conditions.

Finally, while praying to God for all believers, Jesus said,

> *"Then the world will know that you sent me and have loved them even as you have loved me. ... I have made you known to them, and will continue to make you known in order that <u>the love you have for me may be in them</u>." (John 17:23, 26, emphasis added)*

The love God has for Jesus can be *in* us. Think about that for a moment.

Love comes from God

When someone asked Jesus what the greatest commandment is, He answered:

> *"Love the Lord your God with all your heart and with all your soul and with all your mind. This is the first and greatest commandment. And the second is like it: 'Love your neighbor as yourself.'" (Matthew 22:37-39)*

Okay, before getting to what I wanted to say, I feel obliged to point out something. Please read again the first two sentences in Jesus' statement. Now consider the list of priorities for being Christian from the survey results I cited back in chapter 3. Nowhere on that list does it say to love God. Yet, this is the greatest commandment with respect to being Christian, and it's missing!

Anyway, in the verses above Jesus is telling us to love as He loves. Like He also said, *"This is My commandment, that you love one another, just as I have loved you"* (John 15:12 NASB, emphasis added). Maybe prompted by this command, Paul said, *"Therefore be imitators of God, as beloved children, and live in love, as Christ loved us and gave himself up for us"* (Ephesians 5:1-2 NRSV). Be imitators of God—sounds difficult, I know, yet all we have to do is be willing receptacles of God's Spirit, and His love.

In chapter 14 of John's gospel, Jesus said the same thing three times, as if He knew it needed emphasizing:

> "If you love Me, you will keep My commandments. I will ask the Father, and He will give you another Helper, so that He may be with you forever; the Helper is the Spirit of truth." (John 14:15-17 NASB)
>
> "Those who love me will be loved by my Father, and I will love them and reveal myself to them [as the Holy Spirit]." (John 14:21 NRSV)
>
> "Anyone who loves me will obey my teaching. My Father will love them, and we will come to them and make our home with them." (John 14:23)

If we love Jesus, with as much love as we can muster, we can experience the presence of His Spirit in our lives. And because God is love, where there's God's Spirit, there is God's love. We can become the home in which God's Spirit, and love, lives.

On my own, I can't possibly love as God loves, for my love is human and weak. But again, as Jesus said, *"Just as the Father has loved Me, I also have loved you. ... love one another, just as I have loved you"* (John 15:9, 12 NASB). Jesus is saying that as God's love pours into Him, it then flows from Him into us. And from us … well, picture this: God's love is like a three-tiered fountain, with His love pouring from God at the top, down to Jesus, then to us. From us, God's love can spill out to everyone around us. Paul expressed it this way:

> *"God's love has been poured out into our hearts through the Holy Spirit, who has been given to us."* (Romans 5:5)

Also, John said:

> *"Dear friends, let us love one another, for love comes from God. Everyone who loves has been born of God and knows God. ... If we love one another, God lives in us and his love is made complete in us. ... God is love. Whoever lives in love lives in God, and God in them. This is how love is made complete among us. ... We love because he first loved us"* (1 John 4:7, 12, 16-17, 19)

Any love that I feel for someone else, that love originated with God.

Now then, when Jesus instructs us to love one another, I've heard some aspiring Christian's claim that "one another" refers only to other Christians. That sounds conditional. But remember what else Jesus said about love: *"Love your enemies, do good to those who hate you, bless those who curse you, pray for those who mistreat you. ... If you love those who love you, what credit is that to you? Even sinners love those who love them"* (Luke 6:27-28, 32). Yet does loving your enemies sound impossible? Not when it's God's love rather than yours, pouring into you and spilling out indiscriminately to those around you.

Do you seek true love? As with our faith, humility, forgiveness, and all the other virtues of Jesus' Christianity, you can't experience and express God's true love directly, by your own power. Instead, rely on the Holy Spirit, because, *"The fruit of the Spirit is love"* (Galatians 5:22 NRSV).

Fulfillment

So, what does it mean to be a true Christian? Of all the virtues I've mentioned, those virtues that find perfection in the presence of the Holy Spirit—the faith, righteousness, obedience, trust, humility, forgiveness, and love—the greatest is love, because love provides for all the rest.

> "As God's chosen ones, holy and beloved, clothe yourselves with compassion, kindness, humility, meekness, and patience. Bear with one another and, if anyone has a complaint against another, forgive each other; just as the Lord has forgiven you, so you also must forgive. <u>Above all, clothe yourselves with love, which binds everything together in perfect harmony</u>." (Colossians 3:12-14 NRSV, emphasis added)

Love is the mortar, binding everything together in perfect harmony. Love is the fulfillment of God's hopes and desires for His children. As Paul put it:

> "The commandments, 'You shall not commit adultery,' 'You shall not murder,' 'You shall not steal,' 'You shall not covet,' and whatever other command there may be, are summed up in this one command: 'Love your neighbor as yourself.' Love does no harm to its neighbor. Therefore <u>love is the fulfillment of the law</u>." (Romans 13:9-10, emphasis added)

Andrew Murray said this about love and Christians:

> "Their life of love is the chief evidence of Christianity, the proof to the world that God sent Christ and that He has shed abroad in them the same love with which His Father loved Him. Of all the evidences of Christianity, this is the mightiest and most convincing." [3]

Christianity is built on a foundation of faith, held together by the mortar of love. And it's the Holy Spirit, living within us, who can transform us into living evidence of what it means to be Christian. As Andrew Murray also said,

> "With Christ abiding in you, the Holy Spirit sheds abroad the love of God in your heart, and you love the brethren, even the most trying and unlovable, with a love that is not your own but the love of Christ in you." [4]

That's what it means to be Christian.

The greatest of these is Love

Think back to all the ills that plague Christianity, the human flaws and worldly influences that paint the graffiti hiding Jesus' truth. There's disunity, manmade traditions, false teaching, pride, selfishness, judgment, hypocrisy, bigotry, lack of forgiveness, and lack of love. The cure for all of these is love, by the presence and power of the Holy Spirit.

If you asked Jesus what it means to be Christian, He might simply repeat what He once instructed:

> "Love one another. As I have loved you, so you must love one another. By this everyone will know that you are my disciples, if you love one another." (John 13:34-35)

And according to Andrew Murray: *"If we exhibit the love that was in God toward Christ, and in Christ toward us, the world will be obliged to confess that our Christianity is genuine and from above."* [5] How about you? Have you experienced genuine Christianity—Jesus' Christianity?

Love is the conclusion. Love is the one word that sums up what it means to be Christian. So why are there four more chapters in this record of my journey, chapters I added only with the last few revisions of this book? Well, I hadn't yet uncovered answers to all my questions. And we haven't summited this metaphorical mountain we've been climbing, though we're almost there. But before we make our final push to the top …

Dear God, *"Because your love is better than life, my lips will glorify you.* [6] *And I pray that you* [dear reader], *being rooted and established in love, may have power, together with all the Lord's holy people, to grasp how wide and long and high and deep is the love of Christ, and to know this love that surpasses knowledge—that you may be filled to the measure of all the fullness of God.* [7] *May the Lord make your love increase and overflow for each other and for everyone else."* [8] Amen

The Truth Will Set You Free

27. Free From What?

"Wake up CJ, your *self* has you." Like Neo in the movie *The Matrix*, for much of my life I was a clueless prisoner, unaware of my own captivity. We're all prisoners, held captive by such things as painful memories, hurtful relationships, poor health, addiction, lies, conspiracy theories, and poor decisions of work bosses and elected leaders. Mostly, we're unwitting prisoners of ourselves, and the stress, anger, fear, anxiety, frustration, and depression that self wallows in. I've complained a lot about my *self* and the control it has over me. However, as Jesus promised, *"Then you will know the truth, and the truth will set you free"* (John 8:32). Free from what? Free from self.

Now, before you call me delusional, I'd like to remind you of the two sides of our human nature. There's your prideful, selfish, worldly self (lower case s), that conforms to the image of the world. Then there's your humble, loving, spiritual Self (upper case S), who was created in the image of God. I'm talking about freedom from captivity to your worldly self so your spiritual Self can finally live as God originally intended.

We've come a long way together on our journey to uncover the truth of Christianity. We've scaled many obstacles along the way. And on this spiritual mountain we've been climbing, the summit is finally within reach. Waiting for you there, within these next four chapters, are some pinnacle truths about both Christianity, and you. But first, we need to climb over the final barrier that stands in our way.

The exalted self

In the beginning, Adam and Eve had no experience with evil. They didn't know what it was. If someone had said something mean or evil to them, they wouldn't have understood, and they wouldn't have reacted with anger, fear, or defensiveness, as we typically do. The idea of good versus evil was unknown to them, since all they knew was good. Try to imagine how that would feel.

When God created humanity, He poured His image—the image of His character—into Adam and Eve. Initially that image had no rival, no enemy on the other shoulder fighting for control. Then they fell for Satan's temptation to eat from the tree of the knowledge of good and evil. The fruit of that tree poisoned them with evil, since to know evil is to taste it and allow it to become a part of you. Since pride is the root of all evil—as we saw in the chapter about pride—eating that fruit infected Adam and Eve with pride and its companion, self. Achieving its mission of usurping God and taking control, self exalted itself.

I believe our conscience is all that remains of the image of God's character within us, and in some people, it's only a faded shadow of His image. Having inherited the exalted self, a big chunk of humanity is so focused on themselves that they're too blind to see the harm they inflict. Their self-centeredness, arrogance, greed, stubbornness, bigotry, anger, and hatred, blind them from seeing that these aspects of their personality cause all the harm to society, civility, humanity, and our planet. Mass murders, wars, climate deterioration, economic collapse, civil and political chaos prompted by conspiracy theories and lies—these are examples of damage inflicted by the self. And of course there's the closer-to-home self-inflicted damage that many of us suffer from: the stress, anger, fear, anxiety, frustration, and depression.

Our self is greedy, demanding all the attention and all the control. Self expects you to be so full of it, that there's no room left for God—that you exalt self rather than God. As Andrew Murray said,

> *"All the vices of fallen men have their birth and power in the atheism and idolatry of self, for self is both atheist and idolater. It is atheist because it has rejected God; it is idolater because it is its own idol. On the other hand, all the virtues of the heavenly life are the virtues of humility."* [1]

Maybe that's why Jesus calls us to deny self and humbly follow Him:

> *"Whoever wants to be my disciple must deny themselves and take up their cross daily and follow me." (Luke 9:23)*

Of course, self would rather lead than follow. Also, can anyone call themselves a follower of Jesus without having the faith and desire to follow Him all the way? And sorry for bringing this up again, but regarding the survey results with the list of things Christians see as their priorities: even though Jesus requires it as a condition for being Christian, denying self isn't on that list.

> When born-again Christians were asked to list two or three of the most important priorities for being Christian in terms of their faith:
> - 37% said being good and not sinning
> - 31% said learning about Jesus and the Bible
> - 25% said sharing their faith and helping others come to know Jesus
> - 25% said worshiping God and singing
> - 23% said loving others and making friends
> - 18% said helping the poor and serving other people
> - 4% said giving money and time to bless others
> - 1% said influencing and shaping the faith of family
> - 10% aren't sure

From my own experience, the idea of denying self can feel like it's bordering on nonsense, one of those strange things in the Bible we can ignore. Yet self is clever and will use such lies to deceive your better half. Also, self knows it will survive and maintain control only as long as you don't realize that it's holding you captive. For once you recognize self for what it truly is, its days of dominance are limited, unless you choose to remain its prisoner.

The crossroads

I've been at the crossroads many times, staring down the two paths, struggling to decide which to follow. The path on my left is wide, slopes gently downhill, and soon bends out of view. The right-hand path is narrow, level, and straight for as far as I can see. Though that path looks easy, I'd always imagined there was a high price to pay in taking that right-hand path.

Between the two paths stands a large sign that reads, *"What is impossible for mortals is possible for God."* [2] Until recently, I've ignored that sign as I always started down the left-hand path. Then, around that first bend, the path becomes steep, slippery, and lined with deep holes. Soon stumbling, as I always do, there've been times I've spent weeks trapped in one of those holes.

What are these holes? Just negative emotional states, such as anger, frustration, disappointment, anxiety, stress, depression, fear, jealousy, greed, and envy. Yet finally I see that rather than falling, I get pulled into a hole as self reaches up a slimy hand and drags me down. That slimy hand is self, manifested as selfishness, self-centeredness, self-consciousness, self-pity, pride, arrogance, or vanity. In a way, I guess you could say that self *is* the hole I fall into.

By the way, there are signposts for the two choices at the crossroads. The left-hand path is called *self.* The right-hand path is called *God. "What is impossible for mortals is possible for God."*

On our journey through life—which is what each path represents—we can follow the path laid out by self, or the path laid out by God. On the left-hand path we go it alone. On the right path, the Holy Spirit leads us, showing us the way and keeping us safe—safe from self. Where I used to believe that each path led to the same destination, I now see that the path on the left leads to futility, while the path on the right leads to freedom, the freedom I've been seeking.

God has something to say about this:

> "This is what the Lord says: 'Stand at the crossroads and look; ask for the ancient paths, ask where the good way is, and walk in it, and you will find rest for your souls."' (Jeremiah 6:16)

Everywhere I've been on this journey, everything I've discovered, every truth I've uncovered—it all reveals a foundational truth of Jesus' Christianity, the truth that sets you free. We have a choice. We can continue living for ourselves, always following our *self* as it pulls us down that left-hand path to futility. Or, we can follow the Holy Spirit up the right-hand path, to freedom.

Finally, as Jesus said, *"Whoever wants to be my disciple must deny themselves and take up their cross daily and follow me."* By these words, Jesus is calling us to turn our backs on the path laid out by self, and instead follow Him up the path laid out by God. He's standing there now, at the head of the ancient path, holding out His hand to you and saying as He often said, "Come, follow me."

Dying to Self

Humanity is broken. We try to fix ourselves with movements like Me Too and Black Lives Matter. We need such movements because humanity is so screwed up, so filled with self-centeredness, arrogance, greed, bigotry, and all the rest. But it doesn't have to be that way. We have that choice. As Andrew Murray said,

> "There is no other choice for us; we must either deny self or deny Christ. There are two great powers fighting each

> *other—the self-nature in the power of sin, and Christ in the power of God. One of these must rule within us."* [3]

Now check this out from *Dying to Self: A Golden Dialogue*:

> *"Our very life* [aka, self]*, Christ said, must be hated, must be lost. Before a man consents to this, it needs divine teaching to make him see that all our natural life is indeed so incurably evil as to need being given up and parted with. When he does see and consent to this, it needs time and divine teaching to show him what giving up all, this dying to self, really means."* [4]
>
> *"The death of self is something very different from the death to self which God's Word holds out to you. When Jesus died to sin, He did not slay sin in the sense of killing and annihilating it. No, sin is still living and reigning in all who submit to it, whether willingly or reluctantly. He died to it so that it had no more power to tempt or persecute Him. You are partakers of His death to sin, and to self, in which sin works."* [5]

Imagine again your devilish self on one shoulder, and your image-of-God Self on the other shoulder. Your sinful self may be big and strong, having usurped control a long time ago. But, if you choose, the Holy Spirit can overpower your self and kick it off your shoulder, making room for Him to take His rightful place. I like to picture my sinful self all shriveled up and puny, hanging from a thread on my shirt, struggling to hold on.

If that image doesn't work for you, try this one. Picture within your soul—the center of your being—a throne. When God created Adam and Eve, on the throne of their souls sat the Spirit of God. Then, having chosen to listen to Satan, they became inflicted with pride, which resulted in self taking God's place. But again, the Holy Spirit can dethrone the usurper so Jesus can take His rightful place within your soul. And as I quoted Andrew Murray back in the Humility chapter, *"humility is the displacement of self by the enthronement of God."*[6] With this image, I like to picture my shriveled up and puny self as barely visible, nearly outside the frame of the image, groveling at the foot of the throne.

By your death to self, though it will still be present, your self won't have power to influence how you live and experience life. You will have given that power to God. And as William Law said,

> *"The need must be felt of God's light to chase away the darkness of self, of an entirely new life by the Holy Spirit to take the place of the life of self, of an entire death to self to make way for the birth of the Spirit of Love from heaven."* [7]

Whoever loses their life controlled by self will find a new life with the Holy Spirit. That's what Jesus promised, and Paul referred to when they said,

> *"Whoever wants to save their life will lose it, but whoever loses their life for me will find it."* (Matthew 16:25)
>
> *"For we who are alive are always being given over to death* [to self] *for Jesus' sake, so that his life may also be revealed in our mortal body."* (2 Corinthians 4:11)

Finally, regarding when Jesus said, *"Whoever wants to be my disciple must deny themselves and take up their cross daily and follow me,"* Jesus' cross represents death, His death to sin. Our cross represents our own death, our death to self.

Where God is all, self is nothing

I'm back at the crossroads again. I find myself there each morning, and several times throughout the day. Sometimes I just stand there, shackled by *self*-inflicted hesitation. Loitering at the crossroads is stressful, with self lurking nearby. Maybe I worry too much about self. Andrew Murray had something to say about that:

> *"Where God is all, self is nothing. ... Being occupied with self, even amid the deepest self-abhorrence, can never free us from self. ... Not to be occupied with your sin, but to be occupied with God, brings deliverance from self. ... Humility must lead us to die to self. ... Only thus are we freed from fallen nature and find the path that leads to life in God, to*

> *that full birth of the new nature of which humility is the breath and the joy."* [8]

When we're fully occupied with God, there's no room left for self.

By now you'll recognize one of my favorite quotes from John the Baptist. In referring to Jesus he said, *"He must become greater; I must become less"* (John 3:30). I like saying that Jesus must become all; my self must become nothing. About that, Murray said:

> *"It is indeed blessed to be so free from self that whatever is said about us or done to us is lost and swallowed up in the thought that Jesus is all.* [9] *… As the all-pervading life of God possesses you, there will be nothing so natural and nothing so sweet as to be nothing, with not a thought or wish for self, because all is occupied with Him who fills all."* [10]

And where God is all, there's freedom from captivity to self, the freedom I've been searching for.

28. Surrender—Free at Last!

Self can be a monster, a curse, the root cause of all life's problems. Self is so powerful that, as Andrew Murray said in *Dying to Self: A Golden Dialogue*,

> "It is only when the soul is brought to believe in its own entire and utter impotence to deal directly with this monster that it will begin to get an insight into the absoluteness of the surrender to God and the trust in Him, which is needed if He alone is to do the work for us and in us." [1]

We all have that unavoidable choice: to surrender to self and the world, or to God. For most of my life, I didn't realize there was a choice. When I first heard about the concept of surrendering to God, I shied away from it. Such surrender felt like captivity, shackling me to a way of life other than how I hoped to live.

At some point in my personal journey, I finally saw that my *self* was already holding me captive, captive to things like fear, worries, stress, depression—you know the rest. Sometimes feeling overwhelmed by my sense of helplessness and hopelessness, I even considered giving up on the whole thing. But now, instead of giving up on life, I'm finally ready to give up on self. And where surrender to self is captivity, surrender to God is freedom.

I've casually mentioned the idea of surrender throughout this book. Now it's time to get serious. Yet, I understand—surrender to most people feels like loss. However, that feeling is just the voice of self, because from self's perspective, surrender to God *is* loss.

Called to surrender

Jesus encouraged our surrender in how He taught us to pray: *"Our Father ... your will be done, on earth as it is in heaven"* (Matthew 6:10). Jesus got more specific when He called those who want to be His disciple to deny themselves, take up their cross, and follow Him.

Paul encouraged us as well:

> "Therefore, I urge you, brothers and sisters, in view of God's mercy, to offer your bodies as a living sacrifice, holy and pleasing to God—this is your true and proper worship." (Romans 12:1)
>
> "Offer yourselves to God as those who have been brought from death to life." (Romans 6:13)
>
> "And He [Jesus] died for all, so that those who live would no longer live for themselves, but for Him." (2 Corinthians 5:15 NASB)

When Jesus calls us to deny ourselves, He's not expecting us to do anything He hasn't done Himself. Here are some examples of how Jesus lived by His own surrender to God:

> "For I have come down from heaven, not to do My own will, but the will of Him who sent Me." (John 6:38 NASB)
>
> "The words I say to you I do not speak on my own authority. Rather, it is the Father, living in me, who is doing his work." (John 14:10)

Andrew Murray described Jesus' surrender this way:

> "Christ found this life of entire self-renunciation, of absolute submission and dependence upon the Father's will, to be one of perfect peace and joy. He lost nothing by giving everything to God. ... His humility was simply the surrender of Himself to God, to allow the Father to do in Him what He pleased. [2] ... This is true self-denial to which our Savior calls us—the acknowledgment that self has nothing good in it except as an empty vessel which God must fill." [3]

Surrender—to be an empty vessel which God must fill. When the vessel of your being has been filled with God, when self has been pushed off the throne of your soul and replaced by the Spirit of God, you can then become what the Lord originally created humanity to be, a vivid and unblemished image of God. You can then project the love, forgiveness, humility, patience, peace, and kindness of Jesus. This is what Paul was talking about when he said,

> "You were taught, with regard to your former way of life, to put off your old self, which is being corrupted by its deceitful desires; to be made new in the attitude of your minds; and to put on the new self, created to be like God." (Ephesians 4:22-24, emphasis added)
>
> "Therefore if anyone is in Christ, this person is a new creation; the old things passed away; behold, new things have come." (2 Corinthians 5:17 NASB)

The *new creation* Paul mentioned is to be re-created as God originally intended, free from the burdens of self and sin. That's what Jesus is offering us. That's what living "in Christ" means. That's what it means to be a Christian.

Try not

Please consider again Jesus' call for Christians to deny themselves and follow Him. I know that sounds difficult or impossible, but as Paul said,

> "It is God who is at work in you, enabling you both to will and to work for his good pleasure." (Philippians 2:13 NRSV)

And as Andrew Murray said,

> "The death to self is not your work; it is God's work. [4] ... What a hopeless task if we had to do the work! Self can never cast out self. [5] ... Nothing but the presence of God can reveal and expel self." [6]

"Nothing but the presence of God." Where God is all, self is nothing. All I can bring to this battle is my faith, choice, and desire. We also need enough humility to accept our helplessness and rely on God to make our surrender a reality.

There's a lesson for us in *Star Wars: The Empire Strikes Back*. Luke's spaceship sinks in the swamp and Yoda tells him to use the force to raise it out.

Luke says he'll try. Yoda then shoots back, "No! Try not. Do. Or do not. There is no try." Then, after Luke fails and Yoda raises the ship to dry land, Luke says, "I don't … I don't believe it." Yoda replies, "*That* is why you fail."

We, too, are stuck in a swamp, the swamp of our worldly self. In our efforts to surrender to God and free ourselves from the swamp, there is no *try*—there's also no *do*. We don't have the power to make it happen, the force is weak within us. Also, as Luke didn't have enough faith and trust in the force, many of us don't have enough faith and trust in God. The lesson from *Star Wars* is this: all we can do is *believe,* and humbly trust God to breathe life into our surrender, raising us out of the swamp we've been wallowing in.

Fruits of Surrender

The attacks seem to come from everywhere. They attack our emotions, our health, and our sense of well-being. Diseases, politics, bigotry, divisiveness, personal conflicts, anger, hate, war, your job, lack of a job, and more—such are the weapons the world throws at us. However, there is a way to protect ourselves from the impact of these attacks. As Jesus said:

> "I have told you these things, so that in me you may have peace. In this world you will have trouble. But take heart! I have overcome the world." (John 16:33, emphasis added)

I like to picture myself *in* Jesus, as if He's wrapped around me like a magic cloak, shielding me from the troubles of this world. *In* Him I have peace. Such is the life of surrender.

I now see that the fruits of the Spirit—the love, joy, peace, patience, kindness, generosity, faithfulness, gentleness, and self-control—*are* the fruits of surrender. Regarding that last fruit, I'd always believed self-control was me being able to control my words, emotions, thoughts, and actions. Right, like that'll ever happen. Yet, with my surrender, I now see self-control as the Holy Spirit controlling my self, instead of self controlling me.

Terms of surrender

I recently imagined the following conversation between Jesus and me:

Me: "Dear Jesus, I'm ready, I surrender."

Jesus: "Okay. Under what terms? How will the two of us interact in this surrender?"

Me: "Well, I want to live for you, to do everything for your glory. Not my will, but your will be done. You become greater, I become less. I no longer live, but you live—"

Jesus, interrupting: "Hold on. The loosely quoted scripture is nice; however, tell me what surrender means in *your* words?"

Me: "Hmm, my words, let's see."

Jesus, smiling: "Just tell me what you want."

Me: "What I want? Okay. Well, I want to do whatever you want. I mean, I want to put all my trust in you. I want to be empty of my self and filled with You. And peace, no worries, no fears, no more stress, no more nervous stomach, no more tight chest—that's what I want. Whatever happens, whatever I need to say or do in any situation, I want to rely on you to help me deal with it. And freedom from self—I want that too. I want to live as if my self were dead, and in self's place will be You, living through me. I want to be an image of You. I want you to walk the earth again, in me. I just want to always see you sitting on the throne of my soul … with that look on your face that you have right now."

Jesus, again smiling, eyes sparkling: "Okay. Now here are my terms. You'll still have your freedom, freedom of desire and freedom of choice. For without that freedom, there can be no true love, and no true surrender. It's your choice to surrender, and each day you must refresh and affirm your choice. That will show your love for me. And one more thing. Don't try. Just believe, make your choice, and rest in the peace of my presence, trusting *me* to bring your surrender to life."

Back to the choice

Chaos, divisiveness, lies, threats, and wars on the precipice of escalation. If this world feels overwhelming and almost too difficult to cope with, please don't surrender to despair, and please don't surrender to self. Instead, whether stressed out by the world or not, surrender to God and let the Holy Spirit cut the puppet strings of self and the world that have controlled how you experience life. It's God or self—the choice is yours.

By the way, I just looked again at the survey results at the end of chapter 3. It seems implied that those priorities for being Christian, the priorities that many Christians clearly fail to achieve, all rely on self-effort. Many have chosen to rely on themselves rather than God, putting more faith in self than in God. And as Yoda might say, *that* is why they fail.

The garden

Referring to those who love Him, Jesus said, *"My Father will love them, and we will come to them and make our home with them"* (John 14:23). In the beginning, humanity lived with God in the garden paradise, our original home, heaven on earth. Then the devil's curse of pride and self got humanity thrown out of the garden and into the world. But remember Jesus' prayer, *"they are not of the world, just as I am not of the world"* (John 17:14 NASB). This world is not our home. Our home is with God, in the garden, and Jesus came to redeem us and open the way for our return:

> "The reason the Son of God appeared was to destroy the devil's work." (1 John 3:8)

"To destroy the devil's work" means *all* his work, even his most heinous work. Jesus came to destroy the damage inflicted by the curse of pride and self. He then sent the Holy Spirit to set us free from ourselves, take us by the hand, and lead us up that straight and narrow right-hand path. Yes, that path I'd mentioned, the path at our crossroads, is the path leading back home, to the way it was in the garden.

To repeat something Paul said: *"Offer yourselves to God as those who have been brought from death to life"* (Romans 6:13). When humanity got kicked out of the garden, they were doomed to a life of toil, futility, and eventual death. Surrender is more than giving God His rightful place in your life. Surrender to God is leaving our existence often dominated by the fear of death, and spiritually returning home to live with God as it was in the garden. Surrender is being brought from death to life. Surrender is fellowship with God. Surrender is accepting the life that God created us to live.

Free at last!

"Then you will know the truth, and the truth will set you free." Free from what? Free from the self that holds us captive to pride, sin, and the influences of the world. And free to be reconciled with God, to once again be a human image of God, and follow Him as He leads us up the path home. But, there's more.

During the journey that resulted in me writing this book, I found Jesus' Christianity, the Christianity that's been hidden beneath the graffiti and rubble of man. Now, in looking back on the journey of climbing this figurative mountain of truth, I've discovered that there's something else I found freedom from.

I found freedom from the pain of past wounds inflicted by manmade Christianity, and freedom from the sometimes-visible scars those wounds leave behind—like the bad feelings, confusion, self-pity, judgment, and anger. The freedom I found came from finally seeing, recognizing, and embracing the truth of four things: the truth of manmade Christianity, Jesus' Christianity, human nature, and myself. And I came to understand that manmade Christianity is unavoidable, for it's a natural outcome of human nature.

Finally, shortly before His death, Jesus prayed,

> "Father, I want those you have given me to be with me where I am, and to see my glory." (John 17:24, emphasis added)

Living *with* Jesus where He is, He in you and you in Him, free from self and this chaotic world. That's where you'll find peace and rest for your soul. As Jesus also said,

> "Come to me, all you who are weary and burdened, and I will give you rest. Take my yoke upon you and learn from me, for I am gentle and humble in heart, and you will find rest for your souls." (Matthew 11:28-29)

Please read that again, and replace "Come to me," with *Surrender to me*.

Before moving on, I want to recommend an Andrew Murray book that's been invaluable to me on my journey in search of truth, freedom, and surrender. It's appropriately titled *Absolute Surrender*, and if you're hungry for more, I also recommend both *Humility* and *Abide in Christ*, also by Andrew Murray, and maybe *Dying to Self: A Golden Dialogue*, by William Law. You'll find these and other reading recommendations listed at the end of this book.

29. Jesus' Christianity

What else is there for me to do? Having scraped off the graffiti that's been hiding it, I've uncovered the truth of Jesus' Christianity. I even found answers to my *free from what* question. But, from the new vantage point high up this figurative mountain we've been climbing, I look back on the path we've followed, and I see things from a perspective I haven't experienced before. I see things I haven't fully appreciated before. I'd like to show you what I see.

I see the truth of study and reasoning

Have you ever received a text or email that gave you the impression the writer was angry at you, or maybe disappointed? Then later, you discovered that wasn't at all how they felt?

The written word is the lowest, least effective, and most easily misinterpreted form of everyday communication. Verbal is better, like with a phone call, where you can detect the tone of voice along with the words. Face-to-face is better still, as it adds facial expressions and body language. However, the best communication is that which speaks directly to your soul—that is, to your thoughts and emotions.

In our relationship with God and Jesus, we need more than the written word, and to Christians who put too much reliance on such words, here's a reminder of Jesus' warning:

> "You study the Scriptures diligently because you think that in them you have eternal life. These are the very Scriptures that testify about me, yet you refuse to come to me to have life." (John 5:39-40)

However, in looking again at the survey results at the end of chapter 3, almost a third of surveyed born-again Christians say that learning about the Bible is one of the most important priorities for being Christian. I don't disagree. But in considering what's missing from that list of priorities, it looks like many churches and their misinformed members, in their efforts to study the Bible, have refused to come to Jesus to have life.

Look, the Bible doesn't direct us to itself for truth and guidance, nor does it direct us to seminary graduates. The Bible points us to the Holy Spirit, and only the Holy Spirit, who then speaks directly to our souls. As Andrew Murray said,

> *"Scripture ever points us away from itself to the living Word, Christ Jesus, who waits to be formed within us, and to the blessed Spirit who is within us, and is alone able to make what we read or hear 'truth in the inward part.' The Holy Spirit—by whose inspiration the Word was written, and by whose inspiration alone the Word can become life within us, who, as the Spirit of truth, is himself the truth, the power, the life of all that is in the word—dwells within you."* [1]

I'm not saying to ignore the Bible. After all, the Holy Spirit inspired those words. Also, when Jesus walked the roads of ancient Israel, He, too, relied on scripture. However, He relied on His relationship with God more.

In the early days of Christianity, before the creation of the documents that now comprise the New Testament, many believers relied only on the Spirit of God to guide them. They had nothing else. Today, even though most Christians have a Bible, we should rely on our relationship with the Holy Spirit more.

Jesus said, *"I have much more to say to you, more than you can now bear. But when he, the Spirit of truth, comes, he will guide you into all truth"* (John 16:12-13). Like Jesus, the Bible tells us as much as we can handle on our own, as much as we can bear. The Bible then points us to the Holy Spirit, who in speaking directly to our souls—to our thoughts and emotions—will guide us the rest of the way on our journey, to all truth.

Besides, to believe you can truly *know* Jesus by studying books or listening to sermons is probably as fruitful as believing you can nourish yourself by thinking about food. And trusting in reason, intellect, and knowledge is what leads people to rely on doctrine and themselves, rather than the Spirit of God. Study and reasoning won't fill an aspiring Christian with a sense of Jesus' presence in their life. Only the Holy Spirit can do that.

So, while reading the Bible, instead of relying on a study guide, a seminary-taught Bible scholar, or your own intellect, just relax, read, and trust the Holy Spirit to guide you into all truth.

I see the truth about preaching

People usually look to human knowledge for spiritual truth. Andrew Murray warned, *"These thoughts suggest to us the great danger of the Christian life—seeking to know the truth of God in His Word without the distinct waiting on the Spirit of Truth in the heart."* [2] Back in the chapter about prayer, I quoted something else Murray said: *"Jesus never taught His disciples how to preach, only how to pray."* While putting these two comments together, a fresh thought came to me.

Just before Jesus returned to heaven, He instructed His disciples to stay in Jerusalem and *wait* for the arrival of the Holy Spirit (Acts 1:4). He then said, *"You will receive power when the Holy Spirit has come upon you; and you will be my witnesses* (i.e., preachers) *in Jerusalem, in all Judea and Samaria, and to the ends of the earth"* (Acts 1:8 NRSV).

After spending several weeks with the resurrected Jesus, those disciples must have been excited and restless to start preaching. But no, they first had to *wait* for the Holy Spirit. The disciples had to wait because without the presence of the Holy Spirit, their preaching would have been powerless and lifeless, like a spiritless corpse. This could be why many churches today are dying, because absent the life of the Holy Spirit, the preaching itself is lifeless.

It's not ardent study where people learn to effectively preach; it's not eating from that same tree of knowledge that got humanity kicked out of the garden. The power to preach and be witnesses for Jesus comes from the Holy Spirit, whose presence is felt only in prayer. That's why Jesus never taught His disciples how to preach, only how to pray, and *wait* for the power of the Holy Spirit to come upon them.

I see that there's always a chance

In chapter 25, I cited these words from Jesus: *"Whoever speaks a word against the Son of Man* [Jesus] *will be forgiven"* (Matthew 12:32 NRSV). What I left out was the latter half of that verse, which is, *"... but whoever speaks against the Holy Spirit will not be forgiven, either in this age or in the age to come."* Yet, what does it mean to speak against the Holy Spirit? What is the unforgivable sin, as many people call it?

In the beginning, the curse of pride inflicted by Satan upon Adam and Eve plunged humanity into a pit of self and sin. Eventually, Jesus sent the Holy Spirit to reach down, take our hand, and lift us back up. Our only way out of this pit is with the help of the Holy Spirit. Rejecting the Spirit is like slapping His hand away.

Though Jesus has paid the penalty for our sins, rejecting the Holy Spirit is refusing the last help and only hope that God offers for our freedom from the daily grip of self, sin, and the ways of the world. Though Jesus' death on the cross opened the way for our reconciliation with God and fellowship with Him, rejecting the Holy Spirit is rejecting that fellowship. Rejecting the Spirit is refusing God's presence within us, a presence which by definition is salvation. The entity we should be rejecting is self, not the Holy Spirit.

Where Jesus' death on the cross opened the gate for our return to heaven, it's the Holy Spirit who takes us by the hand and leads us there. The unforgivable sin is rejecting the Spirit's hand, and maybe even thinking we can find our own way to heaven. The truly unforgiven are those who, steadfast to the end, refuse to accept the help of the Holy Spirit. In the simplest terms, the unforgiveable sin is refusing the complete fulfillment of God's forgiveness.

But Jesus promises that we can be born again, into a new creation, a new Self with a new chance, who denies our old self and instead of relying on self, relies on the Holy Spirit. So, I believe that until the moment we die, we always have a chance to deny our self, tell Jesus how sorry we are for our past attitude, and welcome the Holy Spirit into our lives, taking His outstretched hand and following Him … all the way to heaven.

I see anew the fear of the Lord

I talked earlier about what the Bible says about fearing God, and that I see it as a fear motivated by love, such that the word *fear* could be replaced with *love* in many verses. For example, "The *love* of the Lord is the beginning of wisdom," and "The Lord has compassion on those who *love* Him." I now see another side to this fear talk. I now see that from self's perspective, there is indeed fear, fear of losing power and control.

So, if you feel hesitant and even fearful about the talk of surrender and denying yourself, maybe that's because your *self* sees that you've been enlightened and alerted to its presence and control. By this, your self feels threatened. And that's a good thing, an indication that maybe you're stepping off on a new journey, to a new life, free from the control of self.

I see new power in prayer

Beneath the graffiti I see a relationship between prayer and self-denial, and a power that comes from merging the two. For there to be power in prayer, there must be self-denial. With self-denial, with Jesus becoming greater within me and my self becoming less, where I'm thus more Jesus than self, my prayers rise to God as if coming directly from Jesus. That's what praying in Jesus' name is all about.

With self-denial, I can fulfill the love Jesus spoke of when He said, *"No one has greater love than this, to lay down one's life for one's friends"* (John 15:13 NRSV). We know how Jesus showed such love in the sacrifice of His life for all of us. I can show my love for my friends by denying my self and my name (laying down my life), and in doing so, truly take Jesus' name. Then, as He said, *"And I will do whatever you ask in my name"* (John 14:13 NRSV).

Here's how Andrew Murray explained much of what I'm trying to say:

> "He who takes the name of another gives up his own as of no value. When I go in the name of another, I deny myself, I take not only his name but himself and what he is, instead of myself and what I am. ... When the Lord Jesus went to heaven, He left His work, the management of His kingdom on earth, in the hands of His servants. He could not do otherwise than also give them His Name to draw all the supplies they needed for the due conduct of His business. And they have the spiritual power to avail themselves of the Name of Jesus just to the extent to which they yield themselves to live only for the interests and the work of the Master. The use of the Name always supposes the surrender of our interests to Him who we represent." [4]

In speaking of Jesus, Murray also said,

> *"In His ascension, He received the Spirit of the Father, through whom He might do what He could not do while on earth. Then He was able to make Himself one with those He loved, and actually live their life for them, so that they could live before the Father in a humility like His, because it was He Himself who lived and breathed in them."* [5]

Jesus living and breathing within you—that's what happens when you die to self and take His name. That's what Paul referred to when he said, *"If anyone is in Christ, this person is a new creation."* And with Jesus' presence and His name, imagine what your prayers can do for your friends. No one has greater love than that.

I see God's image

"God created mankind in his own image." (Genesis 1:27)

At first, Adam and Eve were little human images of God. I suspect that other than physically, they may have been a lot like Jesus. Initially, they knew nothing of hate, anger, fear, greed, selfishness, and all the other afflictions we suffer from. Then pride and self slithered onto the scene and disfigured the image of God in humanity.

However, God wants to help us get His image back. Paul talked about this a lot:

> "You have taken off your old self with its practices and have put on the new self, which is being <u>renewed</u> in knowledge <u>in the image of its Creator</u>." (Colossians 3:9-10, emphasis added)
>
> "And all of us, with unveiled faces, seeing the glory of the Lord as though reflected in a mirror, <u>are being transformed into the same image</u> from one degree of glory to another; for this comes from the Lord, the Spirit." (2 Corinthians 3:18 NRSV, emphasis added)

> *"You were taught, with regard to your former way of life, to put off your old self, which is being corrupted by its deceitful desires; to be made new in the attitude of your minds; and to put on the new self, created to be like God in true righteousness and holiness."* (Ephesians 4:22-24, emphasis added)

Andrew Murray continues this thought:

> *"Let us keep our hearts set on the glory of the image of God in Christ, in the assurance that the Spirit will change us into that image day by day. ... God Almighty, who created mankind in His image, seeks now to work out His purpose in changing you into the image of Christ Jesus by the power of the Holy Spirit."* [6]

This is why Jesus calls us to deny ourselves and follow Him. The replacement of self with the presence of the Holy Spirit will restore the image of Christ within you. This is what Paul referred to when he said, *"It is no longer I* [self] *who live, but it is Christ who lives in me"* (Galatians 2:20).

That's what it means to be born again. I don't know the worldly church definition of that label, yet because of how it's used, I suspect it's not what Jesus meant when He said, *"Very truly I tell you, no one can see the kingdom of God unless they are born again. ... No one can enter the kingdom of God unless they are born of water and the Spirit"* (John 3:3, 5, emphasis added).

Finally, Peter said, *"By his* [God's] *great mercy he has given us a new birth into a living hope through the resurrection of Jesus Christ from the dead"* (1 Peter 1:3 NRSV, emphasis added). Jesus' resurrection was a new birth into a new life. Jesus calls us to follow Him and do as He did, by dying to self and sin, and being reborn into a new life, a Spirit-filled life, in His image.

I see God's Kingdom

Imagine what it would be like if Jesus walked the earth again, though not in His original body, and not necessarily male. Maybe picture someone you know, with Jesus sharing their body with them, where Jesus has influence over what they say and do. Imagine this Jesus person hanging out with you, your family, and friends. How do you think Jesus would interact with everyone, and how might Jesus' presence affect all of you? Please think about this for a moment, creating a scene in your mind.

Since God has no limits, now imagine Jesus walking the earth within millions of people! How would that affect the life we all experience? Imagine that everywhere you go, every situation you find yourself in, there's Jesus, always ready with the right thing to say or do to foster truth, peace, calm, and love.

What I've asked you to imagine is a fulfillment of what Jesus told us to pray for: *"This, then, is how you should pray: 'Our Father in heaven, hallowed be your name, your kingdom come, your will be done, on earth as it is in heaven"* (Matthew 6:9-10). What I asked you to imagine is the Kingdom of God on earth as it is in heaven.

In chapter 15, in my description of Jesus' One True Church, I used His illustration of the vine and the branches, where Jesus is the vine, Spirit-filled believers are the branches attached to the vine, and the entire plant is the Church. God's Kingdom on earth is this Church, consisting of every person who has the Holy Spirit living within them. That's why Jesus said that no one can see the Kingdom of God unless they are born again. Maybe it's also why He said, *"For, in fact, the kingdom of God is among you"* (Luke 17:21 NRSV).

Finally, while praying Jesus said,

> "Holy Father, protect them by the power of your name, the name you gave me, so that they may be one as we are one. ... I have given them the glory that you gave me, that they may be one as we are one—I in them and you in me. ... I have made you known to them, and will continue to make you known in order that the love you have for me may be in them and that I myself may be in them." (John 17:11, 22-23, 26)

What Jesus was praying for is God's Kingdom on earth, as it is in heaven.

I see afresh God's purpose

God didn't create humanity to live independent from Himself. God created His human children to live *with* Him. I now see that God's overarching purpose for fallen humanity is to restore His image within us and bring us back to how it was in the beginning, living with Him in paradise. As William Law said,

> *"For the restoration of fallen man is nothing else but the restoration of him to his first state, under the will and Spirit of God, in and for which he was created."* [7]

Reconciliation and a restored relationship with God are what Christianity is all about. It's why Jesus came to earth, died for us, and then sent the Holy Spirit to live within us.

Yet, in looking back to those well-worn survey results at the end of chapter 3, such a relationship with God is *not* on the list of priorities for being Christian. And like all my other observations about those survey results, the problem isn't with the survey respondents. The problem is with the manmade churches that have misguided those people. The problem is with manmade Christianity.

I found Jesus' Christianity

"What is Christianity, but that which Christ was while on earth." [8]

I hesitate to call Christianity a religion, because *religion* is a manmade word with a variety of manmade definitions. Instead of a religion, I think of Christianity as a way of life, living as Jesus lived while on earth, as a child of God, and an image of God.

So, what's it mean to be a Christian? Jesus might answer that question this way: *"Whoever wants to be my disciple* [aka, a Christian]*, must deny themselves and take up their cross daily and follow me.*[9] *As I have loved you, so you must love one another. By this everyone will know that you are my disciples, if you love one another."*[10] And as Paul said, *"If anyone does not have the Spirit of Christ, they do not belong to Christ."*[11] A life lived as Jesus lived, filled with humility, love, and the Holy Spirit—that's what it means to be Christian.

While climbing my figurative mountain of truth, I finally found Jesus' Christianity, the Christianity I've been searching for. Also, I found freedom from self. And I found Jesus—He in me and me in Him, just as He promised. I hope you've found Him too. You'd think I'd be feeling great right now, but that nagging problem is still troubling me. Yes, the problem of manmade Christianity. Regarding that …

30. Jesus Wants His Christianity Back

As I start on the first draft of this final chapter, there's a rising push by certain politicians to abolish the separation of church and state. Also, CINO extremists are pushing for something called Christian Nationalism, where the church would nearly, or completely, control the state. However, if the wall between church and state comes down any further, that may be the death of Christianity in the US. The question is, will it be the death of manmade Christianity, Jesus' Christianity, or both?

I hadn't planned on this chapter, but this church-and-state conflict convinced me there's more to say. I just needed to define a purpose and outline. So, I closed my eyes and asked Jesus what *He* wants to do with this chapter. What's *His* purpose? Soon a fresh thought drifted into my mind, then another, and another. The ideas kept coming, and like pieces of a picture puzzle, they fell into place until I saw a whole new chapter. Things work out that way sometimes. But be warned—the path ahead may get rough.

I'll begin by repeating something Andrew Murray said, in reference to the experiences of many churchgoing Christians:

> *"They do not see that the spirit of the world permeates the church and takes possession of it to a far greater extent."* [1]

Driven by self and the influences of the world, humanity has often stained Christianity with pride, sin, and the ways of the world. What's left is manmade, feeble, and usually powerless, sometimes causing more harm than good. That's what happens when the world, rather than the life of Christ, rules too much in the lives of Christians.

If the Christian Nationalists have their way, it will only get worse. These extremists want to make the state more Christian, or rather, their view of what it means to be Christian. However, their efforts will also make their version of Christianity more worldly. As manmade Christianity in the US gets more involved in politics, it will become more corrupted by politics. And talk about painting a target on Christianity. If those CINO's thought there was a war against Christianity before, they ain't seen nothin yet.

Here's another warning for such worldly Christians:

> *"Religion that is pure and undefiled before God, the Father, is this: to care for orphans and widows in their distress, and to keep oneself unstained by the world." (James 1:27 NRSV, emphasis added)*

This is only one of several warnings in the Bible cautioning Christians to avoid worldliness and maintain a separation between Church and the ways of the world.

The writer of Hebrews said,

> *"Let's run with endurance the race that is set before us, looking only at Jesus, the originator and perfecter of the faith." (Hebrews 12:1-2 NASB)*

Over the centuries men have tried to improve what Jesus already perfected, as they promoted their worldly versions of the faith. Because of them and people like the Christian Nationalists—who look more to the state and their worldly politicians than to Jesus—it's safe to conclude that Jesus wants His Christianity back, the Christianity He originated and perfected. But roadblocks stand in the way.

The politicization of Christianity

A few years ago, I saw a documentary on the nature of conservative politics in the US over the past 60 years or so. I think it was in the 1960's when conservative Christians began getting more involved in politics. Did this coincide with the beginning of the decline of Christianity in the US? I mean, it looks like some Christians moved their church from the firm foundation of Jesus to the shifting sand foundation of politics. It appears these Christians put more trust in proud politicians, than in God. To this, God might say:

> *"Blessed is the one who trusts in the Lord, who does not look to the proud." (Psalm 40:4)*

Many Christians, especially evangelicals, loyally and very publicly support the Republican Party. How does this look from the perspective of someone who's not a Republican, nor conservative? Might this paint Christianity as the Republican religion; non-conservatives need not apply?

I read an article a while back about how white evangelicals demonized a past US president, apparently because he's not Republican, and possibly because he's not white.[2] Many of these same evangelicals appear to adore the next president in line, their white male Republican, very *un-Christian,* twice-impeached and felony-convicted president. What do non-Christians think about that?

Regarding Christians who put too much trust in proud politicians, Jesus' brother James might say, *"God opposes the proud but shows favor to the humble"* (James 4:6). And the writer of Proverbs said, *"The Lord detests all the proud of heart. Be sure of this: They will not go unpunished"* (Proverbs 16:5). As these verses make clear, God doesn't want me to vote for someone who tops the arrogance chart, regardless of their political party. Yes, to God, character matters.

Now back to that question—what do non-Christians think when they see Christians supporting a man who's so overtly arrogant, conceited, self-centered, and un-Christian? Everyone I know who doesn't support him, whether Christian or non-Christian, is baffled by the widespread Christian support of such a man. In their eyes, these so-called Christians look at best hypocritical, at worst brainwashed (an actual term a friend of mine recently used). Hypocritical and brainwashed—that image certainly won't help make more disciples.

In chapter 18, I presented the idea that the real threat to Christianity is coming from people who call themselves Christian, rather than those on the outside of Christianity. As an example of an internal attack and the harm it inflicts upon Christianity, consider published reports describing the love and devotion many evangelical churches have for their infamous, extremely arrogant, multi-indicted and convicted, very un-Christian, 2024 Republican presidential candidate whose name I've been trying to avoid mentioning. I wish these people could be as devoted to God.

Another related attack was broadcast around the world during the storming of the US Capitol on January 6, 2021. There were highly visible so-called Christians waving Jesus flags, shouting His name, and even kneeling in prayer, (though I can't be sure to *whom* they were praying). By invoking Jesus' name, were they using Him as an excuse for breaking the law and spreading violence?

To the worldly big-name leaders of the manmade Christian establishment, the small-name CINO rioters attacking the Capitol, and to all CINO's in between, Jesus might say,

> "You do not have in mind the concerns of God, but merely human concerns." (Mark 8:33)

Jesus also said, *"In fact, the reason I was born and came into the world is to testify to the truth. Everyone on the side of truth listens to me"* (John 18:37). By putting too much reliance on lying politicians, or failing to take the truths in the Bible literally, it appears that many worldly Christians aren't listening to Jesus. Truth doesn't seem to matter to them. We know it doesn't matter to the politicians some of them adamantly support.

The un-Christian anti-abortion movement

I hadn't planned on this topic, but then the US Supreme Court ended Roe v. Wade and the legally protected right for an abortion. With pro-lifers celebrating, I found myself thinking of aspiring Christians who don't look very Christian when they appear to show no understanding, love, forgiveness, or compassion for the other victim in abortions, the mother. They also seem to ignore the father. Why do you think that is?

Something else bothers me. As Christians push to end abortion, many of them do nothing to deal with the causes of unplanned pregnancies that end in abortion. Outlawing abortion while ignoring the causes of such pregnancies won't make abortion go away. Believing it will is like believing that outlawing heart attacks without addressing the behavior that leads to hearts attacks will greatly reduce the occurrence of heart attacks.

In considering possible causes of unplanned pregnancies, most of them are avoidable and have the same deeper root cause, which has to do with the morality of either the woman, the man who gets her pregnant, or both. However, it seems that many Christians care more about outlawing abortion than promoting moral behavior. As much as I'd love to see an end to all abortions, I have a real problem with how some Christian pro-lifers ignore the underlying moral issues. They seem to be trying to legislate morality via civil laws, which is not what Jesus would do.

Jesus promoted such things as character, morality, self-control, humility, obedience, compassion, and love. Christians should do the same.

However, with many so-called Christians, the picture they paint with their words, actions, and the way they vote, shows that character, morality, and humility does *not* matter. What appears to matter to them is forcing their will upon others. That definitely doesn't help make disciples of all nations.

Taking away free will

Things like love and obedience cannot be forced. In all the ways God and Jesus encouraged us to live, they always left the choice with us. And without free will, without freedom of choice, there can be no real love. That's why God gives us free will. But certain Christians want to take it away.

Regarding the Christian Nationalism movement, in their efforts to force their will upon the rest of society, the CINO's behind this movement are, in effect, trying to take away the free will of others. But God gives us the free will to make our own decisions. He doesn't force His will upon us. The Christian Nationalism CINO's should consider doing the same.

The wall is crumbling

Along with the push for Christian Nationalism, is the Supreme Court ruling on abortion a violation of the doctrine of the separation between church and state?

Pulling down the wall between church and state will further drag manmade Christianity into the politics of the state, making it more worldly than it currently is. Consequently, Christians will end up relying even more on the state and less on God. Yet Jesus calls us to be separated from the ways of the world, to separate church from the state. As He said,

> "If you belonged to the world, it would love you as its own. As it is, you do not belong to the world, but I have chosen you out of the world." (John 15:19)

As reflected in their beliefs and behavior, Christian Nationalists appear to belong to the world. It looks like they've turned their back on Jesus and chosen to stay in the world.

What outsiders see

If I weren't a Christian, just an outsider looking in, what might I conclude are the priorities for being Christian? Though the following list doesn't represent what all outsiders see, it does show what some followers of manmade Christianity display:

- First, from the survey results I cited in chapter 3 showing outsiders perceptions of Christians, the priorities I'd see include: being hypocritical, judgmental, anti-homosexual, unloving, and projecting a negative image of Jesus Christ.
- Be unforgiving.
- Be prideful, conceited, even arrogant.
- Be bigoted towards those who are different.
- Be worldly, and often hard to distinguish from anyone else, except maybe on Sunday.
- Be politically vocal. And you get extra points for voting Republican regardless of the candidates' character.
- Demolishing the separation of church and state and trying to force so-called Christian values upon everyone else. In doing so, try to take away people's God-given freewill.
- In certain extreme-right evangelical communities, being a homophobic white supremacist earns more extra points.

Of course, we don't see these traits in all Christians, though we sure see them in some of the more boisterous and visible ones. Also, because of the images that many so-called Christians display, when we look at this thing called Christianity, what we often see is *not* Christianity. And that's why Jesus wants His Christianity back.

But a word of caution for those whose behavior contributes to the image above. Read what Jesus said about separating the sheep and the goats (Matthew 25:31-46). Jesus looks upon their lack of love for others as a lack of love for Himself.

Manmade Christianity is dying

Looking at manmade Christianity, what else do I see? Well, I see divided and fragmented denominations. I see weakness and failure, and aspiring Christians abandoning a failing religion. I see the rise of Christian Nationalism in the US, and I see so-called Christians exalting proud politicians rather than God. What I see are the dying gasps of a struggling manmade religion.

According to recent survey results, church attendance in the US continues to rapidly decline, as is the number of people who call themselves Christian. What's increasing is the number of churches that are permanently closing. But why? If you do some research, you'll find excuses such as, US society is growing away from religion because the society is becoming more secular. Well, duh. Yet again, why? Though blaming society is a convenient excuse, the source of the decline isn't with the people. It's with the manmade and worldly versions of Christianity.

Other than its worldly nature and the perceptions listed above, why else is manmade Christianity dying? First, the reason Jesus called the Holy Spirit the *Spirit of truth* is that He was directing us to look *only* to the Spirit for spiritual truth. Makes sense. However, manmade Christianity seems to look everywhere *but* the Holy Spirit.

Also, in chapter 11, I cited some Barna Group survey data stating that almost 60% of Christians see the Holy Spirit as "a symbol of God's power or presence but is not a living entity." For most Christians, the Holy Spirit is dead and not a part of their church experience.

When a person's spirit leaves their body, that person is dead. So it is with manmade Christianity. Where God's Spirit is missing and no longer present, that Christianity is dead. What's left, what people often experience, is no more than a rotting corpse. William Law put it this way:

> "For the truth of Christianity is the Spirit of God living and working in it; and where this Spirit is not the life of it, there the outward form is but like the outward carcass of a departed soul." [3]

I've cited other Barna Group survey results showing that 80 percent of adults outside the church see churches as unloving, with 59 percent of churchgoers agreeing. With the Spirit of God missing, His love is also missing. Now picture church and Christianity as a brick building. Since faith is the foundation of Christianity with love as the mortar that holds it all together, it's no wonder the manmade church is crumbling. The mortar is missing.

However, maybe the death of manmade Christianity will open the way for Jesus' Christianity to make a comeback. I mean, most people who stop attending church started out looking for something, something they apparently couldn't find in manmade Christianity, and so they quit. Yet Jesus' Christianity will give them what they were looking for.

God's missing, final thoughts

I've frequently grumbled about the survey results showing the number of de-churched Christians who never found a connection with God while attending church. One reason so many people felt God was missing is that their church wasn't showing them where to look.

As I mentioned in the previous chapter, Jesus told His disciples as much as they could bear. He then pointed them to the Holy Spirit, who would take over their education and bring life to their renewed relationship with God. Churches should do as Jesus did.

Most churches tell people up to the limit of what they can bear—that is, Christianity 1A—though the Holy Spirit is usually missing from the lesson plan. These churches don't often show the people the next path to follow on their spiritual journey, the path that leads to finding and feeling the presence of the Holy Spirit in their lives. These churches should have prioritized prayer as the place to find the Holy Spirit. Yet if you recall, prayer isn't on the survey list of priorities for being Christian, and neither is the Holy Spirit.

John the Baptist directed his disciples to follow Jesus. Jesus then told His followers as much as they could understand and directed them to the Holy Spirit. Like Jesus, the Bible also points us to the Spirit. Therefore, like John, Jesus, and the Bible, all preaching should send us away from itself and to the Holy Spirit. If a church doesn't do that, then God is indeed missing. And where God is missing, it's not Christianity.

The struggle for Jesus' Christianity

Manmade Christianity has been waging an undeclared war against Jesus' Christianity for almost two thousand years. Not many people accept the existence of this war, but it still goes on, acknowledged or not. These days, the manmade side is apparently winning, taking captives and inflicting widespread collateral damage. For those who choose to be on Jesus' side of this war, here's a reminder of Paul's warnings:

> *"I urge you, brothers and sisters, to watch out for those who cause divisions and put obstacles in your way that are contrary to the teaching you have learned. Keep away from*

them. For such people are not serving our Lord Christ, but their own appetites" (Romans 16:17-18 NIV).

"See to it that no one takes you captive through hollow and deceptive philosophy, which depends on human tradition and the elemental spiritual forces of this world rather than on Christ" (Colossians 2:8).

When Jesus was fighting here in the trenches, His priorities—His weapons, if you will—were such things as love, faith, humility, and truth. These priorities helped Jesus win battles. If we're to help Jesus win the war, what would He say should be our priorities?

For one last time, consider the survey results at the end of chapter 3, and the list of priorities born-again Christians gave for being Christian. Along the path we've taken on this journey, you've noticed me pointing out where Jesus gives us a clear priority for Christian living, yet that same priority is not included on the list of survey responses. Here is a summary of Jesus' priorities that are missing from the born-again Christian priorities:

- *Love God with all your heart, soul, and mind. Love your neighbor as yourself, loving even your enemies.*
- *Pray*
- *Be one with the Holy Spirit, as Jesus is one with our Father.*
- *Deny yourself and follow Jesus.*
- *Put all your faith and trust in God.*
- *Be humble*
- *Forgive others as God forgives you.*
- *Be in the world, not off the world.*
- *Hold to the truth, the truth that will set you free.*
- *Whatever you do, do it all for the glory of God.*

Yes, Jesus told us that these are the priorities that define what it means to be Christian. Yet these Christian virtues seem to be missing from manmade Christianity, at least from the perspective of the survey respondents. What's also apparently missing is God, Jesus, and the Holy Spirit. And they still call it Christianity!

A worldly manmade Christianity with manmade priorities is the reason for the growth of the de-churched population, and the death of once-thriving churches. Manmade Christianity is failing God's children and leaving people as wounded and hurting victims of a flawed system.

However, regarding Jesus' priorities listed above, imagine outsider's reactions if these virtues were what they saw when they looked at Christianity. Imagine outsiders looking at Christians and seeing little human images of Jesus. Imagine a Christianity that looks like a refuge and paradise in the midst of this world-in-crisis. Might such an image help Jesus win His Christianity back?

Uncovered truth ... now what?

The Christianity that's often most visible is a religion where Jesus' priorities are blatantly missing; where the majority of followers don't take the words in the Bible literally, the Bible that defines Christianity; where there's more division than unity; where God is missing and the Holy Spirit is dead. This all guarantees that the Christianity we experience in this world is often more manmade than God-made.

Within the pages of this book, I've shown you the path I followed on my search for Christianity—to the peak of the spiritual mountain we've been climbing. But I'm only able to guide you so far. You're not yet at the summit, though it's within reach. The final leg of the climb will begin with your baptism by the Holy Spirit, who will then take you by the hand and lead you the rest of the way, to the top.

Here's a question I've scattered throughout this book that was first asked by God through Jeremiah: *"The prophets prophesy lies, the priests rule by their own authority, and my people love it this way. But what will you do in the end?"* (Jeremiah 5:31). So I ask you the question I've been asking myself: You've come a long way on this journey, where you've seen Jesus, His truth, and His Christianity. Now, what will you do?

In the struggle for Christianity, there's a decision facing all Christians, and outsiders who may be considering Christianity. Whose side will they be on, that of a manmade religion, or Jesus' truth? James said that faith without action is dead.

The same goes for truth without action. Will you act on the truth, or let it die in your hands as you close this book for the last time?

God, by what He said through Jeremiah, is calling us to His side of this war. Maybe your battleground is limited to yourself and your own personal struggles. Or maybe God is calling you to go farther afield. Yet in thinking about what you'll do next, please be careful. Don't let self or the world influence you. With lots of prayer and humility, take your guidance only from the Holy Spirit. And remember something Andrew Murray said,

> "Only when we are filled with the Spirit can we fully experience the spiritual power and truth of the Word." [4]

By the way, Jesus said, *"The reason I was born and came into the world is to testify to the truth. Everyone on the side of truth listens to me"* (John 18:37). If a manmade church or worldly Christian tries to coax you to their side, maybe say to them what Peter said to the religious leaders of his day: *"Which is right in God's eyes: to listen to you, or to him? You be the judges!"* (Acts 4:19). Everyone on the side of truth listens to God.

Now then, before I hand this off to someone else, I hope that, *"My message and my preaching were not with wise and persuasive words, but with a demonstration of the Spirit's power, so that your faith might not rest on men's* [my] *wisdom, but on God's power"* (1 Corinthians 2:4-5). *"...because of the truth, which lives in us and will be with us forever"* (2 John 2).

Also, I offer this prayer for you: *"I pray that out of his* [God's] *glorious riches he may strengthen you with power through his Spirit in your inner being, so that Christ may dwell in your hearts through faith. And I pray that you, being rooted and established in love, may have power, together with all the Lord's holy people, to grasp how wide and long and high and deep is the love of Christ, and to know this love that surpasses knowledge—that you may be filled to the measure of all the fullness of God. Now to him who is able to do immeasurably more than all we ask or imagine, according to his power that is at work within us, to him be glory in the church and in Christ Jesus throughout all generations, for ever and ever! Amen."* (Ephesians 3:16-21)

Finally, if Jesus were to write you a letter, what might He say? Please read the letter that follows as if written especially for you. Try picturing Jesus reading it to you.

****

My dear friend,

Do not be misled by varied and strange teachings.[5] Do not let your heart be troubled; believe in God, believe also in Me.[6] Come to me, all you who are weary and burdened, and I will give you rest.[7]

As the Father has loved me, so have I loved you. Now remain in my love.[8] Love the Lord your God with all your heart and with all your soul and with all your mind.[9] As I have loved you, so you must love one another. By this everyone will know that you are my disciples, if you love one another.[10]

If you ask the Father for anything in My name, He will give it to you.[11] If you remain in me and I in you, you will bear much fruit; apart from me you can do nothing.[12] This is to my Father's glory, that you bear much fruit, showing yourselves to be my disciples.[13] And whoever wants to be my disciple must deny themselves and take up their cross daily and follow me.[14]

And I will put my Spirit in you and move you to follow my decrees and be careful to keep my laws.[15] The Spirit gives life; the flesh counts for nothing.[16] I have much more to say to you, more than you can now bear. But when he, the Spirit of truth, comes, he will guide you into all truth.[17] Then you will know the truth, and the truth will set you free.[18] On that day you will know that I am in My Father, and you are in Me, and I in you.[19] Therefore what God has joined together, let no one separate.[20]

I have told you these things, so that in me you may have peace. In this world you will have trouble. But take heart! I have overcome the world.[21] Peace I leave with you; my peace I give you. I do not give to you as the world gives. Do not let your hearts be troubled and do not be afraid.[22]

I have put before you an open door which no one can shut.[23] Come, follow me.[24]

With all my love for you,
Your friend, Jesus

Notes

Chapter 2

1. C.S. Lewis, *Mere Christianity*, original copyright 1943, renewed 1980 by Arthur Owen Barfield, page 171.
2. Brother Lawrence, *The Practice of the Presence of God*, (New Kensington, PA: Whitaker House), © 1982, page 37.
3. Ibid, page 85.
4. Andrew Murray, *Absolute Surrender*, Bethany House Publishers, © 2003, page 110.
5. Andrew Murray, *The Practice of God's Presence*, collection of Andrew Murray books, quoted from book 3, *Absolute Surrender*, (New Kensington, PA: Whitaker House), © 1999, page 234.
6. Ibid, page 237.
7. Andrew Murray, *Absolute Surrender*, Bethany House Publishers, © 2003, page 52.
8. Charles Spurgeon, *Being God's Friend*, (New Kensington, PA: Whitaker House), © 1997, pg. 108.
9. A.W. Tozer, *Reclaiming Christianity*, Published by Regal, © 2009 by James L. Snyder.
10. A.W. Tozer, *Mystery of the Holy Spirit*, Bridge-Logos, © 2007. Used by permission. All rights reserved. Page 129.
11. Ibid, page viii.
12. A.W. Tozer, *The Pursuit of God*, Christian Publications, Inc., © 1982 Baker Books, all rights reserved. Page 17-18.
13. Ibid, page 38.
14. William Law, *The Power of the Spirit, Extracts From the Writings of W. Law, Selected by A. Murray*, published 1896, reprinted by Scholar Select, reproduction of original work, public domain, pages 7 and 9, slightly modified for readability.
15. William Law, *The Power of the Spirit*, edited edition copyright 1971 by Dave Hunt and published by CLC Publications, Fort Washington, PA. Used by permission. May not be further reproduced. All rights reserved. Page 18.
16. Ibid, page 43.
17. William Law, *The Power of the Spirit, Extracts From the Writings of W. Law, Selected by A. Murray*, page 120.
18. William Law, *The Power of the Spirit*, edited edition, page 83.
19. Ibid, page 86.

20. Ibid, page 87.
21. George Barna and David Kinnaman (Barna Group), *Churchless; Understanding Today's Unchurched and How to Connect with Them*, Tyndale House, © 2014. Used by permission. All rights reserved.
About the Barna Group, from its website (https://www.barna.com): "In its nearly 40-year history, Barna Group has conducted more than two million interviews over the course of thousands of studies, and has become a go-to source for insights about faith and culture, leadership and vocation, and generations. Barna Group has carefully and strategically tracked the role of faith in America, developing one of the nation's most comprehensive databases of spiritual indicators."
22. David Kinnaman and Gabe Lyons, *unChristian; What a New Generation Really Thinks About Christianity*, BakerBooks, © 2007. Used by permission. All rights reserved.
23. From an article by the Schaeffer Institute, written by Richard J. Krejcir, "Statistics and Reasons for Church Decline." © 2007. http://www.churchleadership.org/apps/articles/default.asp?articleid=42346&columnid=4545
24. David Kinnaman and Aly Hawkins, *You Lost Me; Why Young Christians Are Leaving Church ... and Rethinking Faith*, Baker Books, © 2011. Used by permission. All rights reserved.

Chapter 3

1. David Kinnaman and Gabe Lyons, *unChristian; What a New Generation Really Thinks About Christianity*, BakerBooks, © 2007. Used by permission. All rights reserved.
2. George Barna and David Kinnaman (Barna Group), *Churchless; Understanding Today's Unchurched and How to Connect with Them*, Tyndale House, © 2014. Used by permission. All rights reserved.

Chapter 4

1. "U.S. Religious Landscape Survey Religious Beliefs and Practices: Diverse and Politically Relevant," PEW Research Center, Washington D.C., June 2008, https://www.pewforum.org/2008/06/01/u-s-religious-landscape-survey-religious-beliefs-and-practices/
2. "U.S. Public Becoming Less Religious," PEW Research Center, Washington, D.C., November 3, 2015, page 58
3. Ibid, page 179.

4. Brother Lawrence, *The Practice of the Presence of God*, (New Kensington, PA: Whitaker House), © 1982, page 87.

Chapter 5

1. "U.S. Religious Landscape Survey Religious Beliefs and Practices: Diverse and Politically Relevant," PEW Research Center, Washington D.C., June 2008, https://www.pewforum.org/2008/06/01/u-s-religious-landscape-survey-religious-beliefs-and-practices/

Chapter 6

1. Andrew Murray, *Andrew Murray Devotional*, (New Kensington, PA: Whitaker House), © 2006, devotional for February 4.

Chapter 10

1. Andrew Murray, *Andrew Murray Devotional*, (New Kensington, PA: Whitaker House), © 2006, devotional for December 24.
2. Ibid, devotional for May 1.
3. Andrew Murray, *The Practice of God's Presence*, collection of Andrew Murray books, quoted from book 3, *Absolute Surrender*, (New Kensington, PA: Whitaker House), © 1999, page 210.
4. Andrew Murray, *The Practice of God's Presence*, collection of Andrew Murray books, quoted from book 5, *Experiencing the Holy Spirit*, (New Kensington, PA: Whitaker House), © 1999, page 379.

Chapter 11

1. From an article by the Barna Group, "What Millennials Want When They Visit Church," 3/3/15, https://www.barna.org/barna-update/millennials/711-what-millennials-want-when-they-visit-church#.VS5biZN51f0
2. "U.S. Religious Landscape Survey Religious Affiliation: Diverse and Dynamic," PEW Research Center, Washington, D.C., February 2008, pg 5, https://www.pewforum.org/2008/02/01/u-s-religious-landscape-survey-religious-affiliation/
3. Andrew Murray, *Absolute Surrender*, Bethany House, © 2003, page 94.
4. "Most American Christians Do Not Believe that Satan or the Holy Spirit Exist" April 10, 2009, https://www.barna.org/barna-update/faith-spirituality/260-most-american-christians-do-not-believe-that-satan-or-the-holy-spirit-exis#.VTvBjJMYMVQ

Chapter 12

1. "America's Changing Religious Landscape: Christians Decline Sharply as Share of Population; Unaffiliated and Other Faiths Continue to Grow," PEW Research Center, Washington, D.C., May 12, 2015, page 13, https://www.pewforum.org/2015/05/12/americas-changing-religious-landscape/
2. David Kinnaman and Aly Hawkins, *You Lost Me; Why Young Christians Are Leaving Church ... and Rethinking Faith*, Baker Books, © 2011. Used by permission. All rights reserved.
3. A.W. Tozer, *The Pursuit of God*, Christian Publications, Inc., © 1982 Baker Books, all rights reserved.
4. Rose French, "Churches Turning to ad campaigns," Associated Press, 6/1/2009.
5. Cultural Research Center of Arizona Christian University, "Shocking Results Concerning the Worldview of Christian Pastors," Dr. George Barna, May 2022: https://www.arizonachristian.edu/wp-content/uploads/2022/05/AWVI2022_Release05_Digital.pdf.
6. William Law, *The Power of the Spirit*, edited edition copyright 1971 by Dave Hunt and published by CLC Publications, Fort Washington, PA. Used by permission. May not be further reproduced. All rights reserved. Page 155.
7. Brother Lawrence, *The Practice of the Presence of God*, (New Kensington, PA: Whitaker House), © 1992, pg. 85.
8. Andrew Murray, *Andrew Murray Devotional*, (New Kensington, PA: Whitaker House), © 2006, devotional for May 9.
9. William Law, *The Power of the Spirit*, page 43.
10. William Law, *The Power of the Spirit, Extracts From the Writings of W. Law, Selected by A. Murray*, published 1896, reprinted by Scholar Select, reproduction of original work, public domain, page 120, slightly modified for readability.
11. Andrew Murray, *Absolute Surrender*, Bethany House, © 2003, page 22.
12. Ibid, page 23.
13. Andrew Murray, *The Secret of Spiritual Strength*, (New Kensington, PA: Whitaker House), © 1984, pg. 86.
14. "America's Changing Religious Landscape: Christians Decline Sharply as Share of Population; Unaffiliated and Other Faiths Continue to Grow," PEW Research Center, Washington, D.C., May 12, 2015, page 7, https://www.pewforum.org/2015/05/12/americas-changing-religious-landscape/

Chapter 14

1. "Millions of Unchurched Adults Are Christians Hurt by Churches But Can Be Healed of the Pain," Barna Group, April 11, 2010 https://www.barna.org/barna-

update/faith-spirituality/362-millions-of-unchurched-adults-are-christians-hurt-by-churches-but-can-be-healed-of-the-pain#.VTvBVJMYMVQ
2. Quote found here: https://www.gracegems.org/29/entertainment_and_the_church.htm
3. William Law, *The Power of the Spirit, Extracts From the Writings of W. Law, Selected by A. Murray*, published 1896, reprinted by Scholar Select, reproduction of original work, public domain, page 176, slightly modified for readability.
4. Oswald Chambers, *My Utmost For His Highest*, Discovery House, devotion for July 18, © 1935 by Dodd Mead & Co., renewed © 1963 by the Oswald Chambers Publications Assn., Ltd. Used by permission of Our Daily Bread Publishing, Box 3566, Grand Rapids MI 49501. All rights reserved.

Chapter 15

1. MSNBC article titled: "Pope: Other denominations not true churches; Benedict issues statement asserting that Jesus established 'only one church'" 7/10/2007. http://www.msnbc.msn.com/id/19692094
2. Andrew Murray, *Andrew Murray Devotional*, (New Kensington, PA: Whitaker House), © 2006, devotional for April 14.
3. A.W. Tozer, *The Pursuit of God*, Christian Publications, Inc., © 1982 Baker Books, all rights reserved, page 64.

Chapter 16

1. David Kinnaman and Gabe Lyons, *unChristian; What a New Generation Really Thinks About Christianity*, BakerBooks, © 2007, page 32. Used by permission. All rights reserved.

Chapter 17

1. David Kinnaman and Gabe Lyons, *unChristian; What a New Generation Really Thinks About Christianity*, BakerBooks, © 2007, page 25. Used by permission. All rights reserved.
2. Andrew Murray, *Andrew Murray Devotional*, (New Kensington, PA: Whitaker House), © 2006, devotional for December 28.

Chapter 18

1. David Kinnaman and Gabe Lyons, *unChristian; What a New Generation Really Thinks About Christianity*, BakerBooks, © 2007, page 31. Used by permission. All rights reserved.

2. A.W. Tozer, *The Pursuit of God*, Christian Publications, Inc., © 1982 Baker Books, all rights reserved. Page 45.

Chapter 19

1. "America's Changing Religious Landscape: Christians Decline Sharply as Share of Population; Unaffiliated and Other Faiths Continue to Grow," PEW Research Center, Washington, D.C., May 12, 2015, https://www.pewforum.org/2015/05/12/americas-changing-religious-landscape/
2. William Law, *The Power of the Spirit, Extracts From the Writings of W. Law, Selected by A. Murray*, published 1896, reprinted by Scholar Select, reproduction of original work, public domain. Pages 102, 154.

Chapter 20

1. David Kinnaman and Gabe Lyons, *unChristian; What a New Generation Really Thinks About Christianity*, BakerBooks, © 2007, page 48. Used by permission. All rights reserved.
2. Ibid, page 49.

Chapter 21

1. William Law, *The Power of the Spirit, Extracts From the Writings of W. Law, Selected by A. Murray*, published 1896, reprinted by Scholar Select, reproduction of original work, public domain, page 190.

Chapter 23

1. Andrew Murray, *Daily in His Presence: A Spiritual Journey With Andrew Murray*, copyright © 2004 by Exponential, Inc. Used by permission of WaterBrook Multnomah, an imprint of Random House, a division of Penguin Random House LLC. All rights reserved. Devotion for January 5.
2. Andrew Murray; *Abide in Christ*, revised edition copyright 1997 by CLC Publications, Fort Washington, PA. Used by permission. May not be further reproduced. All rights reserved. Pages 135 & 136.
3. Ibid, page 134.
4. Ibid, page 136.
5. Andrew Murray, *With Christ in the School of Prayer*, CreateSpace Independent Publishing Platform, 2018, public domain, page 125.
6. Ibid, pages 100 and 101.

7. Andrew Murray, *The Practice of God's Presence*, collection of Andrew Murray books, quoted from book 3, *Absolute Surrender*, (New Kensington, PA: Whitaker House), © 1999, pages 208-209.
8. Andrew Murray, *With Christ in the School of Prayer*, page 27.
9. Ibid, page 8.

Chapter 24

1. Andrew Murray, *Humility*, (New Kensington, PA: Whitaker House), © 1982, pages 68, 83, 10, 13.
2. Andrew Murray, *Daily in His Presence: A Spiritual Journey With Andrew Murray*, copyright © 2004 by Exponential, Inc. Used by permission of WaterBrook Multnomah, an imprint of Random House, a division of Penguin Random House LLC. All rights reserved. Devotion for September 7.
3. Andrew Murray, *Humility*, pages 24, 59.
4. Ibid, page 18.
5. Ibid, page 87.
6. Ibid, pages 38, 86, 76.

Chapter 26

1. *The Princess Bride*, 1987, Director: Rob Reiner, Executive Producer: Norman Lear, Act III Communications.
2. David Kinnaman and Gabe Lyons, *unChristian; What a New Generation Really Thinks About Christianity*, BakerBooks, © 2007, page 183. Used by permission. All rights reserved.
3. Andrew Murray, *Abide in Christ*, revised edition copyright 1997 by CLC Publications, Fort Washington, PA. Used by permission. May not be further reproduced. All rights reserved. Page 164.
4. Ibid, page 166.
5. Andrew Murray, *Andrew Murray Devotional*, (New Kensington, PA: Whitaker House), © 2006, devotional for January 15.
6. (Psalm 63:3).
7. (Ephesians 3:17-19).
8. (1 Thessalonians 3:12).

Chapter 27

1. William Law, *The Power of the Spirit, Extracts From the Writings of W. Law, Selected by A. Murray*, published 1896, reprinted by Scholar Select, reproduction of original work, public domain, pages 84-85, slightly modified for readability.
2. Luke 18:27 NRSV.

3. Andrew Murray, *The Practice of God's Presence*, collection of Andrew Murray books, quoted from book 3, "Absolute Surrender," (New Kensington, PA: Whitaker House), © 1999, page 213.
4. William Law, *Dying to Self: A Golden Dialogue*, with notes and commentary by Andrew Murray, reprinted 2018, public domain, Andrew Murray comment, page 6.
5. Ibid, page 46.
6. Andrew Murray, *Humility*, (New Kensington, PA: Whitaker House), © 1982, page 59.
7. William Law, *Dying to Self: A Golden Dialogue*, page 34.
8. Andrew Murray, *Humility*, pages 59, 65, 66, 73.
9. Ibid, page 84.
10. Ibid, page 94.

Chapter 28

1. William Law, *Dying to Self: A Golden Dialogue*, with notes and commentary by Andrew Murray, reprinted 2018, public domain, page 41.
2. Andrew Murray, *Humility*, (New Kensington, PA: Whitaker House), © 1982, page 23.
3. Ibid, page 24.
4. Ibid, page 75.
5. Ibid, page 77.
6. Ibid, page 82.

Chapter 29

1. William Law, *Dying to Self: A Golden Dialogue*, with notes and commentary by Andrew Murray, reprinted 2018, public domain, Andrew Murray comment, page 10.
2. Andrew Murray, *Andrew Murray Devotional*, (New Kensington, PA: Whitaker House), © 2006, devotion for August 15.
3. William Law, *The Power of the Spirit, Extracts From the Writings of W. Law, Selected by A. Murray*, published 1896, reprinted by Scholar Select, reproduction of original work, public domain, page 102.
4. Andrew Murray, *With Christ in the School of Prayer*, CreateSpace Independent Publishing Platform, 2018, public domain, page 121.
5. Andrew Murray, *Humility*, page 39.
6. Andrew Murray, *Andrew Murray Devotional*, (New Kensington, PA: Whitaker House), © 2006, devotional for April 1.

7. William Law, *The Power of the Spirit, Extracts From the Writings of W. Law, Selected by A. Murray*, page 173.
8. Ibid page 63.
9. Luke 9:23.
10. John 13:34-35.
11. Romans 8:9.

Chapter 30

1. Andrew Murray, *The Secret of Spiritual Strength*, (New Kensington, PA: Whitaker House), © 1984, pg. 86.
2. "White Evangelicals, This is Why People Are Through With You," John Pavlovitz: https://johnpavlovitz.com/2018/01/24/white-evangelicals-people/
3. William Law, *The Power of the Spirit, Extracts From the Writings of W. Law, Selected by A. Murray*, published 1896, reprinted by Scholar Select, reproduction of original work, public domain, page 151.
4. Andrew Murray, *The Practice of God's Presence*, collection of Andrew Murray books, quoted from book 5, *Experiencing the Holy Spirit*, (New Kensington, PA: Whitaker House), © 1999, page 327.
5. Hebrews 13:9 NASB.
6. John 14:1 NASB.
7. Matthew 11:28.
8. John 15:9.
9. Matthew 22:37.
10. John 13:34-35.
11. John 16:23 NASB.
12. John 15:5.
13. John 15:8.
14. Luke 9:23.
15. Ezekiel 36:27.
16. John 6:63.
17. John 16:12-13.
18. John 8:32.
19. John 14:20 NASB.
20. Mark 10:9 NRSV.
21. John 16:33.
22. John 14:27.
23. Revelations 3:8 NASB.
24. Matthew 4:19.

Reading Recommendations

Other than the Bible, here's a list of the books I've quoted from, plus a few more I'd also like to recommend.

Absolute Surrender, Andrew Murray, Bethany House, © 2003 (also available from other publishers)

Abide in Christ, Andrew Murray; revised edition copyright 1997 by CLC Publications.

The Practice of the Presence of God, Brother Lawrence, (New Kensington, PA: Whitaker House, www.whitakerhouse.com), © 1992 (also available from other publishers)

The Power of the Spirit, William Law; edited edition copyright 1971 by Dave Hunt and published by CLC Publications.

Daily in His Presence: A Spiritual Journey With Andrew Murray, Andrew Murray, copyright © 2004 by Exponential, Inc.

The Pursuit of God, A.W. Tozer, Christian Publications, Inc., © 1982

Humility, Andrew Murray, (New Kensington, PA: Whitaker House, www.whitakerhouse.com), © 1982 (also available from other publishers)

Mystery of the Holy Spirit, A.W. Tozer, Bridge Logos Foundation, © 2007

The Masters Indwelling, Andrew Murray, (New Kensington, PA: Whitaker House, www.whitakerhouse.com), © 1983

The Secret of Spiritual Strength, Andrew Murray, (New Kensington, PA: Whitaker House, www.whitakerhouse.com), © 1984

How to be Filled With the Holy Spirit, A.W. Tozer, Christian Publications, Inc., © 2001

With Christ in the School of Prayer, Andrew Murray, public domain

Waiting on God, Andrew Murray, (New Kensington, PA: Whitaker House, www.whitakerhouse.com), © 1981

Dying to Self: A Golden Dialogue, William Law, with notes and commentary by Andrew Murray, public domain

A final personal message

The effort of writing this book has been a journey that took me farther than I'd ever hoped to go. I found a real and tangible relationship with God, and a commitment to Jesus' Christianity, both of which I previously hadn't imagined. I hope this book has just as powerful an impact on those who read it.

Over the sixteen-plus years I've traveled up the path that resulted in this book, I've come to realize that I, by myself, cannot truly honor and glorify God with anything I might write. With each early draft, of which there were many, I realized how ill-equipped I am to write a book such as this. Accepting that truth only strengthened my resolve to surrender not only the book, but also myself, to God.

Then, with each of the final few drafts, I felt this book becoming more God's and less mine—He became greater, I became less. Purely imagination? Some might think so. All I can tell you is that these words came to me while I read each chapter to the Holy Spirit within me, and trusted Him to alert me when something needed to be changed. As Jesus said, so I hope it has been with me: *"The words I say to you I do not speak on my own authority. Rather, it is the Father, living in me, who is doing his work"* (John 14:10).

Yet know that my own journey's not over. I still feel my self lurking nearby, pestering me, tempting me. However, armed with Jesus' truth and the presence of His Spirit, life for me is new, completely new. I feel peace, and freedom, and sometimes a profound joy.

But please, don't trust me—trust God. Test my words, and rely on God. As the Apostle John advised: *"Dear friends, do not believe every spirit, but test the spirits to see whether they are from God, because many false prophets have gone out into the world"* (1 John 4:1). God will tell you if my words are trustworthy.

Finally, since you've made it this far on your own journey, please consider leaving a review on Amazon.com, or whatever website you may have gotten this book from. I'd greatly value your opinion.

Thank you,
CJ Penn

Website: www.cjpenn.com
Facebook page: https://www.facebook.com/cj.penn4jc740

Printed in Great Britain
by Amazon

60801506R00150